THE RISE AND FALL OF THE
AMERICAN EMPIRE

BY D. S. PRESCOTT

Trilogy Christian Publishers

A Wholly Owned Subsidiary of Trinity Broadcasting Network

2442 Michelle Drive | Tustin, CA 92780

Copyright © 2024 by Douglas S. Prescott

Scripture quotations marked ESV are taken from the ESV® Bible (The Holy Bible, English Standard Version®), copyright © 2001 by Crossway Bibles, a publishing ministry of Good News Publishers. Used by permission. All rights reserved. Scripture quotations marked NIV are taken from the Holy Bible, New International Version®, NIV®. Copyright © 1973, 1978, 1984, 2011 by Biblica, Inc.™ Used by permission of Zondervan. All rights reserved worldwide. www.zondervan.com. The "NIV" and "New International Version" are trademarks registered in the United States Patent and Trademark Office by Biblica, Inc.™ Scripture quotations marked NKJV are taken from the New King James Version®. Copyright © 1982 by Thomas Nelson. Used by permission. All rights reserved. Scripture quotations marked NLT are taken from the Holy Bible, New Living Translation, copyright © 1996, 2004, 2015 by Tyndale House Foundation. Used by permission of Tyndale House Publishers, Inc., Carol Stream, Illinois 60188. All rights reserved. Scripture quotations marked KJV are taken from the King James Version of the Bible. Public domain.

All rights reserved, including the right to reproduce this book or portions thereof in any form whatsoever.

For information, address Trilogy Christian Publishing

Rights Department, 2442 Michelle Drive, Tustin, Ca 92780.

Trilogy Christian Publishing/ TBN and colophon are trademarks of Trinity Broadcasting Network.

For information about special discounts for bulk purchases, please contact Trilogy Christian Publishing.

Trilogy Disclaimer: The views and content expressed in this book are those of the author and may not necessarily reflect the views and doctrine of Trilogy Christian Publishing or the Trinity Broadcasting Network.

10 9 8 7 6 5 4 3 2 1

Library of Congress Cataloging-in-Publication Data is available.

ISBN 979-8-89333-759-4 | ISBN 979-8-89333-760-0 (ebook)

TABLE OF CONTENTS

Preface. 5

Introduction. 9

Chapter 1. Foundations 11

Chapter 2. A Divine Mandate and the Colonization
of Jamestown 17

Chapter 3. Journey to New Plymouth. 23

Chapter 4. The Colonization of America by France, the Dutch,
Portugal, Spain, and Russia 27

Chapter 5. Winthrop's Warning and American
Exceptionalism 35

Chapter 6. Eighteenth-Century British America. 39

Chapter 7. George Whitefield 43

Chapter 8. The Founding Fathers and the American
Revolution. 49

Chapter 9. The Advent of Nineteenth-Century America. 61

Chapter 10. Abraham Lincoln. 75

Chapter 11. The American Civil War 85

Chapter 12. Dwight Lyman Moody .95

Chapter 13. The Dawning of Twentieth-Century America 103

Chapter 14. The Great War 115

The Rise and Fall of the American Empire

Chapter 15. Prophetic Signs 119

Chapter 16. The Tale of Two Cities .127

Chapter 17. The Roaring Twenties 141

Chapter 18. The Great American Depression 157

Chapter 19. Aimee Semple McPherson 165

Chapter 20. Kathryn Kuhlman 175

Chapter 21. America Enters World War II 189

Chapter 22. War in the Pacific 201

Chapter 23. D-Day: The Normandy Invasion. 221

Chapter 24. The Surrender of Germany and Japan. 235

Chapter 25. Faith, Healing, and Salvation 251

Chapter 26. 1950s America. 283

Chapter 27. The End of Innocence, JFK, MLK, Chavez,
     and the 1960s 321

Chapter 28. CBN, TBN, Daystar, and the Close
     of the Twentieth Century 351

Chapter 29. Let the Heroes Arise 371

Chapter 30. Destiny to Win. 375

Epilogue 385

About the Author. 387

Bibliography 389

Onomastic Index. 441

PREFACE

Has America already fulfilled the purpose that God had for it from the beginning and its inception? I think one of those purposes goes back and connects to the Great Commission, which were the final words and instructions of Jesus to His disciples before ascending into heaven.

> Jesus came and spoke to them, saying, "All authority has been given to me in heaven and on earth. Go therefore and make disciples of all nations, baptizing them in the name of the Father and of the Son and of the Holy Spirit, teaching them to observe all things that I have commanded you; and lo, I am with you always, even to the end of the age." Amen.

Matthew 28:18–20 (NKJV)

Pat Robertson recently stated that he thought that "the going forth of the gospel to all nations was just about done" (Robertson, "Abby Robertson's Conversation with Her Grandfather and CBN Founder Pat Robertson: Full Interview," 2023). The gospel came to the shores of America, but it also went forth from the shores of America unto all the nations of the earth. This was a common thread, connection, and motivation of all the colonists of early

The Rise and Fall of the American Empire

North America. The English, French, Spanish, Russian, and Dutch all shared this vision, motivation, commandment, and covenant on one level or another. America, from its founding, went on to be a beacon to the nations and a "city on a hill."

D. S. Prescott

"THE SANDS OF TIME"

The sands of time are shifting, drifting, drawing to a close.

Exactly when that time will come,

There's only one who knows

Since He would,

That none should perish.

With patience, He's holding on because He's waiting,

He's waiting for you.

His hands are reaching.

His voice is calling, with a love undying,

He's knocking at your door….

The sands of time are slipping through this hourglass called life.

The remnant of this age is flowing,

Going past so fast,

The prophetic time clock is about to strike.

The final remaining chord,

A trumpet blast, the signal of our Lord.

He's coming, yeah, He's coming in the clouds.

Like a vapor, the last grain will be gone and, forever,

will be singing the new song.

Hope springs eternal for those who will wait…

The Rise and Fall of the American Empire

Make the decision before it's too late.

There is no time to hesitate.

Don't let yourself be left.

It's true, or you'll be blue and pierced right through.

Oh, the winds will blow,

The storms will rise,

And all will fall that's built on lies…

The sands of time…

D. S. Prescott

November 18, 1989

To hear the audio version of this song and other music, please go to Douglas Prescott's YouTube channel.

INTRODUCTION

I personally believe that almost anyone can see and understand the message and essence of this book, or at least some part of it. It is like the proverbial elephant in the room, and each of us could have a different perspective or angle of view on the subject together, providing a more complete or total picture. There is an array of different things that are out of whack in our country, and I am not sure if we have reached an inflection point or a point of no return.

I had initially written the title and outline and various ideas for *The Rise and Fall of the American Empire* in 1981, about the time that Ronald Reagan took office as the fortieth president of the United States. In his inaugural address, he basically stated that America was in trouble, and forty-three years later, where are we now? Are there fiendish forces attempting to derail our great nation and push it off a cliff to establish an international or global agenda? Or have we been successfully destroying ourselves from within, like the Roman Empire, incrementally tearing down the nuclear family and other vital, core elements of our civilization and infrastructure? Or perhaps it is a little bit of everything, including a culture determined to push God out of its conscience and do what it wants to do.

This book is written with a Christian worldview, combining history, events, and stories about how God has moved in the lives and circumstances of many different individuals in America. The

The Rise and Fall of the American Empire

pen of future history is in the hands of the church and its response to the living God.

D. S. Prescott

CHAPTER 1

Foundations

Deep within the heart of man is a God-given desire for freedom. To be able to pursue life, liberty, and happiness without the interference of a tyrannical government and/or the persecution of a monarchy or state church. It was of paramount importance to the early Puritan pilgrims who settled in America to have freedom of religion. The Founding Fathers of America did a great job laying the foundation and framework for this, as well as for self-governance. The earliest Separatist Pilgrims had a vision for a godly society and a better life in every way.

From the very beginning of human history, men began to multiply and spread out over the whole earth. Long before the European migrations, the Inuit, Yupik, and Native American peoples had come to the North American continent and numbered perhaps in the hundreds of thousands from shore to shore. For example, in the Salt River valley alone, in the area that is now Arizona, there could have been as many as 80,000 Hohokam dwellings ("Hohokam Culture," 2019) along the rivers and the desert at the height of their civilization. Later, when the Europeans began to explore and arrive, they brought a silent and invisible enemy in the form of disease, which decimated significant portions of the native populations. God had always had a purpose and plan for mankind and the nations of the earth. And at the very center of that plan was Jesus and His redemptive role in human history. One of the very first men that God revealed Himself to was Abraham. There were others also, like Adam of the first generation, Noah of the tenth generation, and even Enoch, whom God translated directly to heaven without seeing death.

Abraham was the father of the Jews, the chosen people, chosen to make known the knowledge of the one true God who made heaven and earth to all the peoples of the earth. They were also chosen to make known the knowledge of the Messiah, the Savior of the world. The plan of God for humanity was further clarified and made manifest when Moses and other holy men, moved and inspired by the spirit of God, wrote the sixty-six books of the Bible. Abraham was father to both the Jews and the Arabs through Isaac and Ishmael, which really was a type of the natural and supernatural, the effort of man and the intervention of God. The birth of Isaac was a miracle, and throughout the history of the Jews, many miracles have been recorded, including their very existence and preservation.

Fast forward from 1492 to 1504, Christopher Columbus made four different voyages in an effort to find an all-water route to Asia. There is no indication that Columbus made it to the shores of North America but landed on various Caribbean islands and the coasts of Central and South America.

It is more likely that the first European explorers to discover the North American continent were Leif Erikson (Groeneveld, 2018) and the Icelandic Norsemen Vikings. Although the histor-

Foundations

ical evidence and research are a little light, I believe that there is enough that it is worth noting. There are two main sagas or stories that are similar in nature. A ship trying to reach Greenland and being blown off course, reaching lands beyond Iceland and Greenland. So, let's start with Bjarni Herjolfsson. According to another Greenlander saga or story some fifteen years prior to Leif Erikson, Bjarni and his crew, on a voyage from Iceland to Greenland, were overtaken by wind and fog, missing the southern tip of Greenland, reaching an unknown coast and lands beyond. According to *The Saga of Erik the Red*, Leif's father, Leif discovered an unknown coast of land after being blown off course on his way from Norway to Greenland. He so named the land Vineland or Wineland because of the many vines of grapes they saw. Before this voyage, Leif had spent time at the court of Norwegian King Olaf Tryggvason, where he had been converted to Christianity. Leif Erikson was so moved by his conversion to Christianity that he had a vision to go to Greenland to introduce the people there to Christianity. But en route, he encountered a storm blowing him off course, reaching the unknown coast of the land he so named Vineland. According to *The Saga of Erik the Red*, Leif never returned to Vineland but stated that others from Greenland and Iceland did, establishing settlements. In the 1960s, explorers and archaeologists Helge and Anne Ingstad identified a Norse site located at the northern tip of Newfoundland, further corroborating the evidence of the Norse's discovery of North America. The dates of these early Norse expeditions would have been about AD 980 to 1021 (Boissoneault, 2015).

Back to the time of Columbus, Amerigo Vespucci was born

on March 9, 1454, in Italy. Amerigo was the first explorer to propose the idea that the New World discovered by Columbus was a completely different continent and not the East Indies. Thus, the origin of the name that stuck for the new continent, America, was attributed to Amerigo Vespucci (Almagia, 2023).

Early historical records about the initial explorers and expeditions to the New World are few and far between. Many European powers were trying to find the eastern or western passages to Asia and discovered new and different lands along the way. One of the threads of commonality that I observed among many of the early pioneers and pilgrims was their faith in God. Many different Europeans brought various levels of Christian influence and vision to the New World, especially the English, which we will take a closer look at in Chapter 2.

There was always a purpose and a plan in the heart of God for America, and this is the foundation for America, despite what has been built on that foundation. The early Puritan Pilgrims desired to create a new society with freedom of religion, no longer under the rule of a monarch, where they created and agreed the laws between themselves. They experienced the exciting discovery of the Native Americans, who were integral to their survival in the early years. But sadly, as there were disagreements and conflicts, trust was eroded, and both sides experienced the horrors of the Indian wars for centuries.

Foundations

One of the most difficult things was the establishment of the first successful forts, settlements, or colonies. There were various explorations and attempts in the 1500s, such as Roanoke in 1586 and 1587, which became known as the Lost Colony ("What Happened to the 'Lost Colony' of Roanoke: How Could 115 People Just Vanish?" 2012). In 1602, a fort was established at Cuttyhunk, but then it was soon abandoned. In 1603, Martin Pring ("In 1603, Martin Pring Escaped New England with His Tail between His Legs," 2022), an explorer from Bristol, built a fort at Cape Cod, which was later discovered by the Pilgrims' first expeditions ashore at New Plymouth. Well, they found the remnants of what was left of it anyway. Many other world powers had varying degrees of success colonizing America through the centuries, which we will examine in greater detail in Chapter 3. The first successful English colony became Jamestown in 1607 (Price, 2023), established by the London Virginia Company. Later, when Captain Jones came in 1620, this was where he was attempting to go, but the wind and the weather, and perhaps Providence itself, drove them and the *Mayflower* (Fraser, 2017) to New Plymouth instead. Although Jamestown had some very godly individuals who dedicated the New World to God and his purposes, the Puritan Separatists at Plymouth took it to another level of dedication and commitment. And they would need all of that and more to establish their vision of a New Jerusalem and a Godly society in the New World, pretty much starting out with nothing but their faith and determination. And in the next two chapters, we will see how England, France,

The Rise and Fall of the American Empire

the Netherlands, Portugal, Spain, and even Russia all played very important roles in the development and colonization of America.

a government based on the values of liberty, equality, and a new form of justice. They did a great job creating a government with separation of powers, having a system of checks and balances to prevent tyrannical rule.

Jamestown Established

Jamestown Colony was established in 1607, prior to Plymouth Colony in 1620. On December 20, 1606, 105 daring settlers and forty brave seamen set out from the River Thames Estuary near London, England. They embarked on a mission to the New World of America after receiving a charter from King James. A significant aspect of the stated mission of the Virginia Company included concern for spiritual things. One printed declaration of the Virginia Company consisted of the following proclamation (Price, 2023).

The True Declaration of the State of Virginia

First, to preach and baptize into Christian religion and by the propagation of the gospel, to recover out of the arms of the devil a number of poor and miserable souls wrapped up into death in almost invincible ignorance, to endeavor the fulfilling and accomplishments of the number of the elect that shall be gathered from out of all corners of the earth, and add to our myth the treasury of heaven. ("A True Declaration of the Estate of the Colonie in Virginia, with a Confutation of Such Scandalous Reports as Have Tended to the Disgrace of So Worthy an Enterprise," n.d.)

CHAPTER 2

A Divine Mandate and the Colonization of Jamestown

God has a purpose for every individual, family, people group, and nation, including the United States. In the beginning, the Bible was translated from the original languages, such as Hebrew, Aramaic, and Koine Greek, into Syriac, Latin, Ge'ez, Gothic, and Slavonic languages. The Bible has been translated into more than 3,580 languages, including the main ones like Spanish and English. The United States has been used by God as one of the main launching pads for the spread of the gospel into all the nations of the earth. Throughout its history and existence, America has been the "city on a hill." I believe that since the inception of America, there has been a divine mandate, a Sovereign call upon this country to finish and fulfill the work of the gospel to the ends of the earth. From the beginning, most early colonists believed in God and understood the importance of having the freedom to follow and worship Him. God raised up armies of evangelists and missionaries from America who not only influenced its inhabitants but, from its shores, the nations of the earth. Throughout its history, America has been a beacon of democracy and freedom, shining in a world with ever-increasing oppressive governments and ideologies. Athens is often regarded by Western scholars as the birthplace of democracy, but America took it to another level. The Founding Fathers of America took the brave steps of creating

dedication remain to all generations as long as the earth remains, and may this land, along with England, be an evangelist to the world. May all who see this cross remember what we have done here, and may those who come here to inhabit join us in this covenant and in this most noble work that the Holy Scriptures may be fulfilled (Eisenger, 2023). Then they read Psalm 22:27–28 (NIV), which states, "All the ends of the earth will remember and turn to the Lord, and all the families of the nations will bow down before him, for dominion belongs to the Lord and he rules over the nations."

It is difficult to imagine just how hard it must have been for the first settlers and colonists. It took faith and vision and a sense of destiny to endure the hardships like the peril and the incredible duration of the voyage, having to build the first structures from the wood of the forest on arrival, also trying to learn how to farm, fish, and hunt in an entirely new environment and land. It was the new, great, unknown territory with mysterious natives, unpredictable weather, and harsh New England winters. They were driven by fate and survival, and perhaps it was a miracle that anyone survived those grueling first months, years, and winters. On October 8, 1607, Christopher Newport sailed from England to Jamestown with two supply ships and approximately one hundred additional colonists. In 1610, additional settlers brought from the island of Bermuda were shipwrecked there. Besides other interventions in 1619 and prior, the Virginia Company shipped about ninety women who had volunteered to go to Jamestown to start families and

A Divine Mandate and the Colonization of Jamestown

Jamestown

Crossing waters that they did not know, with poor trade wind conditions and ocean currents, it took a grueling, remarkable 144 days to cross the Atlantic Ocean. They finally made shore on April 29, 1607, with the three ships, the *Discovery*, the *Godspeed*, and the *Susan Constant*. Whether it was Mary Chilton, who took the first step on Plymouth Rock, or another member of the party, they all disembarked (Price, 2023).

Reverend Robert Hunt stood as a representative of the king, the church, and the people of England in a sacred moment and dedicated the new continent to the purpose of God. He raised his hand to heaven and claimed the land for country and king and consecrated the continent to the glory of God. Reverend Hunt then planted a seven-foot cross on the wind-swept shore of Virginia. He then declared, "From these very shores the gospel shall go forth to not only this new world, but to all nations." Jamestown became the first permanent English colony on April 29, 1607. Reverend Robert Hunt prayed for America at Cape Henry (later Virginia Beach, Virginia) ("The Reverend Robert Hunt: The First Chaplain at Jamestown," 2022).

Prayer for America

We do hereby dedicate this land and ourselves to reach the people within these shores with the gospel of Jesus Christ and to raise up godly generations after us, and with these generations, take the Kingdom of God to all the earth. May this covenant of

A Divine Mandate and the Colonization of Jamestown

grow the colony. In 1619, adding to the mix of Europeans and natives, the first documented Africans were brought to Virginia to work the tobacco fields. They had been captured and were essentially slaves. On July 30, 1619, newly appointed Governor Yeardley called for the first representative Legislative Assembly. This was the beginning of the representative government in what is now the United States of America ("A Short History of Jamestown," 2022).

signed a Covenant Agreement among themselves and began their own church. They were very happy about getting out from under the Church of England, but for most of the Scrooby group, there were severe economic issues, assimilation issues, and others. They decided amongst themselves that they had to go; having heard of Jamestown, the first colony settled by the English in Virginia, they decided to go there. It would be a fresh start for them and their Puritan church in the New World. They felt a sense of destiny and the hand of God leading them. William Bradford continued to develop into an important leader among the Scrooby group. The King of England's view of them changed because, in this circumstance, he saw them as useful in their desire to help settle and establish an English colony in the New World. So, in this instance, instead of being persecuted, they were viewed by the king as resources and gained a sponsor in the Virginia Company that held a charter. There were only around forty Separatists who were willing to go to the New World, largely due to the difficulties of the two-month voyage and the harsh realities of what they might face starting out in the new colony. To ensure that their plan worked, they signed up others—non-Separatist English people. They also hired the professional soldier Miles Standish and barrel maker John Alden to assist on the long, arduous journey. After two attempts to start off and launch with the *Speedwell*, they found that it was leaking and had to set off alone, only using the *Mayflower*. The *Mayflower* was not in very good condition either and was scrapped not long after its return to England. At first, it was very exciting to set sail from England, waving goodbye to family and friends. Soon, however,

CHAPTER 3

Journey to New Plymouth

A Pilgrim, by definition, is someone who journeys to a sacred place for religious reasons. Another name for the English people who left Scrooby, England, and other areas for Leiden, Holland, was "Separatists." They came to conclude that it was impossible to change the Church of England, and they began to form their own. They were attempting to more closely follow the early teachings and doctrines set forth by the first apostles of the church and separate themselves from the errors, pretense, and traditions that they felt were inherent in the Church of England. After persecutions by the Church of England and arrests made by King James I and his government, they decided to leave England and move to Leiden, Holland. They knew that in Holland, the Dutch allowed people to worship as they wished. Although things were far from perfect for the Separatists in Leiden, this first step to freedom further set the stage to eventually make the decision to leave and go to the new world. William Brewster was one of the key individuals who, in the beginning, was elected an elder in the Separatist church and helped members of the church escape from England to Holland. William Bradford was about seventeen years old when he joined the Scrooby Separatists. He developed into a Pilgrim leader and helped organize the Mayflower Trip to America. By 1609, most of the Scrooby group, along with Separatists from other parts of England, had settled in Leiden, Holland. There, they

the cramped quarters and the wet and cold began to wear on everyone. There were 102 passengers and thirty sailors. Of the 102 passengers, thirty-four were children, and there were also two dogs. Of the sixty-six days at sea, most of the passengers were seasick, cold, wet, and hungry. It was almost impossible to keep anything dry, and many became tired, weakened, and sick. It was no wonder that most of the sailors on the crew were short-tempered with the passengers and children. During one wild storm, John Howard fell overboard, but amazingly, they were able to get him back aboard with ropes. There was a mixture of the Puritan Separatists and "the others." The others were mostly younger, English, daring, and bold, looking for a new and better life. They did not hold the same zealous religious views as the Puritan Pilgrim Separatists. After over two long months at sea, they beheld the most glorious sight. On November 10, 1620, they sighted land, but they did not realize it was not Virginia. They had landed at Cape Cod instead. Largely due to fatigue and the threat of storms possibly blowing them back out to sea, they set anchor and remained at Cape Cod despite the initial resistance of the others. On November 11, 1620, they signed the Mayflower Compact, which was essentially an agreement for governing the settlement that they all would accept. It began with the words "In the name of God," recognizing Him and His provenance and guiding them to where they were and into the future of the colonies of New England.

Elizabeth Hopkins was one of only four women who survived the first winter. Perhaps it was a miracle that no one at all survived the first winter. They had all been weakened, half-starved, trudging through a mile of icy cold seawater each time they went ashore. Because it was not a deepwater bay, that was as close as they could get the ship to shore. During the voyage, Elizabeth Hopkins gave birth to a child whom they named Oceanus. The sailors and crew kept the *Mayflower* moored there for months before leaving to go back to England. This enabled the men to at least begin to build the first rough structures and allowed the women and children to shelter aboard the *Mayflower* until this was done. Many of the crew and sailors had also become sick and ailing, so this was another reason that Captain Christopher Jones opted to remain longer so they could recover. Even Captain Jones died shortly after returning to England in March 1622 at age fifty-two. He had also become so weakened by the whole ordeal that he never fully recovered. Yes, there would be more colonists besides the English to come to the New World, including the French, Dutch, Portuguese, Spanish, and even Russians, but the role of the first New England colonies and their importance in the early foundation and development of America cannot be underestimated (Eliot Morison, 2011).

were hindered by disease, weather, and conflict with other Europe-an powers and sometimes different tribes. Samuel de Champlain, considered the founder of New France, established a settlement at what is now Quebec City in 1608. At its peak in 1710, the French colonial empire stretched to over 3,900,000 miles, which was the second-largest colonial empire in the world after the Spanish Em-pire (Hornsby, 2004).

Dutch Colonization

In 1602, the Republic of the Seven United Netherlands char-tered a young Dutch East India Company, VOC, with the mission of exploring North American rivers and bays for a direct passage through to the Indies. By 1610, the Dutch East India Company, or VOC (Vereenigde Oostindische Compagnie), had already com-missioned Henry Hudson to try and find the Northwest Passage. Hudson entered the upper New York Bay by sailboat, heading up the Hudson River, which now bears his name (Henry Hudson, 2023). In 1614, Adriaen Block led an expedition aboard the *On-rust*, becoming the first known European to navigate the *Helle-gat* to gain entrance into Long Island Sound. Upon his return to Amsterdam in 1614, Block compiled a map of the area between English Virginia and French Canada for the first time and named it New Netherland (Block Island, 2019). The first Dutch settlement in America was founded in 1615. It was called Fort Nassau, and it was along the Hudson on Castle Island near present-day Albany. By 1621, the United Provinces had chartered a trading monopoly in the Americas: The Dutch West India Company. In 1623, they

CHAPTER 4

The Colonization of America by France, the Dutch, Portugal, Spain, and Russia

France

France also began exploring and colonizing the North American continent in the sixteenth century, creating fur trading posts and later settlements. Also, like other European powers, France continued to try to find a trade and travel passage to Asia through the New World. Because of this and the fur trade, they continued to discover new areas and push the boundaries of their exploration. As early as 1534, Jacques Cartier began the French colonization of North America (Eccles, 2022). Some French missionaries made their way to North America to convert Native Americans to Catholicism. More intermarriages took place between French settlers and Native Americans than with any other European group. They respected the natives, their territories, and their ways and treated them like fellow human beings made by God. The natives, in turn, treated the French as trusted friends. Part of my ancestry consists of both the French and Micmac tribe, who lived in regions in eastern North America. My ancestors departed New Rochelle, France, some as early as 1604, and began to settle on what is now Prince Edward Island and adjacent areas. The French viewed indigenous natives as allies and relied on them not only for fur trade wealth but also for survival and help in the New World. In the 1500s, the initial attempts by the French to create colonies in North America

Portuguese Colonization

Portugal also attempted to colonize North America with expeditions by Joao Vaz Corte Real as early as 1473. The Corte Real brothers attempted to claim the Canadian provinces of Newfoundland and Labrador as early as 1501 and 1502. In 1521, they were able to establish fishing outposts in Nova Scotia and Newfoundland. The Portuguese were successful in establishing several North American towns that continue to remain but largely abandoned their efforts of North American colonization to focus on Brazil and South America (Deak, 2023).

Colonization by Spain

While the French, English, and Dutch began to explore and colonize the eastern half of North America, the Spaniards were well underway in the West. Hernan Cortes and a small group of Spanish soldiers conquered Mexico in 1521, just two years after they had landed near the modern-day city of Veracruz. The swift conquest of Mexico was made possible by the armies of native Mexicans, enemies of the Aztecs that Cortes enlisted as his allies. Like the French and English, Spain's purpose in colonizing Mexico and the other colonies was to get new lands and resources and to spread Christianity. Sadly, one silent and invisible weapon that the Spanish brought, like other Europeans, were the diseases that they carried and that decimated many of the native Mexican people. Hernan Cortes's victory at Tenochtitlan set in motion the rapid collapse of the Aztec Empire. After the Aztecs, they systematically took down one tribe and area after another. Within three

founded another Fort Nassau on the Delaware River near Gloucester City, New Jersey (Fort Nassau, n.d.). In 1624, additional colonists arrived to strengthen and develop the settlements in the New
Netherlands. The Dutch Reformed Church was the official religion
of the colony and the early settlers. An interesting footnote to New
Netherlander history is that, just as they were tolerant to the Puritans who came to Leiden to live, they were historically tolerant to
diverse flows of various peoples and migrants who settled there.
For example, one of the largest populations of Jews in the world
emigrated there ("Netherlands Reformed Church: Dutch Protes-
tant Denomination," 2010). In 1626, director of the WIC, or Dutch
West India Company, purchased the island of Manhattan from the
Lenape Indians and began the construction of Fort Amsterdam.
It grew to become the main port and capital of New Amsterdam.
The colony continued to grow and expand to Pavonia, Brooklyn,
Bronx, and Long Island.

The province then took the name New York about 1664 from
Prince James's English title. After three Anglo-Dutch wars, many
of the Dutch settlements were lost or abandoned by the end of the
seventeenth century. Although Dutch colonial rule in the area was
relatively brief, their footprint and influence remained. Incredibly,
400 years later. The New York, Newark, Jersey City metropolitan
area holds about 20 million people. Countless thousands flowed
through Ellis Island, New York, into all parts of America. In 1907
alone, 1.25 million immigrants passed through and were processed
at Ellis Island, New York (Howe, 2012).

years, the Conquistadors brought the whole of Mesoamerica under Spanish rule and established the colony of New Spain. In the early years, the northern boundary of New Spain remained largely indeterminate, with populations small and scattered in those regions. These northern areas of New Spain would eventually become what was to be much of the future western United States of America. Texas, New Mexico, Arizona, California, Nevada, Utah, and western Colorado were later gained from Mexico by the United States in agreements. Spanish conquistadors and priests first came to what is now Arizona with Coronado in 1541. Spaniards established a presence in Arizona and other areas beginning in the late 1600s, endeavoring to spread the Catholic faith, search for gold and mineral wealth, and claim the land for Spain (Nowell, 2023). On July 16, 1769, Father Junipero Serra founded California's first mission, which was called Mission San Diego de Alcala. Over the following decades, it evolved into the city of San Diego, California (Bolton, n.d.). For nearly 300 years, from 1521 to 1821, Spain ruled the Empire of New Spain. When the Mexicans gained independence from Spain on August 24, 1821, they renamed New Spain the Mexican Empire. The oldest continuously occupied settlement in what would become the United States was probably St. Augustine, Florida, founded by the Spanish in 1565. Saint Augustine came under British rule for the first time and served as a Loyalist colony during the American Revolutionary War.

The Rise and Fall of the American Empire

Caption: *The Grand Canyon, located in the western United States, is considered one of the seven natural wonders of the world.*

In 1821, the Adams-Onis Treaty peaceably turned the Spanish provinces in Florida, and with them Saint Augustine, over to the United States ("Our History," n.d.).

Russian Colonization

The Russian Empire had also begun to colonize North America from about 1732 to 1867. Russian explorers had been pushing eastward across the interior of their continent in the 1500s and 1600s until they reached the coast and the Pacific Ocean. Then, they further began to explore the Pacific in ships. Peter the Great of Russia, at the end of his life, drew up a charter commissioning Vitus Bering, a Dane, to explore Siberia and discover where Asia left off and North America began. In August of 1728, Russian explorers set off on their first expedition and at least determined the

The Colonization of America by France, the Dutch, Portugal, Spain, and Russia

fact that there was clear sea between Asia and America. Although they did not sight land on the first expedition, it helped them to be much better prepared for the next. Once again, Russian explorers set off with two ships in 1741, determined to go all the way, and were exhilarated to finally sight the southern coast of Alaska. It did not take them long to realize that there were other people who had arrived long before them. The Yupik and the Inuit had crossed over from Asia generations previous and had already established a civilization in Alaska and the North American continent. The first known permanent Russian settlement was established in 1784 at Three Saints Bay near present-day Kodiak. The Unangan people lived in this area, and they were pushed by the Russians to help them in the hunting of fur seals. Although one of the main reasons for colonizing Alaska was the fur trade, as stocks had been depleted in Siberia, the Russian Orthodox Church had great spiritual interests and motivations. Many people do not realize that prior to the Bolshevik Revolution in 1917, Russia was a predominantly Christian nation. The Bolsheviks systematically and brutally eradicated this. In 1794, the first group of Russian Orthodox Christian missionaries began to evangelize thousands of Native American Alaskans. This is one of the greatest and lasting impacts to the area as many of the descendants of those native Alaskans still believe and follow Christianity to this day. New Archangel, which is present-day Sitka, was the capital of Russian America in the 1800s. The Russians had settlements as far South as the Fortress Ross Outpost, north of San Francisco Bay, California, in about 1812. At about this time, while Russia was pushing colonization of North America south, Spain was competing by pushing colonization north.

With most settlements abandoned by the 1860s, Russia sold its last remaining possession, Alaska, to the United States on October 18, 1867. Besides now owning the vast resources of the region, this purchase effectively ended Russia's presence in North America and ensured United States access to the Pacific Northern Rim. The purchase of Alaska was an unusually peaceful transition, and despite criticism of what many said to be a high cost, it was actually a great bargain at $7.2 million. The value alone of the future critical and strategic military location cannot be underestimated (McGee, 2022).

CHAPTER 5

Winthrop's Warning and American Exceptionalism

After Jamestown and Plymouth colonies were established, approximately 20,000 English Puritans migrated to America between 1630 and 1640. And one of the leading figures of that time and the great migration was John Winthrop, born at Edwardstone, Suffolk, England, on January 12, 1588. Plans were set to depart England with a fleet of eleven ships, including the *Arbella*, with 700 immigrants on board, in the spring of 1630. Prior to their departure on March 21, 1630, John Winthrop issued a warning at Holyrood Church and repeated it again later. The title of his sermon that day was "A model of Christian charity." He quoted from both Matthew 5:14 and Deuteronomy chapter 28, declaring that what they would be building would be like a city on a hill and that the whole world would be watching. He proclaimed the blessing of the Lord over them if they followed and obeyed the Lord. But he also warned them that if they failed to follow and obey the Lord, they would be cursed and become a byword of the nations. In his sermon, John Winthrop outlined plans and ideas to keep Puritan society strong in faith, a vision that echoed in New England's colonial development, influencing the government and the people for generations to come. He drew a parallel and comparison to the struggles and the hardships that they would face to the story of the exodus of the Jews from Egypt to the Promised Land. Once again, he emphasized to them that if the Puritans failed to uphold their covenant with God, then their sins and errors would be exposed for all the world to see, and God would begin to withdraw His hand and His help. John Winthrop, an English Puritan lawyer, was one of the most influential voices of his time and served as a governor of the Massachusetts Bay Colony for twelve of his first twenty years. The echo of his warning to not turn away from God reverberated among the people and the colonies for years and generations to come. Winthrop's warning and message of a city on a hill was rediscovered in twentieth-century America and was used frequently by Ronald Reagan and others in speeches (Dunn, 2023).

American Exceptionalism

I have a simple belief that God created man and that over time, man spread out over all the earth, forming the nations of the earth, including America. Americans are not only the descendants of Puritan English immigrants but really come from just about every continent and nation on the earth. But we all, as Americans, share the common bond of being part of a unique and distinctive nation we now call America. Well, does God have His favorites? Does He somehow love America and Americans more than other nations or people? Was God and the message of the Bible suddenly a new discovery of the English and Europeans that they were trying to introduce to Native Americans? As previously noted, long before the Europeans, God began to reveal Himself to Abraham and the Jews, and they meticulously recorded the Bible, which was a revelation of God and His purpose for mankind. The nations of the earth are like children to God. He loves them all, and they all have different talents, giftings, abilities, purposes, and destinies to fulfill. The rise and fall of nations are in God's hands. America was not an accident. It was meant to be, to be born, and to fulfill the divine purpose God had for it all along. If God is real, does man have an accountability to Him? Or can man just do whatever he wants? What happened to the nation of Israel when they would forget about God and cease to follow or obey Him? The United States has clearly held a special place among the countries of the world, and it possesses qualities that make it different, unique, and exemplary. It was the land of opportunity for generations of immigrants who came here for a better life. It was the development of the American Dream, which was created by visionaries and dreamers who believed that you could accomplish anything you put your heart and mind to. It was the rugged mindset of the expansionists who had a simple faith in the promise of God in Genesis 1:28a (NIV): "Be fruitful and increase in number; fill the earth and subdue it." Many believed it was a manifest destiny to spread and possess the whole of the continent, which Providence gave for the development of the great experiment of liberty and federated self-government. America rose to be the greatest superpower in the history of the world, a leader and titan in every sphere. There are countless stories of the risk-takers and visionaries who propelled America to prominence and prosperity through the eighteenth, nineteenth, and twentieth centuries. Growing and expanding like a giant in industry, agriculture, business, and finance, America became the greatest economic and military power in the world. Its footprint and influence on culture have been remarkable and worldwide. Our nation is still relatively young, being only 247 years old since July 4, 1776. The nation has become increasingly diverse, mixed, and international, yet retaining that distinctive element of Americana and being an American. So, what is an American, and what is America? Americans are all the Native Americans, Europeans, Asians, Africans, Middle Easterners, South, Central, and North American peoples, and all the various mixtures thereof who share this wonderful and amazing land of opportunity and freedom. America is the beacon to the world, a city on a hill, and the foundation thereof is the fearless faith in God of the English, French, Spanish, Russians, Dutch, Portuguese, and all people who shed their precious blood, sweat, and tears to make this great nation what it is today (Van Engen, 2020).

Caption: *The Founding Fathers.*

CHAPTER 6

Eighteenth-Century British America

A great nation was slowly taking shape as the eighteenth century dawned on British America. The French, Spanish, British, Dutch, and Native Americans had battled for control of America for half a century of almost continuous wars, then at that time, a new entity emerged, "the Americans." By the end of the eighteenth century, the Americans created the greatest experiment in self-government the world had ever seen, and it would prove to be successful.

The foundation of higher education continued to be laid and expanded beyond the establishment of Harvard in 1836. Yale College was founded in 1701, then Princeton in 1746, and Columbia University in New York City was chartered in 1754. Many of the Founding Fathers who went on to become presidents attended these schools. John Adams graduated from Harvard, James Madison from Princeton, and Thomas Jefferson attended the College of William and Mary. George Washington's formal education ended when he was fifteen, and he did not attend college. Benjamin Franklin's father wanted him to attend school with the clergy but only had enough money to send him to school for two years. He continued to self-educate through different ways, including voracious reading. Seventeen twenty-three marked the beginning of free public school education in Maryland and other colonies. In 1701, the royal colonies were created, and more were added until

The Rise and Fall of the American Empire

there was a total of 13. In 1709, Pennsylvania Colony was established, and Baltimore and Georgia were added in 1729 and 1732, with Georgia becoming the thirteenth and final colony.

More roads were established, connecting the colonies with the first stagecoach line beginning in 1732. American innovation grew as Captain Robinson designed the schooner in 1713. In 1750, American enterprise was further helped by the more advanced Conestoga wagon and the flatboat. American art and artists continued to develop their own style and uniqueness, and painters like John Singleton Copley began to capture American life. The literary field grew with new books and authors covering a wide array of subjects, including, in 1702, the ecclesiastical history of New England, elaborating on the church and documenting its development. Many new towns and settlements were established, including New Orleans in 1718. There were many new and exciting firsts in eighteenth-century colonial America. Benjamin Franklin, always the inquisitor, conducted an unusual experiment on June 10, 1752. He flew a kite with a metal key attached to it during a thunderstorm to attempt to collect an ambient electrical charge in a Leyden jar. This scientific experiment demonstrated the connection between lightning and electricity. Another relatively simple experiment Franklin conducted was using sound and mathematical calculations. He had heard stories of how loud George Whitefield's voice was and felt that they had to be exaggerated. So, he went to see his friend Whitefield while he was preaching an open-air sermon. Franklin slowly walked away and was still able to hear

Eighteenth-Century British America

his booming voice clearly at 500 feet. Combining the distance and the arc of audibility circumference, Benjamin Franklin calculated that as many as 30,000 people could potentially hear his voice in the open air. This, of course, without the assistance of modern amplification. In 1764, in Lewiston, New York, the first American railroad track and line was laid. This was the beginning of connecting the towns and colonies economically and socially with railroad, spawning exponential expansion. French traders Paul and Pierre Malay, along with explorers like Vitus Bering, continued to expand the frontiers of colonial America. Also, in 1750, the Pueblo Indian Revolt led to the creation of the American Indian horse culture of the eighteenth century. Not only did this further the future equine industry, but horses were also a very big part of the culture in general, with riding, breeding, racing, and companionship. And as the tensions between British America and England grew, the Revolutionary War loomed in the distance, and yet this unstable environment stirred the great statesmen and thinkers of the time to emerge and arise, such as the Founding Fathers (Gopnik and Owen, 2023).

CHAPTER 7

George Whitefield

One of the most extraordinary and influential individuals of the eighteenth century was George Whitefield. He was born on December 16, 1714, in Gloucester, United Kingdom, and lived fifty-five remarkable years until he was buried on September 30, 1770, at Newburyport, Massachusetts. He truly was the Billy Graham of the eighteenth century. Just prior to the onset of the American Revolution and the signing of the Declaration of Independence, he had ignited the fires of revival throughout England, the United Kingdom, and British America. Historians later termed this the Great Awakening of the eighteenth century. I find it interesting that in John 4:35 (KJV), Jesus said, "Behold, I say unto you, Lift up your eyes, and look on the *fields*; for they are *white* already to harvest."[1] And that's exactly what Whitefield did. After having an amazing life-changing encounter with God, he spent the remainder of his life sharing this with the world. He became the father of the modern evangelical movement and, along with John Wesley, a founder of the Methodists. When George Whitefield was born at the Bell Inn, which was the family business on Southgate Street, his beginnings were particularly modest. He was born the seventh child of his family, and they were struggling financially. Then, his father died when George was age two. Yet, as poor as his family was, his residence at Gloucester provided him with the advantage of a free and good education at the Crypt

1 Hereinafter, emphasis added.

Grammar School of that city. Here, he was a day scholar until he was fifteen. One notable fact about his school days is that he stood out and was noticed for his excellent elocution. He was selected to recite speeches before the Corporation of Gloucester at their annual visitation of the grammar school. There was a period when he dropped out of school to help his mother with the family business. But after an old schoolmate revived his dream of going to Oxford, he returned to finish grammar school and then was able to move on to college. Although he had no money for tuition, he made it in as a servitor, the lowest entry level. In addition to his regular studies, he would have to tutor fellow students, carry their books, clean their rooms, and perform other duties. Whitefield's residence at Oxford really was the great turning point in his life. There, he was introduced to John and Charles Wesley, with whom he would work closely in his later ministry. At Oxford, he joined the Holy Club and eventually became its leader after John Wesley left the school. Whitefield related that when he was younger, he was naturally inclined to lie, profanity, and other issues of a youth without God. Great conviction came upon him as a member of the Holy Club. He sought God in every way he knew how, wearing the worst clothes and eating the most terrible, modest food, all intentionally, trying to get closer to God. He began to read the Bible on his knees, sometimes praying over every word and line, asking for fresh light, life, and power from above. About this time, after going through various stages and phases of his spiritual journey, George Whitefield had a deep revelation of the doctrine of free grace and experienced a strong religious awakening that he called

George Whitefield

a new birth. It is recorded in John 3:3 (ESV): Jesus answered him, "Truly, truly, I say to you, unless one is born again, he cannot see the kingdom of God." This became a foundational belief of Whitefield and his future ministry. George Whitefield matriculated at Pembroke College at the University of Oxford, graduating in 1732. In 1736, Whitefield was ordained deacon of the Anglican Church and earned his bachelor of arts degree. Although Whitefield had already been developing his skills, preaching to the prisoners and reading the Bible to them at the jail, his first official sermon came one week after his ordination, aged twenty-two. It was at Saint Mary De Crypt Church, Gloucester. He was nervous when he began to preach but then began to feel a fire inside and in his words. He became an itinerant preacher and evangelist, preaching both in churches and sometimes, by necessity, open air. He developed a desire, even at an early age, to go onto all the highways and byways to reach people who did not ordinarily go to church. From the very beginning, he obtained a high degree of popularity, such as no preacher before or since. Wherever he would go, the churches were packed, and an immense sensation was produced, as he was an eloquent extempore preacher of the pure gospel with most uncommon gifts of voice and manner. George Whitefield became increasingly famous in both England and British America. He preached about 18,000 sermons to as many as 10 million people over a period of thirty-four years, which was extraordinary for the 1700s. He also utilized printed media and pamphlets through which half of the population of British America had the opportunity to see a clear presentation of the gospel message. Seventy-eight

The Rise and Fall of the American Empire

of his sermons and forty-five of his autobiographical journals were published to his posterity. He influenced nobility and many of the Founding Fathers, including Benjamin Franklin. But he was at his best, connecting with the common man and people, igniting the Great Awakening of British America. He traveled to America seven different times, sometimes staying for months and years. He would travel British America on horseback, record distances, speaking to thousands. One of his great passions was Bethesda Orphanage, which he founded in 1740. Bethesda means "house of mercy." Although Bethesda was very demanding of his time and energy, as he began to wear out, it established a foundation for the care of orphans in Georgia and other colonies in British America. There were periods of time when he had considerable pushback from the established status quo church leaders, especially regarding his doctrine of the regenerative birth, which later became foundationally accepted and understood in most Christian circles. Whitefield believed that every true believer in God needed to experience a spiritual rebirth in Jesus and be born of the Holy Spirit, a personal conversion beyond church attendance and tradition. He rocked the boat of the established clergy, engaging in numerous debates and disputes, often telling them that their sermons were pathetic and that it would be a miracle if anyone made it to heaven listening to them.

Some historians endlessly debate the purpose of America. I simply believe that the purpose of man is to glorify God and that the purpose of the nations, including America, was to carry out the

George Whitefield

Great Commission as instructed by Jesus prior to His ascension into heaven. George Whitefield was one of the instruments that God used in America and Europe to continue to fulfill that purpose in the eighteenth century. Another notable contribution to America by Whitefield was the big role he played in the establishment of African American Christianity. In all altar calls, he would request the Africans to come forward also at the end of his sermons.

During his short yet remarkable life and ministry, Whitefield once again redirected the focus and the hearts and minds of British America back to God. Whitefield's preaching bolstered the evolving Republican ideology that sought local democratic control of civil affairs and freedom from monarchical and parliamentary intrusion preceding the American Revolution ("George Whitefield: British Clergyman," 2021) (Fairchild, 2019).

CHAPTER 8

The Founding Fathers and the American Revolution

Was America founded as a Christian nation, and is this the thesis that I am trying to put forth with this book? No, not necessarily, and yet the connections are undeniable by recognizing the ever-present hand of God in human affairs, weaving together the destinies of mankind and civilization, whether we acknowledge it or not. And there are those who are content to attempt to remove God entirely from American history to complement the current culture, as they have already made up their minds to not believe in God. You cannot perceive and understand the spiritual and supernatural with the natural mind and intellect. I once met the professor of religious studies of a leading, prestigious American University. He smugly related to me how he had read the New Testament over one hundred times. And as he continued to talk about his vast religious and biblical knowledge, I quickly realized and perceived that he neither believed in God nor the truths of the Scripture. Unfortunately, this is commonplace. It is often now a miracle for a young person to make it through college with their faith intact. It is written in 1 John 4:1–3 (NIV):

> Dear friends, do not believe every spirit, but test the spirits to see whether they are from God, because many false prophets

have gone out into the world. This is how you can recognize the Spirit of God: Every spirit that acknowledges that Jesus Christ has come in the flesh is from God, but every spirit that does not acknowledge Jesus is not from God. This is the spirit of the antichrist, which you have heard is coming and even now is already in the world.

The War Begins

The Revolutionary War from 1775 to 1783, also referred to as the American Revolution, began as skirmishes between the British troops and colonial militiamen. But the seeds of dissent had been growing for decades. Perhaps even being planted by the Native Americans themselves, who repeatedly asked the English and Europeans, "What right do you have to rule over us?" After hearing it so many times, they began to ask the same question: "What right does England have to rule over the colonies of America?" Tensions continued to rise over numerous issues. The British government had spent so much money funding the French and Indian War that they attempted to raise new revenues from the colonies by harsh and unpopular taxes. The Stamp Act of 1765, the Tea Act of 1773, and the Townshend Act of 1767 were all met with resentment and heated protests by the colonists. By the summer of 1776, the rebels were waging a full-scale war for their independence. Leaders such as George Washington began to emerge, demanding representation in parliament and equal rights commensurate with

The Founding Fathers and the American Revolution

British subjects. Another issue raising tensions was the practice of illegal searches of colonist's homes by the British government. Other leaders like Patrick Henry, Samuel Adams, and the Sons of Liberty began to arise and foment rebellion (P. J. Kiger, 2019). Another terrible incident was the Boston Massacre, when British soldiers opened fire on angry colonists. On the night of April 18, 1775, British troops marched from Boston to Concord to seize an arms cache. Paul Revere, Samuel Prescott, William Dawes, and other riders sounded the alarm, and colonial militia began to mobilize to intercept the redcoats. As the colonial militia began to clash with British soldiers on April 19, 1775, was the shot heard around the world, and the Revolutionary War had begun. For the ragtag American colonists to take on the greatest navy and empire in the world of that time and century and to even believe that they had a chance was extraordinary. And as you read these inspiring and heroic tales of overcoming and standing up to the impossible, remember that there is a hero inside of you, too, to make a difference in this time and in this generation.

The Revolutionary War was epic in its reach and in its span, both politically and with rifles and cannons. It would eventually become more of a global conflict as France and even Spain entered the conflict and gave assistance. Some of the colonists leaned loyalist toward Britain, and even high-level traitors like General Benedict Arnold switched sides and conspired later (Seven, 2018). The Native American tribes were divided in allegiance but more actively sided with the British. Spain had already engaged with

Britain in the War of Jenkins' Ear fn 1739 to 1742 and felt that the American colonists had a rig o independence. The War of Jenkins' Ear had far-reaching ets throughout Europe and British America.

The Founding Fathers a he Sons of Liberty had reached the point where they felt that had to break free from the tyrannical rule of Britain (P. J. Kig 2019). It was all or nothing from there on out. On March 23, 5, Patrick Henry gave his fiery "give me liberty or give me de speech. If there were any Americans who were undecided, th changed after the battles of Lexington and Concord. Nearly British and ninety American colonists died that day alone re were many instances of heroism, including the story Margaret Cochran Corbin (Michals, 2015). Not only did M et follow her husband into battle, but when he fell wounded essian and British forces attacked Fort Washington, she ster behind her husband's cannon and continued to fire on advar forces. It took a concerted effort from everyone and ther e, but there were no guarantees of victory, for they were at with the mighty British Army and Empire.

Signing the Declaration of Independence.

There were also many privateers who continued to harass British shipping throughout the war. And there were many noteworthy contributions to the war effort by various Native American tribes. Five thousand African Americans entered the conflict, wielding swords, courage, and rifles (Zielinski, 2020). Many women assisted the cause, giving support on various levels. Even the French and Spanish secretly supplied arms and assistance until later, when they declared war and officially entered the conflict.

The Declaration of Independence

After much debate, the Second Continental Congress agreed upon the Declaration of Independence and signed it. The colonists had only been fighting the Revolutionary War for one year, and the War for Independence would continue for another seven years after that. But this profound action and resolution of independence demanded careful consideration and deliberation. Prior to the signing of the Declaration, Congress appointed a five-member committee to draft a public statement explaining the reasons for declaring independence should Congress decide. The Committee of Five who prepared the draft of the Declaration of Independence were as follows: Benjamin Franklin of Pennsylvania, John Adams of Massachusetts, Robert R. Livingston of New York, Roger Sherman of Connecticut, and the fifth member, Thomas Jefferson of Virginia, was chosen to be the document's principal drafter. As Congress debated the resolution, only nine colonies were prepared to vote in favor. But between July 1 and 2, the situation changed, including Caesar Rodney racing on horseback to Philadelphia from Dover, Delaware. When the vote was called for July 2, the resolution proposed by Richard Henry Lee passed by a vote of 12 to 0, with New York abstaining (L. Kennedy, 2020).

The Founding Fathers united the thirteen colonies, oversaw the War of Independence, established the United States, and created and crafted a framework of government. Seven of the key founders who had signed the United States Declaration of Independence, Articles of Confederation, the United States Constitution, and others demonstrating longevity, leadership, and statesmanship were as follows: George Washington, Benjamin Franklin, Thomas Jefferson, John Adams, Alexander Hamilton, John Jay, and James Madison. George Washington was the commanding general of the Continental Army and a Revolutionary War hero. Presiding over the Constitutional Convention, he became the nation's first president in April of 1790 ("The Founding Fathers," 2019). The Constitutional Congress adopted the Declaration of Independence on July 4, 1776.

The Revolutionary War and Its Culmination

After Thomas Paine's pamphlet *Common Sense* was published in 1776, selling more than 100,000 copies, it clearly unified the public mindset to agree for independence from Britain (P. Kiger, 2021).

Washington Crosses the Delaware

In December of 1776, the British forces drove General Washington and the Continental Army out of their positions in New York City and then across New Jersey. The Continental Army struck back in the most unimaginably difficult circumstances on the night of December 25, 1776. The men were exhausted, hungry, and freezing cold as they crossed the Delaware in the intense wind and snowstorm. The river itself was packed with pockets of ice, but fortunately, that point on the Delaware River was only 300 yards across. Their objective was to attack the Hessian Garrison at Trenton. The English had hired some 30,000 German Hessian soldiers to assist in the war. One advantage they had was the element of surprise, as the commander of the Hessian Garrison felt the Continental Army couldn't possibly attack in that weather. Washington and the Continental Army marched all night and continued to work at crossing the river in a nor'easter. They were utterly exhausted and freezing but, with a final determined burst of energy, attacked the Garrison as one at the break of dawn, gaining victory and 900 prisoners. The triumph at Trenton and later at Princeton roused the morale of the country and the Continental Army.

The Surrender of Burgoyne

The surrender of British General John Burgoyne at Saratoga, New York, on October 17, 1777, occurred after battles with American General Horatio Gates in September and October of 1777. By the time General Burgoyne had retreated to Saratoga, he had been weakened and lost many men. It was one more important turning point in the war as it prevented Britain from separating New England from the rest of the colonies. And it was also a deciding factor in bringing active French support.

Washington Winters at Valley Forge

In December of 1777, General George Washington moved the Continental Army to their winter quarters at Valley Forge. It was probably the steady, stable leadership of General George Washington that halted desertion or, worse, a mutiny. It was a perfectly miserable winter there, but out of these very real adversities came very strategic and critical improvements for the Continental Army. It was an absolute and constant challenge to obtain food and keep them fed. There were never enough lodges, and many had to sleep outdoors. The temperatures were often well below freezing, and many did not have winter coats, blankets, or shoes. Two individuals were indispensable in helping transform this ragtag army into a far better-drilled, prepared fighting machine. Baron Friedrich Wilhelm von Steuben and the Marquis de La Fayette, primarily, and Alexander Hamilton and Nathaniel Greene played a big role in the transformation of the Continental Army. Von Steuben was astonished and appalled at the Continental Army's lack of skills and training. First, Baron von Steuben formed a model company of soldiers and trained them to march, use the bayonet, and execute orders quickly on the battlefield. And in turn, this company began to train the other able-bodied soldiers at Valley Forge. Despite the incredible hardships and adversities of that winter at Valley Forge, the Continental Army emerged in June of 1778, a much better trained, skilled, and disciplined fighting force.

Alliance Formed with France

Other European allies, such as Spain, had been assisting the Americans with armaments, supplies, and clothes, but the French were of primary help. On February 6, 1778, France and the United States formed an alliance. The French had been secretly supplying aid since 1776 but formally declared war on Britain in June 1778. This was a significant turning point in the war, boosting morale and taking what seemed an impossibility to gaining a vision for victory. With the signing of the Treaty of Amity and Commerce and the Treaty of Alliance, the Franco-American Alliance was formalized. France prepared fleets and armies and strategized with the Americans how to defeat the British.

Commander John Paul Jones

Sighting two enemy ships of war with merchantmen and naval military stores, Commander Jones's *Bonhomme Richard* engaged the British frigate *Serapis* in an epic three-and-a-half-hour duel. Jones was ordered to surrender but answered, "I have not yet begun to fight." Even though the Bonham Richard was indeed sinking, Commander John Paul Jones outlasted his adversary and forced the *Serapis* to surrender before the *Bonhomme Richard* sank. Commander Jones and his remaining men were able to board the *Serapis* and take the ship over. Approximately 300 men were killed in the battle (John Paul Jones, 2009).

General Benedict Arnold

After being passed over for promotion to the post of major general, Arnold tried to resign from the Continental Army. George Washington refused to accept the resignation. In 1778 and 1779, Arnold expressed disappointment and pessimism about an American victory, and evidence mounted that he was conspiring with the British military to give them sensitive information for money. He was almost court-martial but was ironically cleared at least the first time. But then he did it again. After gaining command of West Point Fort, he once again entered secret negotiations with the British military. He passed on information to assist the British capture of West Point. John Andre, Arnold's British contact, was captured and hanged. Arnold narrowly avoided capture and eventually fled to England. Arnold served in the British Army for the duration of the war and died in 1801, his name becoming synonymous with treachery, betrayal, and self-interest (Seven, 2018).

Articles of Confederation Ratified

On March 1, 1781, the Articles of Confederation were ratified and served as a bridge until the United States Constitution was established in 1787. Although the articles were written from 1776 to 1777 and adopted on November 15, 1777, they were not fully ratified until March 1, 1781.

Siege of Yorktown

After Lord Cornwallis set up a base at Yorktown with other British forces, Washington's army and the French army led by Count de Rochambeau placed Yorktown under siege, and Cornwallis and his army of 7,000 surrendered on October 19, 1781. After French assistance helped the Continental Army to force the British to surrender at Yorktown, the Americans had effectively won the war and gained their independence, although fighting did not formally end until 1783.

Treaty of Paris on September 3, 1783

After the British defeat at Yorktown, the land battles in America largely died out, but fighting continued at sea, primarily between the British and America's European allies, which came to include Spain and the Netherlands. By the terms of the Anglo-American Peace Treaty of 1782 and Treaty of Paris 1783, Britain recognized the independence of the United States, with the Mississippi River being the western boundary. Britain kept Canada but ceded East and West Florida to Spain ("Revolutionary War," 2009).

Religious Beliefs of the Founders and Delegates

As we wind up the events of the eighteenth century and move into the nineteenth, let's take a little look at the spiritual beliefs of the delegates and some of the founders. God can work through anyone, including non-Christians. For example, Winston Churchill really was not a devout Christian, but God worked through him in remarkable history-shaping ways.

Of the fifty-five delegates to the Constitutional Convention in 1787, twenty-eight were Anglicans (Church of England or Episcopalians), twenty-one were different types of Protestants, and three were Catholics. Among the Protestant delegates to the Constitutional Convention, eight were Presbyterians, seven were Congregationalists, two were Lutherans, two were Dutch Reformed, and two were Methodists. Although Orthodox Christians participated at every stage of the New Republic, Deism influenced most of the founders. Deism believes in the existence of a supreme being, yet believes that this supreme being, or God, did not interact with mankind or intervene in the affairs of the universe. John 3:16 (KJV) states, "For God so love the world, that he gave his only begotten Son, that whosoever believeth in him should not perish, but have everlasting life." I think God the Father did intervene in mankind's affairs by sending Jesus to the earth to atone for mankind's sins. And Jesus, who was God in the flesh, interacted with mankind for the thirty-three years that He was on the earth prior to His ascension into heaven. Now, after the ascension of Jesus, the Third Person of the Trinity, the Holy Spirit, continues to intervene and interact in the affairs of mankind (Leidner, 2012).

CHAPTER 9

The Advent of Nineteenth-Century America

Charles Grandison Finney

Charles Finney was an American Presbyterian minister who has been called the Father of Old Revivalism. He was born at the end of the eighteenth century, August 29, 1792, in Warren, Connecticut, and was raised in Oneida County, New York. He was a leader in the Second Great Awakening in nineteenth-century America. He rejected a lot of traditional Reformed theology. So, he taught that people have complete free will to choose salvation. Nobody was born destined to be lost but had complete free will to choose Jesus, to believe in and follow Him. He helped transform Christian values into American values. He was also a devoted abolitionist and encouraged Christians to see it as a moral issue rather than a political or economic issue. One of the great things that he helped to end was slavery. His belief in free will ran against the grain of some theology that stated that only the elect would be saved. He taught that all people were sinners separated from a holy God, but they could have peace with God by repenting from their sins and accepting Jesus Christ as their savior.

In the early nineteenth century, America was going through a period of intense change and reform. America was still a young country, having just gained independence from Britain. They found their own identity apart from that of England in many ways, including their own church, which was separate from Anglicanism. Leaders like Charles Finney and Lyman Beecher rose up to affect a generation in the Second Great Awakening of America. After being a teacher for a short time, Finney studied law and then became an attorney in New York. References in his study of law to Mosaic institutions and law prompted him to a more in-depth examination and study of the Bible. In 1821, Charles Finney had a profound religious conversion that affected the remainder of his life. Finney dropped his law practice and, after being licensed by the Presbyterians, became an evangelist. Spirited revivals broke out in the villages of upstate New York. He would take the truths of the scriptures and the skills that he had developed in persuading juries to communicate and convince the congregants of the necessity to decide for God. Combined with his keen intellect and the spirit of God working through him, he continued to flourish and develop his preaching skills, perhaps smoothing them out and refining them in time, still making his points but not perhaps so harshly. He continued to preach in larger towns and churches, and his revivals achieved spectacular success. In 1832, he held an almost continuous revival in New York City as minister of the Second Free Presbyterian Church. Apparently, Finney and a few of his congregants didn't feel that the Free Presbyterian Church was all that free, and in 1834, after issues with doctrine and theology, they built an entirely new church in New York called Broadway Tabernacle. The following year, he became a professor of theology in the newly formed School of Theology in Oberlin, Ohio. He split his time between his post as professor of theology at Oberlin and minister at Broadway Tabernacle. Perhaps to simplify matters, he left New York in 1837 to become minister of Oberlin's First Congregational Church, close to and closely related to Oberlin College, where he was the president from 1851 to 1866. Charles Finney's theological views and teachings influenced a generation of ministers. He believed humanity was incapable of reforming itself without the transforming power of God. In 1835, he published his *Lectures on Revivals of Religion*, and in 1847, he published *Lectures on Systematic Theology*. Charles Grandison Finney, considered by many to be the father of modern evangelism, whose revival sparked the Second Great Awakening in America, died on August 6, 1875, aged eighty-two, in Oberlin, Ohio ("Charles Grandison Finney: American Evangelist," 2020) (Finney G., 1988).

In the year 1800, the United States was still a fledgling nation, developing and finding its way. By the time the century ended, America had expanded westward exponentially, had become a world power, revolutionized our economy from mostly agricultural to significant manufacturing, and suffered the divide of a civil war that nearly brought the nation to an end.

The Louisiana Purchase

Signed on April 30, 1803, the United States successfully purchased 828,000 square miles of land from France for only $15 million. This equates to roughly four cents an acre, effectively doubling the land size of America and expanding the nation westward. It was an enormous piece of land that extended Mississippi to the Rockies and from the Gulf of Mexico to the Canadian border. This providential purchase continued to open many possibilities for American growth and expansion. Perhaps one of the reasons Napoleon gave up his plans for Louisiana was the threat of looming war with England. Napoleon surprised Robert Livingston and James Monroe with an offer of $15 million for the entire deal and territory. This marked the first time that the United States had acquired territory by treaty with another nation. As great of a deal and opportunity as it was, some leaders opposed it because it would greatly extend the liability and responsibility financially of the United States. The United States had to borrow from two European banks at 6 percent, and it took until 1823 to finally pay it off at a final total cost of $23 million ("Louisiana Purchase," 2019).

The Great American West.

The Advent of Nineteenth-Century America

Lewis and Clark

From May 14th, 1804, to September 23, 1806, Merriweather Lewis, Lewis Clark, and the Corps of Discovery, which was composed of forty men, traveled on an expedition exploring thousands of miles of the West. The Corps of Discovery left from the northern plains of the area just outside Saint Louis, called Camp Wood, to officially launch their expedition. Amazingly, they traveled from there through the Rocky Mountains, all the way to the Pacific Ocean, and then back. The remarkable expedition was organized by President Thomas Jefferson, who hoped to not only explore the recently acquired territories but also to determine once and for all if a Northwest Passage to the Pacific existed or not. They also hoped to establish a trade network and befriend the different Indian tribes as they traveled. They determined that there was no Northwestern all-water passage but that it was possible to reach the Pacific overland. They had an impressive record of peaceful cooperation with the different native tribes that they met along the way. Also, Sacagawea, a Lemhi Shoshone in her teens, helped to guide the corps of discovery along the approximately 5,000-mile journey. Her help was indispensable for Lewis and Clark to be able to communicate with other Native Americans and trade for horses and supplies along the way. Perhaps some of the most valuable information they obtained was the scientific and anthropological data. They took notes and filled journals with all the information about the different Native American tribes they encountered and the plants, animals, fish, and reptiles. They also made a systematic record of the meteorology (weather patterns). The weather that they encountered was sometimes extremely harsh, and some of the men had frostbite. Often, mosquitoes were a big problem, as were boils and foot sores. When they finally reached the Pacific Ocean in mid-November, they were ecstatic and proclaimed, "Ocean in view! Oh, the joy!" The journey strengthened the claims to future states, such as Washington and Oregon, for America. They did extensive mapping along the way, especially the Missouri River and its tributaries. One thing they did for sure was bring back tales and stories of the amazing West, inspiring thousands of people to eventually go there, realizing the great dream of heading West. Above all, the Lewis and Clark Expedition set the stage for further land expansion for America in the future ("Lewis and Clark Expedition," 2009).

The War of 1812

Perhaps the United States had many reasons for going back to war with Britain in 1812. Britain's interference with its trade and seamen, American desire to expand settlement, aspirations to conquer Canada and end British influence and meddling in North America, upholding the nation's sovereignty and honor. While the war hawks were pushing to go to war, the two presidents of that era, Thomas Jefferson and James Madison, were not convinced that it was a good idea. They thought that it would be better to just let Britain and France slug it out in the Napoleonic Wars. However, war hawk John C. Calhoun felt that the United States needed to finish its struggle for liberty and independence. When Britain began to capture American seamen off merchant ships and forced

The Advent of Nineteenth-Century America

them to serve in the British Navy, this angered the US so much and became the official cause of initiating the War of 1812.

A War Begins and Ends Inconclusively

Britain effectively won the War of 1812 by successfully defending its North American colonies, but they were far from getting everything they wanted. To Britain, the American conflict was secondary as they were already locked into a do-or-die battle with Napoleon and France in Europe. The British mood was such that they were already tired of being at war and were unwilling to maintain a protracted battle with the United States. York (now Toronto), Niagara, and Washington, DC, were all torched and burnt to the ground. In many areas, the war caused chaos and destruction to families, homes, and towns. The human cost was steep, with some 35,000 people losing their lives, being wounded, or missing by the war's end. Americans looked on the conflict as a victorious second war of independence because they had felt bullied and oppressed by the British Empire. As they resorted to war and asserted themselves, they compelled Britain and the world to acknowledge American sovereignty and power. Native Americans who had fought as British allies were bitterly disappointed with the war's outcome. They had hoped to push back American frontier settlement and expansion. Instead, at war's end, they felt abandoned by the British and suffered catastrophic defeat. Britain agreed to maintain the previously established boundaries as it was completely engrossed with its conflict with France, so the old lines between British North America and the United States were reconfirmed and kept by the Treaty of Ghent, signed December 24, 1814, ending the war ("War of 1812," 2023).

Harriet Tubman

Harriet Tubman, whose birth name was Araminta Ross, was probably born about March of 1822, as exact records are unknown, in Dorchester County, Maryland. The amazing stories and life of Harriet Tubman have taken on legendary proportions. Despite the early years of abuse, whippings, beatings, and being struck in the head with a heavy piece of metal by her slave owners, Harriet had a deep and profound faith in God that would truly carry her throughout her life. When Harriet was still very young, she watched her mother stand up to the slave owner who was going to sell her brother Moses and separate him from the family. That definitely had a big impact on her and stayed with her.

The first time that Harriet tried to escape, it did not go very well. She had left with her brothers Henry and Ben, and they began to worry about and think of the rest of the family and decided to go back. The second time, she left alone, and with the aid of the Underground Railroad, she made it all the way successfully. The Underground Railroad, which Harriet later led, was a secret network of people, places, and routes that provided shelter and assistance to escaping slaves. She left Maryland in the fall of 1849 and found freedom in Philadelphia, Pennsylvania. The journey to freedom was no less than exhilarating when she crossed the line. Her journey to freedom inspired her to go back to Maryland to

The Advent of Nineteenth-Century America

help free her family and others. One of her strategies was to execute the rescues in the winter and travel at night to draw less attention. From 1851 to 1862, Harriet completed about thirteen rescue expeditions, repeatedly going back to the shores of eastern Maryland. She was also able to get her brothers Henry, Ben, and Robert, their wives, and some of the children. Harriet and the fugitives that she assisted to escape were never captured. Years later, she told an audience, "I was the conductor of the Underground Railroad for eight years, and I never lost a passenger or derailed the train." Frederick Douglass, the Martin Luther King of the 1800s, worked for slavery abolition alongside Harriet Tubman. He worked by day in the open in the political and governmental sphere, whereas Harriet was effective working at night, in the dark, in secret with the Underground Railroad. As she led escapees across the border to freedom, she would cry out, "Glory to God and Jesus, too; one more soul is safe." This was Harriet's calling and destiny, and she would also do other notable exploits in the future. Her friend Thomas Garrett once said of Harriet, "I never met anyone who had more confidence in hearing the voice of God in her soul." Harriet Tubman said that she had an open vision once when God showed her that the Civil War would bring about the end of slavery in the United States. During the Civil War, Harriet was an armed scout and nurse and even operated as a spy for the Union Army.

Later, she helped to start a home for the aged, and ironically, that is where she spent the last couple of years of her life. The last thing Harriet Tubman said was a quotation from Jesus's words in

The Rise and Fall of the American Empire

John 14:3: "I go away to prepare a place for you" (paraphrased). A very brave woman who led a remarkable life. She died on March 10, 1913, and was buried at Fort Hill Cemetery in Auburn, New York (Dawson, 2015).

Invention of the Typewriter

The invention of the typewriter may seem like a small thing, but it actually was very important in many ways. It led to the computer keyboard of the modern computer. The first American typewriter, called a typographer, was invented by William Austin Burt. Burt was brilliant and had many new inventions, including the solar compass. Although Pellegrino Turri had already made a topographer in Italy in 1808, W. A. Burt had designed the first working American model and patented it in 1829. Sadly, Burt's first working model was burned up in the 1836 Patent Office fire. The typographer was slow and initially not very successful. Christopher Latham Sholes invented the first modern typewriter in 1867, which revolutionized the office and office work. Shoals invited Thomas A. Edison to see his invention, the "miracle machine," and Edison said that one day soon, it would be operated by electricity. In 1914, they brought the electric-operated typewriter to a consistent and practical level and value with the introduction and development of the electric IBM typewriter. Although no record or description of the invention survived, Queen Anne of England granted a patent to Henry Mills on January 7, 1714, for a typography device that neatly printed characters (Tolentino, 2023).

The Advent of Nineteenth-Century America

The California Gold Rush

The next segment could have been taken from Ripley's Believe It or Not! as sometimes reality is stranger than fiction. What in the world would compel Americans from the eastern United States to uproot, leaving everything that they know, from 1848 through the 1850s, to go to the unknown distant territory of California! Besides the Americans, people from China, Europe, South America, and from all over the globe began to go to California, most disembarking ships in San Francisco. Prior to 1847, San Francisco was the small, sleepy settlement called Yerba Buena. Most of the migrants traveling to California came from the eastern United States and could basically get there by one of three routes. The so-called safest route was a nearly 18,000-mile journey sailing around Cape Horn, the southernmost tip of South America. Besides the trip itself taking approximately five months, the waters around Cape Horn are very dangerous due to strong winds, icebergs, large waves, and strong ocean currents. And then there was the Panama shortcut, where you could potentially cut a few months off the trip and reduce the distance by about 8,000 miles. However, there were several serious obstacles with the Panama shortcut, including yellow fever and malaria and the uncertainty of being able to find another ship on the other side of the Ismith to continue the journey to California. Then, the other option was the overland routes using covered wagons pulled by oxen, covering thousands of miles and easily taking four to six months. Disease was the biggest killer on this route. Travelers fell victim to cholera, mountain fever, pneumonia, and diphtheria. Hundreds of gold

The Rise and Fall of the American Empire

seekers died and were buried along the trail. The strain took a toll on the oxen and mules as well.

So, what was this euphoric dream that triggered the California Gold Rush starting in 1848? Perhaps it was the tales and true stories of gold holes, large nuggets, and abundant veins discovered. They had been bitten by the gold bug and now had gold fever. It is recorded that nearly 300,000 people descended upon California from all over the globe, primarily Americans from the east, from 1848 to 1855. This great influx of people permanently changed the landscape and demographics of California. But let's take a step back to how this all started.

In 1848, John Augustus Sutter was having a water-powered sawmill built along the American River in Coloma, California, where modern-day Sacramento now is. On January 24, 1848, his carpenter, James W. Marshall, found flakes of gold in a streambed. They agreed to become partners and tried to keep the discovery a secret but to no avail. Perhaps it was Henry Bigler, who was working at Sutter's mill and who routinely kept a journal of daily activities, including the discovery of the gold, that got the word out. Sutter's mill was first invaded by hundreds of locals, then besieged by thousands of fortune seekers thereafter. With his property continuing to be overrun, plundered, and destroyed, John Sutter and the mill were bankrupt and ruined by 1852. The miners and prospectors who began to descend upon the area in 1849 were called forty-niners. But the truth is, very few of the individual miners and seekers became wealthy or rich, with the inflated cost of everything: food, shelter, tools, provisions, et cetera. And the fact that corporate mining operations backed by government and law enforcement quickly began to move in. Up until that time, it had been somewhat of a free-for-all in the Wild West California Gold Rush. Some 750,000 lbs. of gold were extracted from 1848 to 1853, and, by today's value of 22.4 thousand per pound, would have put the value in the billions of dollars.

Prior to the influx of people, most of the population of the territory of California was primarily Native Americans, with a smaller number of Mexican and American residents. By 1860, the Gold Rush was all but over, but the population of California had swelled to 380,000 people by that time. California was admitted to the Union on September 9, 1850, and became the thirty-first state ("California Gold Rush," 2022).

Abraham Lincoln

CHAPTER 10

Abraham Lincoln

Abraham Lincoln came from the humblest of beginnings to go on to be the sixteenth president of the United States of America. Twice elected to the highest office, he basically had about one year total of formal education but continued to self-educate. He pressed on through law school and eventually to a most remarkable political career. And as exceptional as this was, what was even more impressive was Abraham Lincoln's spiritual journey. When he was very young, he had just a few different books to read, including the family Bible and John Bunyan's *The Pilgrim's Progress*, written in 1678. Abraham had always believed in God from the time he was a small boy, but things changed and became clearer as he neared the end of his life. The immense pressures of the presidency and the Civil War caused Abraham to fervently pray and seek God for wisdom and guidance. It was as if his eyes began to increasingly be opened to the reality that there was a bigger battle going on in Washington, DC, the Civil War, and for the very soul and survival of the nation. Lincoln had always held the belief that slavery was wrong, but he began to see more clearly just how evil it really was. Abraham Lincoln was shot on Good Friday, April 14, 1865, and then died the following day. But not before God had used him as an instrument to end the Civil War, preserve the Union, and issue the Emancipation Proclamation, effectively ending slavery. Now, let's go back to the beginning of Abraham Lincoln's journey back

The Rise and Fall of the American Empire

to Larue County, Kentucky, on February 12, 1809.

Abraham was born on a Sunday in a backwoods cabin three miles South of Hodgenville, and winter still had its grip on Kentucky that cold February 12. Today, Larue County was Hardin County in 1809, and baby Lincoln lived there at his father's sinking Spring Farm for just two years. In 1811, the Lincoln family moved to the adjacent valley of Knob Creek to that farm just ten miles away. Lincoln, later describing his early years, said he was raised to farm work (Lincoln, 2013). Some of Abraham's earliest memories were of planting pumpkin and corn seeds at this farm with his father and then how a heavy rainstorm came, causing a flash flood that would wash away all their work and seeds.

His father, Thomas Lincoln, was the descendant of a weaver's apprentice who had migrated to Massachusetts in 1637. Perhaps some of Thomas's European predecessors were more well-to-do, but he was a sturdy pioneer of early America. On June 12, 1806, Thomas Lincoln married Nancy Hanks. She was said to be melancholy but fervently religious. They had three children together: Sarah, Abraham, and Thomas Junior. In December 1816, Thomas and Nancy moved from Kentucky to southwestern Indiana out of necessity. They needed to find a new home because of legal issues over the title to their current farm. Like dozens of others, Thomas Lincoln fell victim to Kentucky's chaotic land laws, and on three separate occasions, defective titles caused him to lose his farm. They hoped to solve these problems with the move to Indiana, but starting out there was anything but easy. Just imagine this: when

Abraham Lincoln

the Lincoln family first arrived in December of 1816, there was no home to live in. Starting out, Thomas built a temporary structure until he could complete the fully enclosed permanent cabin. The first crude structure, made of logs and bows, was completely open to the air and the elements on one side. The best that they could do in the freezing winter temperatures, to stay warm and to keep wild animals away, was to maintain a blazing campfire. This was early Indiana frontier living. Seven-year-old Abraham did the best that he could to help his family clear the fields, construct the enclosed cabin, and take care of the crops. After the fall of 1818, it took everything Thomas Lincoln had to keep going. His faith in God, determination, and the love of his children, Sarah and Abraham. At the age of eight, Thomas Lincoln Sr. had witnessed the murder of his father by the Native Americans. Then his son Thomas Jr. died in infancy, and now his wife, Nancy, died after drinking tainted milk. Abraham had to endure the sad, cold winter of 1818 without the love and warmth of his mother. But the hand of Providence was upon Thomas and the Lincolns, as he swiftly found a great new wife in Kentucky the following year. The cheerful, energetic Sarah Bush Johnston had also recently lost her spouse; she was raising three children alone, and they needed each other. She loved all the blended family equally, as if she had borne them all, but Sarah was especially fond of Abraham. Suddenly, most of the sadness was gone, and it was a new chapter and beginning for the seven members of the blended Lincoln family on the Indiana frontier. Abraham was already nearly as tall as his stepmother, Sarah, and he was learning invaluable life lessons from both her and his father, Thomas, that continued to build his character. But perhaps it was the hand of God Himself who slowly began to awaken the greatness and destiny inside young Abraham.

Once again, in the spring of 1830, the Lincoln family moved, this time to Illinois, and with a full-grown twenty-one-year-old Abraham driving the team of oxen. Abraham was just about ready to leave his family and go out on his own. He tried a variety of different things, including tug boating and rail splitting. He had developed a reputation for how hard he could swing a large, heavy axe with his lengthy, muscular six-foot-four frame. During the Black Hawk War of 1832, he enlisted as a volunteer and was elected captain of his company. He later joked that their biggest battle was with the mosquitoes. Something within him continued to drive him to learn, read, and self-educate, and soon, he was elected to the State Assembly as a legislator. He taught himself grammar and mathematics and then began to diligently study law books. He took the bar examination in 1836, passed, and began to practice law.

The following year, he moved from New Salem to the new state capitol, Springfield, Illinois. The capital opened new doors and opportunities with different partnerships until, finally, he formed a very successful law partnership with the younger William H. Herndon in 1844. He continued to blossom both in his career as an attorney and in his eloquence as a speaker. Abraham was a very hard worker, and not only did he develop his practice in the capital, but he was willing to travel the circuits by buggy or

Abraham Lincoln

horseback throughout the state. He handled both small and large cases for banks, insurance companies, and mercantile and manufacturing firms. Lincoln rose to become one of the most distinguished and successful lawyers in Illinois. He was well known for his shrewd, practical common sense, possessing a unique ability to see to the heart of legal cases but also demonstrating fairness and complete honesty. About twenty years after launching his legal career, Lincoln became increasingly prominent in national politics.

While Lincoln was living in New Salem, he had just the beginning of a romance with Ann Rutledge, but sadly, she died at the young age of twenty-two. A year after that, he courted Mary Owens, but it did not work out. Later, after he had moved to Springfield, he met the well-educated, quick-witted, and high-spirited Mary Todd. Her distinguished family and Springfield relatives belonged to the social hierarchy of the town, and frankly, Abraham was a little intimidated by her and her family. He broke off their engagement in January of 1841. He was terribly sad and despondent, but Mary smoothed things over with her parents and assured Abraham that he was the one she wanted to marry. After the two reconciled, they were married on November 4, 1842. Abraham was the steady, stable one, and she was the spitfire who had what it took to be the first lady of the White House in the future. She unquestionably encouraged her husband in the early years and served as an inspiration to his own ambitions. During the later years, her often erratic behavior tested his innate qualities of tolerance and patience. They had four children, all boys, but only Robert Todd,

The Rise and Fall of the American Empire

the eldest, lived to adulthood. There were times when Lincoln seemed to be put off by the religious hypocrisy that he observed, both in the church and politics. But Mary would continue to steer them back to attendance at the Presbyterian churches in Springfield and Washington. Perhaps there had always been some innate mental health issues with Mary Todd, but a lifetime of stress took it to another level. She had witnessed and experienced the death of three of her sons and lived through the agony of the Civil War, with friends and family often taking the Confederate position and point of view. She had felt the pressures and criticisms of being the first lady, as if no matter what she did, there were many who were not happy with her. Sometimes, she extravagantly overspent to impress people, but that created other problems. Finally, she accompanied her husband to the Ford Theater the night his assassin shot him in the back of the head. She stayed at his side throughout the night, but he died in the morning. Whatever his motives and anxieties for his mother were, Robert Todd Lincoln had his mother placed into a mental asylum for three months in 1875 until she was declared sane and obtained her release. Mary Todd Lincoln died at the home of her sister in Springfield, Illinois, on July 16, 1882.

When Abraham first entered politics, Andrew Jackson was the sitting president, and Jacksonian politics was the order of the day. Lincoln agreed with much of Jacksonian politics but disagreed with the idea that the government should be divorced from economic enterprise. He felt that the government should help the community of people accomplish things that need to be done,

Abraham Lincoln

things that they are unable to do by themselves. He also admired Henry Clay and Daniel Webster and associated himself with their party, the Whigs, from the outset. The Whigs advocated using the powers of the federal government to encourage business and aid economic development. In Lincoln's view, Illinois and the West needed such government help for economic development. Lincoln was elected four times, from 1834 to 1840, as a Whig to the Illinois State Legislature. Lincoln also served one term in Congress, from 1847 to 1849, as the lone Whig from Illinois. He also took great interest in and devoted considerable time to presidential politics while James K. Polk was in office. He held considerable influence in the election of war hero Zachary Taylor and hoped to be appointed the commissioner of the general land office, but it did not work out. By the age of forty, he was frustrated with politics and seemed to be in the twilight of his public career. For about five years, Lincoln took a big step back from politics but was watching things closely the whole time. A sectional crisis occurred in 1854 when his political rival, Stephen A. Douglas, maneuvered through Congress a bill reopening the entire Louisiana Purchase to slavery. The Kansas-Nebraska Act ignited violent opposition in Illinois and the other states of the Old Northwest. All this political pushing and pulling gave rise to the Republican Party and accelerated the disintegration of the Whig Party. Lincoln, along with thousands of other Whigs, soon became Republican in 1856. Shortly after, a group of prominent Eastern Republicans lobbied the idea of attracting Douglas to the Republican fold, but Lincoln was adamantly against it. He was determined that he would be the

The Rise and Fall of the American Empire

leader of his state and section, not Douglas. Lincoln and Douglas went head-to-head for election to the Senate seat in 1858 and engaged in a series of debates of the highest political oratory and order. Although Lincoln lost that election, his prose and speeches were remarkable, pithy, and powerful and gained him national attention. That, together with a best-selling biography of Lincoln, soon had his name circulating as the next possible president. On May 18th, 1860, after lengthy preparations, Lincoln was nominated on the third ballot at the Republican National Convention in Chicago. He then set aside his law practice and gave full-time attention to his presidential campaign. Even though Lincoln and Douglas were pretty close in their basic political views, Lincoln held that Congress must exclude slavery from the territories. And in one of his most famous speeches, Lincoln said, "A house divided against itself cannot stand. I believe the government cannot permanently endure half slave and half free." He predicted that the country would become one or the other. He insisted that the civil liberties of every US citizen, White and Black, were at stake. During the campaign, he wisely counseled all party workers to say nothing on points where it was probable we would disagree. With the Republicans united, the Democrats divided, and a total of four candidates in the field, he carried the election and won on November 6, 1860.

Even from the outset of Lincoln's presidency, there was serious trouble in the water as the state of South Carolina proclaimed its withdrawal from the Union. To stop other Southern states from following in the footsteps of South Carolina, various compromises were proposed in Congress, including the Crittenden Compromise. Lincoln was adamantly against the latter half of the Crittenden Compromise and said that it was putting us again on the high road to a slave empire. He advised Republicans to vote against it, and the Crittenden compromise was killed in committee. Six additional states succeeded, and with South Carolina, they combined to form the Confederate States of America ("Abraham Lincoln," 2009) (Current, 2023).

CHAPTER 11

The American Civil War

Throughout history, God has often raised up a Cyrus, that is, a key individual leader placed strategically by God in the middle of a national or international mess or crisis to help fix or solve it. Cyrus the Great himself lived from about 600 to 530 BC, and in his lifetime, he set the Jews free from their Babylonian captivity and facilitated their return to the Promised Land. He, in essence, became a type of savior and deliverer who also helped the Jews to build the second temple in Jerusalem. Winston Churchill was another Cyrus, raised up by God to stop Kaiser Wilhelm in World War I and Adolf Hitler in World War II. Another way that Churchill was used, which fewer people are aware of, is that while he was colonial secretary, he secured the League of Nations Mandate, prompting the formal adoption of Zionism into British foreign policy and consequently enabling Jewish nationhood. Another Cyrus was Harry Truman, who helped arrange the unconditional surrender of Germany in May 1945 and then the surrender of Japan, effectively ending World War II.

And God raised up another Cyrus in Abraham Lincoln. He was successful in ending slavery and maintaining the Union of the United States. When Lincoln became president and faced the profound difficulties of the Civil War, he developed a deep religious sense and came to look at himself quite humbly as an instrument of Providence and to view all history as God's enterprise. And that

The Rise and Fall of the American Empire

God sometimes used people to write that history. Lincoln knew the Bible well and was consistently praying while president.

Before Lincoln had even moved into the White House with Mary Todd and his family, a disunion crisis had descended upon the nation. Also, Fort Sumter in Charleston Harbor, South Carolina, came under threat by the Confederate army, who claimed it. This fort was still under construction, garrisoned by US troops under the command of Major Robert Anderson. Right away, President Lincoln could foresee trouble and confidentially communicated with the general in chief of the US Army, Winfield Scott, to be prepared to either hold or retake the forts, as the case may require, at and after the inauguration. In his inaugural address, he restated his Sumter policy, upheld the Union's indestructibility, and appealed for sectional harmony. Then, near the end of the address, he spoke to the absent southern leaders and said you can have no conflict without being yourselves the aggressors. No sooner than Lincoln had just begun his presidency, the Confederate authorities demanded Fort Sumter's immediate evacuation, which Commander Major Anderson refused.

On April 12, 1861, at dawn, the Confederate batteries in the harbor opened fire. When Congress had convened, Lincoln informed them that, then and thereby, the Confederates began the conflict of arms by their aggression. Lincoln was determined to preserve the Union, and to do so, he thought that he must take a stand against the Confederacy. He decided that this stand might as well start at Fort Sumter. After the attack on Fort Sumter, Lincoln called upon the state governors for troops, and Virginia and three other states of the Upper South responded by joining the Confederacy. He then ordered a blockade of the southern ports.

On July 21, 1861, the Union army made a direct advance on the Virginia Fort at Bull Run, but it resulted in defeat for the Federal forces. Lincoln had several sleepless nights trying to think of better ways to succeed and move forward. For better or worse, Lincoln had little or no experience in military command. On the positive, he held no outdated concepts of military strategy. It was a learning curve, but one of the indicators of Lincoln's military genius was his assembly of a very capable war cabinet. Thus, Lincoln pioneered the creation of a high command, an organization for amassing all the energies and resources of a people in the grand strategy of total war. Month by month and each year, they improved the effectiveness, overall success, and direction of the armies.

Over a period of four years, Union and Confederate forces met in more than 10,000 armed confrontations across the nation, ranging from small clashes to full-scale battles involving tens of thousands of soldiers and locations from Vermont to Arizona. If anyone was under the illusion that the Civil War would be short and quick, including President Lincoln, it wasn't, and it took a massive toll. According to National Park Service statistics, 110,100 men on the Union side were killed in action, and another 275,174 were wounded in action. Ninety-four thousand Confederate soldiers were killed in action, and another 194,026 were wounded.

The Rise and Fall of the American Empire

Still, more soldiers died of disease, starvation, and accidents, and many of the wounded later died. The death toll for the Civil War could have been more than 700,000. There were stories of families, cousins, and sometimes brothers being on either the side of the North or the South, fighting directly with one another. When Mary Todd Lincoln moved into the White House with her husband, many friends and family suddenly became adversarial.

Sometimes, Lincoln was wrong about a general, and they would prove to be better, smarter, and more capable than he realized. And sometimes, he made changes. He accepted the resignation of General Winfield Scott in November of 1861 and then tried General George B. McClellan for a while but was disgusted eventually with how slow he was to make decisions and move. Eventually, he placed General Ulysses S. Grant as his top general over the Union forces. Lincoln finally found in General Grant, along with solid subordinates William T. Sherman, Phillip Sheridan, and George H. Thomas, a capable war cabinet that could put into effect those parts of Lincoln's concept of a large-scale coordinated offensive that still needed to be carried out. Taking the responsibility for men and supplies was Secretary of War Edwin M. Stanton. Henry W. Halleck, chief of staff, served as a presidential adviser and as a liaison with military officers in the field. General in Chief Ulysses S. Grant directed all the armies while accompanying General Meade's army of the Potomac.

Bull Run

The Civil War's first major battle began on July 21, 1861, at the First Battle of Bull Run. Marching out of Washington, DC, into Virginia, Union General Irvin McDowell was intent on seizing the Confederate capital of Richmond and ending the conflict quickly. Most of General McDowell's men were naive ninety-day volunteers, inexperienced farmhands who were barely past being boys. They came up against the powerful force commanded by General P. G. T. Beauregard, and with their zeal and intensity, they drove them back and thought that they were winning. And they were, that is, until Brigadier General Thomas Stonewall Jackson arrived with another wave of reinforcements, tenaciously holding their ground. The Union forces were routed, with thousands on both sides killed in action, missing, wounded, or captured. The struggle ahead would be longer and far more costly than Americans had expected.

Fort Donelson

One of the first major Union victories was the capture of Fort Donelson, February 11 to 16, 1862, along with the capture of nearby Fort Henry, opening the state of Tennessee to Union invasion and helping General Ulysses S. Grant become a national hero. Fort Donelson was located along the Cumberland River in Tennessee. The Confederates initially repulsed an attack by Union gunboats and planned a bold counterattack to escape and avoid capture. The Confederates seemed to be on the verge of success when suddenly they retreated and returned to the fort. Confederate Generals Gideon Pillow and John B. Floyd defeatedly fled the fort, leaving behind 13,000 soldiers who waved a white flag above their fortifications. When the rebels asked for terms of surrender, General Grant informed them that there would be no terms except immediate and unconditional surrender. General Ulysses S. Grant's brilliance and the genius of Lincoln and his war cabinet began to slowly gain traction, cohesion, and effectiveness.

Antietam

On September 17, 1862, General Robert E. Lee and his army of Northern Virginia invaded Maryland to drive the Union forces back and break their morale. President Abraham Lincoln sent Major General George McClellan and the Potomac army to stop him. The two forces initially engaged at dawn in a cornfield in Sharpsburg, Maryland. Their movements were obscured by the tall corn fields, and it was possible friendly fire occurred. The battle shifted to a stone bridge along Antietam Creek, where Union troops had to charge Confederate positions repeatedly before finally capturing it. An estimated 22,717 soldiers on both sides were killed in action, wounded, captured, or went missing. Though the battle ended in a stalemate, the Union army had effectively stymied General Robert E. Lee's invasion. That gave Lincoln enough confidence to issue the Emancipation Proclamation, which redefined the Civil War from a struggle to persevere the Union to also focus on ending slavery. With thousands of bodies strewn on the battlefield at Antietam, it brought home to both sides the brutal cost of war.

Chancellorsville

General Robert E. Lee gained one of his greatest triumphs at Chancellorsville, Virginia, on May 1st, 1863. General Lee had divided the forces and sent Lieutenant General Thomas J. Stonewall Jackson to push his way, one of the directions, through a rough forest to outflank units led by Union General Joseph Hooker. After several days of fighting, the Union forces had to retreat. It was a decisive victory for General Lee and the South, but it came at a very high cost. Thirteen thousand Confederate soldiers had died in the conflict, including one of their finest, Lieutenant General "Stonewall" Jackson.

Vicksburg

Confederate President Jefferson Davis viewed Vicksburg, Mississippi, a port fortress and railroad hub along the Mississippi River, as a strategic center point that held together both sides of the South. That made it even more of an important target, the Gibraltar of the Confederacy, for the Union army to take. In mid-May of 1863, General Ulysses S. Grant sent forces repeatedly to attack the city but was unable to penetrate the Confederates' defenses. That forced him to settle into a long siege. The Union army even used miners to dig tunnels to reach fortifications to blow them up, but that didn't work very well. But by July of 1863, the Union forces had worn them down, and Confederate Lieutenant General John C. Pemberton and his 29,000 soldiers could not hold out any longer and surrendered to General Grant and the Union army. The victory gave the Union control of the critical supply line of the entire Mississippi River, and the Confederacy was effectively split.

The Rise and Fall of the American Empire

Gettysburg

General Robert E. Lee once again invaded July 1 to 3, 1863, hoping he could beat the Union on its own soil, threaten Washington, DC, and possibly force President Lincoln to agree to a peace treaty. Virginia had been devastated by the war, and he also desperately needed supplies for his soldiers. General Lee's army was pursued by Major General George Meade and the Union forces, who caught up with them at Gettysburg in what was one of the fateful battles of the American Civil War. On July 3, Lee attacked the middle of the Union army at Cemetery Ridge, South of Gettysburg. After two hours of nonstop shelling, Confederate General George Pickett led a charge of two brigades and an assault of the Union positions. It was a disaster for the Confederate forces as they suffered 60 percent casualties, and General Lee was forced to retreat and abandon the invasion. The battle was a major victory for the Union army, yet casualties exceeded 50,000 total for both North and South. Demoralized, General Robert E. Lee offered his resignation to President Jefferson Davis, but he refused it. In November of 1863, President Lincoln traveled to the site and delivered the Gettysburg Address.

A Portion of the Gettysburg Address

Four score and seven years ago, our fathers brought forth on this continent a new nation, conceived in Liberty, and dedicated to the proposition that all men are created equal. From these honored dead, we take increased devotion to that cause for which they gave the last full measure of devotion, that we here highly resolve, that these dead shall not have died in vain, that this nation under God shall have a new birth of freedom, and that government of the people by the people for the people, shall not perish from the earth.

President Abraham Lincoln

November 19, 1863

Atlanta

As the Civil War was nearing its end, a trio of Union armies led by General William T. Sherman converged upon Atlanta on July 22, 1864. Outside of the city, they were met by a desperate Confederate counterattack that failed. Sherman's forces continued their advance and finally surrounded the city, besieging it for the entire month of August. At last, on September 1, 1864, Lieutenant General John Bell Hood, a Confederate veteran of both Antietam and Gettysburg, gave up abandoned Atlanta, allowing General William T. Sherman to enter. With the capture of Atlanta, it crippled the Confederate war effort, helping the Union army pursue the war to its conclusion ("Civil War," 2023) (Hassler, 2023).

Assassination

On April 14, 1865, Abraham Lincoln, the sixteenth president of the United States, was assassinated by John Wilkes Booth while attending the play *Our American Cousin* at Ford's Theater in Washington, DC. He was shot from behind while he watched the play and died the following morning in the Peterson house. He was the first US president to be assassinated, and his funeral and burial were marked by an extended period of national mourning. He had been shot on Good Friday, the same day that Jesus was crucified. He died the following day, April 15, 1865, but not before he successfully stopped the destruction and disunion of the United States and put an end to slavery in America ("Abraham Lincoln's Assassination," 2022).

CHAPTER 12

Dwight Lyman Moody

D. L. Moody was an ordinary farm boy born February 5, 1837, in Northfield, Massachusetts, who remarkably rose up to be the greatest evangelist of the latter nineteenth century. Many Americans today might not even be familiar with the name D. L. Moody, yet in the time that he lived, he was internationally renowned. And if Moody becomes obscured by time, his message cannot. He often spoke to crowds of 10,000 and 20,000, and during his ministry, he presented the plan of salvation by voice or pen to at least 100 million people, changing American culture. Dwight Lyman Moody died just nine days before the start of the twentieth century, December 22, 1899, in Northfield, Massachusetts. He lived during a period of dramatic industrial expansion, urbanization, and economic growth. After the Civil War, America began to slowly coalesce into a giant. During the evolving sophistication of the Gilded Age, D. L. Moody was successful in continuing to point the nation back to a simple faith in God.

Early Years

D. L. Moody was born the sixth child of Edwin and Betsy Holton Moody in Northfield, Massachusetts. His formal education ended after the fifth grade, and he helped his family with the chores and farm work until he was able to strike out on his own. His early learning about seeds, harvesting, planting, and sowing would help later in the development of some sermons. When Dwight turned seventeen, he dreamed of going to Boston to seek his fortune. He tried to find work, but finally, his uncle, Samuel Holton, reluctantly hired him to help in his shoe store. There was one condition for young Dwight's employment, and that was his attendance at Mount Vernon Congregational Church. Moody's first spiritual mentor there was Edward Kimball, who taught Sunday school classes. On April 21, 1855, Kimball made the effort to personally visit Dwight at the Holton shoe store. D. L. later recalled, "I can't remember exactly what he said, but I will never forget how I felt the spirit of God when he placed his hand on my shoulder..." (Laird Simons, n.d.) From that experience and time, D. L. Moody accepted the love of God and devoted his life to serving Him. The following year, Moody moved to Chicago, hoping to make his fortune selling shoes. While selling shoes, he provided a Sunday school class for Chicago's children at the local Young Men's Christian Association. During the revival of 1857 and 1858, Moody became more involved at the YMCA, performing jobs and serving wherever they needed him. In 1860, he felt called to leave the shoe business and more fully dedicate himself to ministry work. He continued to increase his time at the YMCA, although they could not pay him while working in a missionary role in the city. D. L. Moody came from very humble beginnings, and he truly cared about people, and it showed. Moody's Mission Sunday School flourished and soon evolved into his own church. His approach was different, as he had a desire to reach the lost youth of the city and help poor families with difficult circumstances to get strong in God. With encouragement from his associates, on February 28, 1864, they opened the doors to the Illinois Street Church with D. L. Moody as pastor.

As the American Civil War began to set in, the Union army mobilized volunteer soldiers across the North. Then, they set up and established Camp Douglas outside of Chicago. With help from the YMCA, Moody created the Committee on Devotional Meetings to minister to the seventy-second Illinois Volunteer Regiment stationed at Camp Douglas. D. L. Moody was great at reaching his hands across both denominational and military lines. From 1861 to 1865, he ministered to thousands of Union and Confederate soldiers across the country and on the battlefields. All this time, he continued to maintain the Mission Sunday School and, later in the war, the Illinois Street Church. There were times during the Civil War when he arrived at scenes of apocalyptic destruction that looked like the end of the world.

While D. L. Moody was ministering in Chicago, he and his wife met an impressive woman named Emma Dryer, who was a teacher and administrator. Moody was moved by her zeal for ministry as well as her educational acumen. He knew that women held unique giftings and talents to minister to and evangelize mothers and children in a way that men could not. Moody asked Dryer to oversee a ministry specifically to train women for evangelistic outreach and missionary work. Under Dryer's leadership, the training program grew rapidly, and Emma Dryer then had an expanded vision to see this training program include men as well.

After much time, prayer, and effort, this training program evolved into the Chicago Evangelization Society and is now called the Moody Bible Institute.

On Sunday, October 8, 1871, a terrible disaster descended upon Chicago. The city fire bells began to ring, but it wasn't until Tuesday that the Great Chicago Fire had finally burned itself out. Much of the buildings Moody had constructed were burnt up, along with the city. During this deep and profound time of loss for him and his neighbors, D. L. Moody searched his heart and called on the Lord for wisdom and guidance. He had stated at that time, "I knew from that point on my call was to preach the Word of God to the world." It was as if, at this terrible low point, God redirected his focus and priorities.

Travel to England and the UK

In June of 1872, D. L. Moody made his first trip to England and the United Kingdom to visit the land he had heard so much about. This first visit planted the seeds for his return the next year, which was providential. In June of 1873, Moody and his wife and family, as well as good friend and musician Ira Sankey, all traveled from New York to Liverpool, England. Revival had been slowly sweeping the region, and Moody and Sankey traveled the UK, fueling the fires of revival. For two years, D. L. Moody remained in the UK, refining his oratory skills and salvation message. His time there made a lasting impression and inspired both lay and church people to begin children's ministries and ministry training schools for women. Moody even preached in Ireland while he was there, at a time when there was great tension between Catholics and Protestants, effectively communicating the message of Christ. As a result, the revival swept into Ireland as well as England, and D. L. Moody was esteemed by both the Catholics and Protestants. Moody and his family returned to the United States in 1875, and by that time, he was a much more famous and skillful preacher and evangelist. Moody and Sankey began to develop the early foundations for modern Christian music, which Thomas Dorsey and others later took to another level and was called gospel music.

It is possible that after all that travel, D. L. Moody was longing for a sense of home and roots and moved back to where he was born and raised in Northfield, Massachusetts. As Moody's family was enjoying the friendly small-town farm atmosphere, D. L. Moody was already busy planning his next round of evangelistic city campaigns. From October 1875 to May 1876, Moody and three other evangelists toured through the major cities of the Midwest and Atlantic Coast, powerfully preaching the message of salvation. They did it again up until 1878 when the desire to train and equip young Christian workers once again became his focus. How much more effective if one hundred ministry workers, 1,000 or even 10,000, were doing the works of the ministry instead of only Moody's efforts. D. L. Moody had become one of the most effective ministers of his time, and he began to pour this experience into his schools. In 1879, Moody opened the Northfield Seminary for Young Women to provide the opportunity for the poor and minorities to obtain an education. Not long after, D. L. Moody started the Mount Herman School for Boys with essentially the same goal. The schools were comprised of a diverse cross-section of students, both racially and denominationally, all obtaining a Christian-based education.

In 1886, with a lot of help, prayer, and hard work from Emma Dryer, the Chicago Evangelization Society was founded, which was later renamed Moody Bible Institute. Moody had been concentrating on ministry near his home in Northfield, but he came out to Chicago to raise money and support the birthing of a vision that he had held for a long time. It may have been initially Moody's vision and dream, but without Emma Dryer, it would have never happened. Also, in 1886, Moody assembled at Mount Hermon a large group of college students for summer school. This conference would birth the student volunteer movement for foreign missions. By 1911, 5,000 student volunteers from America alone came out of the program. Missionaries were sent around the world, and the program itself developed missionaries, grew, and spread to Europe and South Africa.

In his later years, D. L. Moody continued to evangelize throughout America, often preaching in major cities and at various universities. Yet his heart was for his schools, and he spent much of his time in Northfield, Massachusetts. Moody, who himself had only a fifth-grade education, rose up to be a great educator, training both young men and women, many of whom became ministers and missionaries, impacting America and the world. Dwight L.

Dwight Lyman Moody

Moody's life and legacy lived beyond him, and as one of the greatest evangelists, educators, and ministers of the nineteenth century, he served as a remarkable inspiration to the next generation. D. L. Moody died on December 22, 1899, at the same place that he was born, Northfield, Massachusetts. What an incredible journey and life well lived (Dwight L. Moody, 2021) (D. L. Moody, n.d.).

CHAPTER 13

The Dawning of Twentieth-Century America

The Great Migration

The arrival of the twentieth century also brought new hope and different challenges for many Americans. African Americans may have been granted freedom from slavery in nineteenth-century America, but they were still dealing with a litany of issues and problems, especially those living in the South. One of the largest movements of people in United States history occurred roughly from 1910 to the 1970s when approximately 6 million African Americans relocated from the South to Northern, Midwestern, and Western states. They had become increasingly fed up with racial violence, oppression, and injustice and sought greater economic, educational, and social opportunities. They succeeded on some levels but also encountered other problems. Perhaps in this present world, we will never be fully free from hatred, division, and prejudice. But God can begin to transform and change, one person at a time. The former mayor of Jerusalem once asked me what I thought might solve the Arab-Israeli conflict, and I responded, "The Messiah changing one heart and life at a time."

During the time and life of D. L. Moody, he preached to both North and South soldiers, to both Irish Catholics and English Protestants, the same message of love and salvation in Jesus. Moody also endeavored to elevate women and minorities. Later in the twentieth century, Martin Luther King poignantly preached unity for all people under God. Once again, here in America, we are facing the tempests of racial tensions and division. The historical wounds of slavery in America are deep and painful generational scars that remain in the national psyche, wounds that only God Himself can heal. And all the while, during the Great Migration of African Americans from the South to other parts of the country, millions of new immigrants arrived at Ellis Island and America each year ("The Great Migration," 2010). The population of the United States increased from 76.1 million in 1900 to 282.2 million by the year 2000. And there it stood, that great symbol of American liberty and freedom, the Statue of Liberty, standing in New York Harbor, beckoning and greeting the new arrivals. By the year 1900, the United States already consisted of forty-five states, with Oklahoma, Arizona, and New Mexico being added in 1912 and Alaska and Hawaii receiving statehood in 1959 to make it an even fifty states.

The Dawning of Twentieth-Century America

The Statue of Liberty, which stands on Ellis Island, beckoned millions of new arrivals to the New World

Dawning of the Twentieth Century

Back in 1752, Benjamin Franklin clearly demonstrated that lightning was electricity with his famous key and kite experiment. Thomas Edison began to conduct various experiments, and by May 29th, 1879, he had invented the light bulb. The first home to be fully electric was in Appleton, Wisconsin, in September 1882, powered by hydroelectricity. By 1925, about 50 percent of American homes had electricity; by 1945, 85 percent, and by 1960, nearly all homes in the United States had electricity. Many of the everyday things that American consumers had taken for granted by the twentieth century had been made and invented in the nineteenth century and continued to be refined and improved by electricity and combustion engines. Inventors continued to develop the farm combine from 1911 to 1915 until they were self-propelled and had onboard threshing motors. These were revolutionary improvements to the agriculture and farm industry. The electrical telegraph led to the telephone, and by 1920, 35 percent of all Americans had one. By the year 1900, there were 193,000 miles of train tracks throughout the country connecting commerce and the cities and towns. With the introduction of the mass-produced automobiles, Americans began to live in the suburbs, travel from farm to farm, and began to roam the country along the newly constructed highways. By 1930, 23 million cars were on the roads, and more than half of American families owned one. On December 17, 1903, all of Wilbur and Orville Wright's hard work and determination paid off, and they got an airplane off the ground for a sustained flight. World War I pushed flight technology and engineering to a more advanced level. Modern fighter jets reached 2,000 mph by the end of the century, and the X-15 experimental rocket jet exceeded 4,500 mph. By the 1920s, rocket research accelerated with the advancement of modern military warheads and, later in the century, space exploration. In 1867, Alfred Nobel invented dynamite, a stabilized form of nitroglycerin. Scientists and researchers continued to develop new and more powerful explosives until July

The Dawning of Twentieth-Century America

16, 1945, when they were able to detonate the first nuclear weapon under the Manhattan Project. America had already seen the first industrial revolution during the nineteenth century, and the second industrial revolution was well underway by the beginning of the twentieth century. Many historians also refer to the computing, communication, and information revolution, which began in the 1950s and 1960s as part of the third industrial revolution. There were massive cultural, social, technological, and economic changes associated with the development of the World Wide Web and the digital revolution.

One of the favorite national pastimes was sports, and they really began to take off in the twentieth century, with many professional leagues being formed. The first professional baseball team was the Cincinnati Red Stockings, founded in 1866. Churchill Downs and the Kentucky Derby were founded in 1875. The National Basketball League was formed in 1891 and was a great indoor sport during the cold of winter. The Green Bay Packers were founded in 1919 and were the new hybrid of rugby and soccer, called football. The National Boxing Association was founded in 1921, and America became the Center for sport. The Fox Burg Country Club golf course in Pennsylvania was designed in 1887 and played a role in the exploding popularity of the sport over the next century ("Early Twentieth Century US," n.d.) (Overview, n.d.) (Brill, *America in the 1900s*, 2010).

William Ashley Sunday

Billy Sunday was born on November 19, 1862, in Story County, Iowa. His father, William Sunday, was the son of German immigrants whose name was Sonntag until it was changed and anglicized to Sunday. William Sunday Sr. was a bricklayer who worked his way from Chambersburg, Pennsylvania, to an area near Ames, Iowa, where he met and married Mary Jane Corey. William Sunday Sr. enlisted in the Iowa Twenty-Third Volunteer Infantry on August 14, 1862. William Sr. died just four months later of pneumonia at an army camp hospital in Patterson, Missouri, five weeks after the birth of his youngest son, William Ashley. Mary Jane Sunday and her children moved in with her parents for a few years, and young Billy became close to his grandparents, especially his grandmother. Billy Sunday recalled years later that some of his earliest memories were of his mother and grandmother singing hymns. Mary Jane Sunday later remarried, but her second husband was an irresponsible alcoholic and soon abandoned her and the family. Ten-year-old Billy simply could not grasp what his mother was trying to tell him. She had sat him and his older brother down and told them that she had to take them to the Soldiers' Orphans' Home because she could no longer care for them. She tried to be strong and told them that everything would be okay. But was she okay? Her husband had died, and the second one abandoned her, and now she was taking her two boys to the orphanage because she was out of money and out of options.

One thing Billy Sunday discovered about himself at the or-

The Dawning of Twentieth-Century America

phanage was that he was strong and could outrun anyone in a foot race. The orphanage also taught him discipline and gave him a good primary education. By the time Billy was fourteen, he was on his own and working. In Nevada, Iowa, he worked for Colonel John Scott, a former Lieutenant governor, tending to the horses and farm chores. He was able to get a bunk and two meals a day, and he had the opportunity to go to Nevada High School and get additional schooling. In 1880, Billy Sunday moved to Marshall-town, Iowa, where, because of his athleticism, he was picked for a fire brigade team. He also worked different jobs and played for the town baseball team.

In 1883, on Hall of Fame Cap Anson's recommendation, A. G. Spalding, president of the Chicago White Stockings, signed Bil-ly Sunday to the defending National League champions. Sunday played for eight years in the major leagues for different teams, where he was an average hitter, a good fielder, and a great base runner. In 1885, the White Stockings arranged a race between Billy Sunday and Arlie Latham, the fastest runner in the American As-sociation. Sunday easily won the one-hundred-yard dash by about ten feet. This was still the period when the outfielders did not have gloves but caught the balls bare-handed, and Sunday often would perform incredible diving catches. Sunday's personality, demean-or, and amazing athleticism made him popular with both the fans and his teammates. He was a diving and sliding marvel.

Born-Again

One Sunday afternoon in Chicago, during the 1886 baseball season, Sunday and several of his teammates were out in the town on a day off. At one street corner, they stopped to listen to a gospel preaching team from the Pacific Garden Mission. Attracted by the hymns he had heard his mother sing when he was a boy, Sunday began attending services at the mission. After talking with a former society matron who worked there, Sunday prayed to receive Jesus and became a Christian. Yet there was a very big struggle for Sunday leading up to that decision. He began to attend Jefferson Park Presbyterian Church, which was close to the ballpark and his rented room. Following his conversion, Sunday stopped drinking, swearing, and gambling, and his change of behavior was noticed by both his teammates and fans. Shortly thereafter, Sunday began speaking in churches and at the YMCA.

Later, in 1886, Billy Sunday met Helen Amelia "Nell" Thompson while attending Jefferson Park Presbyterian Church. Although they were both, at the time, involved in other serious relationships, they ended up getting married on September 5, 1888. Sunday was perfectly smitten by Nell from the moment he met her. Nell's father owned a large dairy product business in Chicago and strongly discouraged the courtship, stating, "Professional baseball players are transient ne'er-do-wells who are unstable and destined to be misfits once they are too old to play." Even though she was the wealthy girl from the other side of society, fortunately for Sunday, both Nell and her mother persuaded her father until he changed his mind about their marriage. She ended up making a big difference in the trajectory of his life and future ministry, and she eventually became the primary administrator of the ministry and handled things very well.

And in the spring of 1891, Sunday turned down a lucrative baseball contract and began to increasingly answer the call to ministry. Billy Sunday was hired at the YMCA as assistant secretary, yet the position also involved a great deal of ministerial work. For three years, Sunday visited the sick, prayed with the troubled, counseled the suicidal, and visited saloons to invite patrons to evangelistic meetings. All the while, Billy Sunday and his wife grew in their faith and their knowledge of the Bible, and by the end of Sunday's life, he had accumulated a vast library of well-used biblical books. One evangelist who had a great deal of influence on Sunday was Dwight L. Moody. In 1893, Sunday became the full-time assistant to Jay Wilbur Chapman, one of the best-known evangelists in the United States at that time. Chapman was well-educated, brought a certain sophistication to the pulpit, and commanded great respect with both his strong voice and demeanor. Billy Sunday's job was to go ahead of Chapman to the cities where he would be preaching and preparing and taking care of everything. He would organize prayer meetings and choirs, help put up tents when necessary, and, in general, take care of all necessary details. It was actually a great apprenticeship for the evangelism that he himself would soon be doing. He would listen to and watch Chapman closely, his preaching, his prayer life, and his ministry in general. Chapman encouraged Billy Sunday's theological development and reinforced his understanding of and commitment to conservative biblical Christianity. There was, on different levels, a certain transference of mantles and anointing from Chapman to Sunday. Some things are more caught than taught.

When J. Wilbur Chapman unexpectedly returned to Pastoring a church in 1896, Billy Sunday struck out on his own. Although he had been preparing and training in the ministry for years, his first official evangelistic meeting was in the tiny town of Garner, Iowa. For the next twelve years, Billy Sunday preached in approximately seventy communities, most of them in Iowa and Illinois. Sunday referred to this time and these towns as "the kerosene circuit" because, unlike Chicago, most of these smaller towns did not yet have electricity. They also coined the term "hitting the sawdust trail," meaning those who would walk forward at the preacher's invitation. The tabernacle floors were covered with sawdust to dampen the noise of shuffling feet, hold down the dust from dirt floors, and provide a pleasant smell. Apparently, hitting the sawdust trail had first been used by loggers in the Pacific Northwest to describe following home a trail of previously dropped sawdust through an uncut forest, described by Nell Sunday as a metaphor for coming from "a lost condition to a saved condition."

William Sunday preached almost continuously up until his death on November 6, 1935, in Chicago, Illinois. From 1896 to 1935, he was America's best-known evangelist, with the height of his popularity being around 1917 in New York City. For almost

The Dawning of Twentieth-Century America

the entirety of his career, he had used no electric voice amplification. He may have preached as many as 20,000 sermons and conducted more than 300 revivals, some lasting months. Millions of people attended the meetings through the years of his ministry, with thousands of people coming forward for salvation. He was devoted to his wife, and she played a huge role in his success as a person and as a minister. He used both his celebrity as a baseball player and as an evangelist to campaign against alcohol and its destructive effects on families. He always spoke in a language that the common man could understand and would tell stories to communicate to the people the importance of a relationship with God.

Few people know that Billy Sunday's amazing wife, Helen Amelia "Nell" Sunday, the indefatigable organizer of his huge evangelistic campaigns, went on after his death to be an evangelist also. When Billy Sunday died in 1935, Nell became the guardian of her husband's ministry legacy while also embarking on her own twenty-two-year ministry. She spent the rest of her life preaching, encouraging young evangelists, and raising money for Christian organizations such as Pacific Garden Mission, where her husband had been saved. She had a great sense of humor that helped her through many tragedies and difficulties, including the suicide of her son. Nell Sunday lived long enough to speak at the early Billy Graham Crusades, and she frequently visited Bob Jones College, where she was given an honorary degree in 1940. In 1957, Helen Thompson Sunday died in Phoenix, Arizona, while spending the winter with her grandson ("William Ashley [Billy] Sunday: 1862–1935," n.d.) (Billy Sunday, 2022).

CHAPTER 14

The Great War

World War I Begins

Tensions had been brewing throughout Europe, especially the Balkans, for years before World War I started. And one turn of events that exacerbated the already existing tensions was the assassination of Archduke Franz Ferdinand of Austria. The archduke, who was heir to the Austro-Hungarian Empire, was shot to death along with his wife, Sophie, by Serbian nationalist Gavrilo Princip on June 28, 1914. Princip and other nationalists were struggling to end Austro-Hungarian rule over Bosnia and Herzegovina. Not only was Archduke Franz Ferdinand's trip to Sarajevo ill-advised, but even after the Serbian nationalists had made one assassination attempt by throwing a bomb at their car, they made the bad decision to go back out again, driving their car. At that time, the archduke's driver inadvertently made a wrong turn, and the Serbian nationalists spotted them again and shot both him and his wife, Sophie, point blank. The assassination of Franz Ferdinand was like lighting a fuse, pushing over a row of dominoes, setting off a rapidly escalating chain of events. Because Russia supported Serbia, Austria-Hungary waited to declare war until its leaders gained assurance from Kaiser Wilhelm II that Germany would support their cause. On July 5, Kaiser Wilhelm II secretly pledged his support, giving Austria-Hungary a complete assurance of Germany's backing in the case of war.

Convinced that Austria-Hungary was readying for war, the Serbian government ordered the Serbian army to mobilize and appealed to Russia for assistance. On July 28, Austria-Hungary declared war on Serbia, and the tenuous peace between Europe's great powers quickly collapsed. Within one week, Russia, Belgium, France, Great Britain, and Serbia had lined up against Austria-Hungary and Germany, and World War I had begun.

America Enters the War

At the outbreak of fighting in 1914, the United States remained on the sidelines of World War I, adopting the policy of neutrality favored by President Woodrow Wilson while continuing to engage in shipping and commerce with European countries on both sides of the conflict. It became increasingly difficult for the United States to remain neutral with Germany sinking commercial and passenger vessels, including some US ships. American and British citizens were outraged by the sinking of the Lusitania by a German U-boat. Germany had declared the waters around the British Isles a war zone, but the problem was that they were sinking much more than military vessels. Germany sank four more US merchant ships in March 1917, and on April 2, Woodrow Wilson appeared before Congress and called for a declaration of war against Germany. Germany was even trying to entice Mexico to join into an alliance with them against the United States. Germany promised the Mexican government that it would help them get back the territory that they had ceded to the United States in return for their assistance and support in the war. This information was obtained

The Great War

on January 19, 1917, via the infamous "Zimmermann telegram" intercepted and decrypted by British Naval Intelligence.

The German government also had every intention of resuming unrestricted submarine attacks on all Allied and neutral shipping within prescribed war zones, hoping that German submarines could end the war before the first US troop ships began to land in Europe. German Chancellor Theobald von Bethmann warned that it was a big mistake that would lead to the defeat of Germany.

The most critical role in the war was that of Russia. Despite the end of their participation in 1917, they had given great sacrifice and effort, had sustained the most casualties, and ground down the German army on the Eastern Front, just prior to the American entry into the war. The Russian economy was in shambles, the soldiers and people were starving and discontent, and the Bolsheviks, led by Vladimir Lenin, pushed out Czar Nicholas II. The Bolsheviks' priority was winning the civil war in Russia, so they pulled all the soldiers back in 1917 and signed a treaty with the Central Powers on March 3, 1918, ending their participation in World War I. On the Western Front was an enormous system of hundreds of miles of trenches stretching from the English Channel to the Swiss Alps. Although this was not a new military strategy, it created the most hellish and hideous of conditions for soldiers. On one side were the Germans, and on the other side were the French, the British, and later the Americans. Casualties were very high, as in one day alone, July 1, 1916, in the Battle of the Somme, there were almost 60,000 British casualties. They endured days

The Rise and Fall of the American Empire

and weeks of being shell shocked, machine-gunned, hit with poisonous gasses, and the secret night assaults by the Germans at any perceived weak points. And if that wasn't enough, the Spanish flu, or the Great Flu of 1918, began to break out. It was an avian type of flu with origins possibly from Fort Riley in Kansas on March 11, 1918. As the soldiers were transported to Europe, the influenza began to spread throughout Europe, the United States, Africa, and the world. As much as one-fifth of the world's population was attacked by this deadly virus. The total casualties from World War I were approximately 41 million dead and 21 million wounded, with many of these being civilian casualties. Germany, Russia, France, and England suffered the greatest losses, while US casualties numbered 116,000. Centers for Disease Control and Prevention state that the number of deaths worldwide attributed to the 1918 Great Influenza was estimated to be at least 50 million, with 675,000 deaths occurring in the United States. World War I was finally over at 11:00 a.m. on November 11, 1918. On the eleventh hour of the eleventh day of the eleventh month, the guns fell silent. Yet there was smoldering resentment in Germany, especially with one young officer named Adolf Hitler. And just two decades later, Germany built up the biggest war machine the world had ever seen (Wagner, 2017) ("US Entry into World War I," 2022).

CHAPTER 15

Prophetic Signs

There are many places in the sixty-six books of the Bible that talk about prophetic signs and or future events. So, let's look at some and see what they say. In Luke chapter 21, Mark chapter 13, and Matthew chapters 24 and 25 (NIV), Jesus privately talks to Peter, James, John, and Andrew about signs preceding the end of the age.

In Mark 13:1–2 (NIV), it is written,

> As Jesus was leaving the temple, one of his disciples said to him, "Look, Teacher! What massive stones! What magnificent buildings!"
>
> "Do you see all these great buildings? replied Jesus. "Not one stone here will be left on another; everyone will be thrown down."

And in verse 4 (NIV), they asked Jesus, "Tell us, when will these things happen? And what will be the sign that they are all about to be fulfilled?" So, then Jesus began to break it down and teach them.

In these three books, the writers tell the same stories from different angles, but let's look at all three to gain a fuller teaching and perspective. One of the first things that Jesus said was to watch out for deception. See Luke 21:8, Mark 13:5, Matthew 24:4, and Mathew 24:24. Jesus said in Mark 13:6 (NIV), "Many will come in my name, claiming, 'I am he,' and will deceive many." He also warned of false teachers, prophets, and messiahs leading people astray. See Mark 13:21–23, Matthew 24:5, 24:11, and 24:24. He also warned of false signs and wonders in Matthew 24:24.

One of the most effective ways to safeguard against deception is to know the Bible well, especially the words and teachings of Jesus, and continue to read and study it. Make sure that you have a personal relationship with God, ask Jesus into your life, and stay in prayer. Jesus also stated in Matthew 24:6–7a (NIV), "You will hear of wars and rumors of wars, but see to it that you are not alarmed. Such things must happen, but the end is still to come. Nation will rise against nation, and kingdom against kingdom."

The United States fought in five major wars in the 1900s, including World War I, World War II, the Korean War, Vietnam, and the Gulf War. See Luke 21:9–10 and Mark 13:7. Jesus also said in Matthew 24:7b–8 (NIV), "There will be famines and earthquakes in various places. All these are the beginning of birth pains." Also, see Luke 21:11 and Mark 13:8. There have been many famines in the history of the world and the United States, and sometimes the poor, the indigent, and the homeless do not have the money or resources for food and other necessities. For example, the struggle for survival in America during the Great Depression.

Prophetic Signs

Since the year 1900, there have been more than 10,000 strong earthquakes throughout the world with a magnitude of 6 or greater. We will take a closer look at the San Francisco earthquake of 1906 in the next chapter. Certain areas seem to have a higher incidence, like California or Alaska. On March 27, 1964, Alaska had a 9.2 magnitude earthquake, which was one of the biggest in history. Perhaps there has also been an increased frequency and or intensity of earthquakes over the last generations.

It is interesting how Jesus stated in Matthew 24:8 (NIV), "All these are the beginning of birth pains." When a woman is getting closer to the birth and delivery of her child, the frequency and intensity of the labor pains occur. Only Luke used the word "pestilence" in Luke 21:11, and pestilence can be used synonymously with famine, death, contagion, plague, disease, or virus. For example, the Black Plague in Europe, which killed over 30 percent of the population during the late Middle Ages, was a pestilence. Also, the Spanish flu of 1918 and the pandemic of 2020. Jesus also stated in Luke 21:25b (NIV), "On the earth, nations will be in anguish and perplexity at the roaring and tossing of the sea."

Hurricanes, cyclones, volcanic eruptions, and seismic activity can also cause tsunamis. He also referred to "fearful events and great signs from heaven" in verse 11 (NIV). Right now, while I am writing this, a super blue moon is coming into view; a hurricane is pounding Florida on one side, and on the other side of Florida, three more storms are headed their way. And in the United States alone, we had approximately 167 hurricanes reach land in

The Rise and Fall of the American Empire

the 1900s, causing catastrophic damage. On September 8, 1900, a hurricane packing 145 mph winds with a fifteen-foot storm surge struck Galveston, Texas, destroying the area and killing 8,000 people. They had dozens more sea storms hit Galveston in the 1900s, but they had constructed a sea wall, which did help. We have approximately 1,200 tornadoes striking the US yearly. In 1925, the tristate tornado tore through Missouri, Illinois, and Indiana, packing 300 mph winds, and was a mile wide at times, killing 695 people and wounding 2,000.

Jesus spoke of cataclysmic signs in the stars, heavens, and sky preceding His return. See Luke 21:11, 21:25–26, Mark 13:24–25, and Matthew 24:29. Jesus also talked to His disciples about being hated and persecuted, being betrayed by family, friends, and relatives, being interrogated by the authorities, with some being imprisoned or put to death for their faith. Jesus also spoke of an increase in wickedness, with the hearts and love of many growing cold and many falling away from their faith. See Matthew 24:9–12, Luke 21:12–17, and Mark 13:9–13.

Jesus told of a time of great distress and trouble preceding the end of the age. See Mark 13:19–20 and Matthew 24:19–22. Jesus also taught the parable of the fig tree. See Matthew 24:32–34 (NIV):

> "Now learn this lesson from the fig tree:
> As soon as its twigs get tender and its
> leaves come out, you know that summer

Prophetic Signs

> is near. Even so, when you see all these things, you know that it is near right at the door. Truly I tell you, this generation will certainly not pass away until all these things have happened."

Also, see Mark 13:28–30 and Luke 21:29–32.

Most biblical scholars and rabbis believe that the fig tree refers to Israel and that summer means the end or the end of the age. We are now living in the generation that has seen the reestablishment and sprouting up of Israel as a nation, once again on May 14, 1948, and all the prophetic signs that Jesus referred to culminating and coming to pass. Jesus also said in Luke 21:24b (NIV), "Jerusalem will be trampled on by the Gentiles until the times of the Gentiles are fulfilled." The non-Jews occupied Jerusalem and trampled on it until the Jews took it back over in 1948. I believe it is very important to understand that Jesus said that His words were eternal and that they would stand forever. Luke 21:33 (NIV) states, "Heaven and earth will pass away, but my words will never pass away." See also Mark 13:31 and Matthew 24:35.

Who was Jesus? Jesus is the third member of the Godhead, and everything that He said and did reflects the Father. See John 14:1–30. Another very powerful sign is the completion of the Gospel going forth to all nations. Jesus stated in Matthew 24:14 (NIV), "And this gospel of the kingdom will be preached in the whole world as a testimony to all nations, and then the end will

The Rise and Fall of the American Empire

come." See also Mark 13:10. Many Bible scholars, pastors, and teachers state that there is nothing prophetically left to fulfill and that Jesus could come back at any time.

It is true that the media can be a dual-edged sword for either good or evil, as it all depends on whose hands it is in. Yet in the last one hundred years, radio, television, satellite television, film, the World Wide Web, social media, et cetera, have all dramatically accelerated the preaching of the gospel to all the nations and people of the earth. Jesus stated in Matthew 24:36 (NIV), "But about that day or hour no one knows, not even the angels in heaven, nor the Son, but only the Father." See also Mark 13:32–37. And the point here that He was really trying to drive home was to remain ready and watchful because, just like in the time of Noah, most people will not be ready at the time of the Lord's return. See Luke 21:34–36 and Matthew 24:36–44. Jesus said to remain ready, vigilant, wise, faithful, working, and about the Father's business at His return. See Matthew 24:45–47 and Luke 21:34–36.

He said that when He comes back, the people on the earth will mourn because they were not ready. See Matthew 24:30–31 and Luke 21:35. Jesus also said, "But the one who stands firm to the end will be saved" (Matthew 24:13, NIV). See Mark 13:13, Matthew 24:13, and Luke 21:19. Jesus also forewarned not to listen to people who say that Jesus has already come back because His coming will be known, obvious, and apparent to all. See Matthew 24:26–28. Jesus said in Luke 21:27–28 (NIV), "At that time they will see the Son of Man coming in a cloud with power and great

Prophetic Signs

glory. When these things begin to take place, stand up and lift your heads, because your redemption is drawing near." See also Mark 13:26–27 and Matthew 24:30–31.

The great evangelist Billy Graham would talk about the brevity of life. Yes, there will be the final generation who sees the return of Jesus, and it is possible that it is this generation, but it is of paramount importance that we are ready for His return (*Life Application Study Bible*, 2019) (B. Graham, *Till Armageddon: A Perspective on Suffering*, 1981).

CHAPTER 16

The Tale of Two Cities

San Francisco, 1906

On the morning of April 18, 1906, before the sun had even risen, one of the worst disasters in American history began. First, there were some tremors and some shaking, and San Francisco quickly began to awaken. Then, at 5:12 AM, coming from the ocean offshore, a deep roaring sound began, followed by violent shock waves and shaking that lasted sixty seconds. Buildings began to collapse, and gas lines began to explode and ignite fires all over the city.

The epicenter of the massive earthquake was offshore, two miles West of San Francisco, and could be felt as far away as Oregon, Los Angeles, and the middle of Nevada. The earthquake devastated the city, and then the subsequent fires throughout the city, caused by the ruptured gas lines, decimated it. The Queen of the West and the pride of the Coast was a bustling city of 400,000 residents, but in a matter of days, it was reduced to a pile of ash and rubble. Eighty percent of the city was leveled and burned. Three hundred thousand people were homeless and slept outside in parks and anywhere they could find for days and weeks. More than 3,000 people died, and many more were seriously injured.

In the aftermath of the quake, the fire department found that

The Rise and Fall of the American Empire

the city water lines were also broken. Tragically, there were very few rescuers in the searing heat, and there was no water available to put out the fires. Twenty-five thousand buildings were destroyed, and most of the evacuees never returned to the city. There were some interviews with remaining survivors, though they are all gone now. Survivor Bill Bon Barton said, the night before the quake, "I kissed my mother goodnight, and she said, 'Be sure to say your prayers before you go to bed.' Little did I know at that moment that I would never see my family again." Barton also said that he was thrown through the window, cot, and all, sustaining many injuries, but he survived.

Agnes Singer said, "The earthquake came in with the roar of the ocean, a tremendously loud roar." She also said that the first night after the quake and the fire, her father woke her up in the middle of the night to show her the panorama of the entire city up in flames. And he said to her, "Agnes, I hope you never see a thing like this again." Another man said that he ran out of their building with his mother and that there were people everywhere on the street praying, thinking it was the end of the world. And it was the end of the world for all those who perished in the flames and rubble of the Great San Francisco earthquake of 1906 (Brill, *America in the 1900s*, 2010) (Greenspan, "Remembering the Great San Francisco Earthquake of 1906," 2018) (Miguel, 2016).

Los Angeles, 1906

The Azusa Street Revival

One of the most important and powerful revivals in the history of the world began in a modest clapboard building at 312 Azusa Street in Los Angeles in April 1906. The area is now part of the Japanese Village downtown, north of Skid Row, and was a rough area of Los Angeles in 1906. From Azusa Street, a revival exploded that spread throughout Los Angeles, all of California, the United States, and the world over the following century, affecting 600 million people.

But the reality was that God had been moving for years in many ways, places, and people leading up to Azusa. One such move was an outpouring of the Spirit in Russia in the 1800s, followed by another in Armenia twenty-five years later. Due to a prophetic warning of a coming persecution that absolutely came to pass, thousands of Armenians left to go to Canada, Mexico, and the United States, and especially Los Angeles, California.

One of the families that arrived in Los Angeles was Demos Shakarian and his family, and his grandson, also named Demos Shakarian, would later establish the Full Gospel Businessmen's Association (Bakalian, 2023) (De Arteaga, 2019). Another move was the Welsh Revival of 1904 to 1905, which saw some 100,000 converts and a reformation in the culture of Wales. That revival triggered revivals in several other countries and was also another influence leading up to Azusa.

The Rise and Fall of the American Empire

Christians took the Welsh revival and other similar events to be a sign that the prophecy of Joel 2:28–29 (NIV) was about to take place: "And afterward, I will pour out my Spirit on all people. Your sons and daughters will prophesy, your old men will dream dreams, your young men will see visions. Even on my servants, both men and women, I will pour out my Spirit in those days." ("The 1904 Welsh Revival," 2016).

With everything that was going on, there seemed to be a growing and increasing sense of expectation leading up to the Azusa Street Revival. Joseph Smale, pastor of the First Baptist Church in Los Angeles, went to Wales personally to experience and witness what was going on in the revival. Upon his return to Los Angeles, he attempted to ignite a similar event in his own congregation (Martin, n.d.).

Another very important central figure leading up to Azusa was Charles F. Parham. In America, before the turn of the century, Charles F. Parham and many from the holiness groups were seeking more from God. Many, like Parham, strongly believed in divine healing and prayer for the sick. Others were asking God for a Pentecostal outpouring of holiness and power. Just prior to Parham starting the Bethel Bible School in Topeka, Kansas, in 1900, it had come to his attention that one individual who had been working with the ministry of Frank Sanford received the gift of glossolalia, or tongues. Parham had also worked with and studied under the ministry of Sanford in the past.

The Tale of Two Cities

Parham came to the belief and conclusion that there was more to a full baptism in the Holy Spirit than others were aware of or acknowledged at the time. By the end of 1900, Parham had led his students at Bethel Bible School through his belief and understanding that there had to be a further experience with God. The students had several days of prayer and worship and held a New Year's Eve watch-night service at Bethel on December 31, 1900. Then, the next evening, on the first day of the first month of the new century, during a worship service, many of the Bethel Bible School students received the baptism of the Holy Spirit with the evidence of speaking in tongues, including Agnes Ozman.

Parham ministered until his death on January 29, 1929, seeing many healings and salvations in his meetings. So, it was Charles F. Parham who connected and associated glossolalia, or tongues, with the baptism of the Holy Spirit, a theological connection crucial to the emergence of Pentecostalism as a distinct movement. Parham was the first preacher to articulate Pentecostalism's distinctive doctrine of evidential tongues and to further set the foundation for Azusa (King, 2021).

William J. Seymour

William Joseph Seymour was one of the most influential African American religious leaders of his time, and he also was the leader and Pastor of the Azusa Street Mission later in his life. Seymour was born on May 2, 1870, in Centerville, Louisiana. His parents, Simon and Phyllis Seymour, were both recently freed slaves.

The Rise and Fall of the American Empire

He was raised in poverty and received little formal education. In 1895, at age twenty-five, William left Louisiana for Indianapolis, Indiana, possibly to get away from the racial issues of the South and go to a Northern state. He joined the Simpson Chapel Methodist Episcopal Church while he was there, continuing to learn more about the Bible.

In 1900, he moved to Cincinnati, Ohio, where he joined the Church of God Restoration Movement. The group was also part of the growing holiness movement that believed in the imminent return of Christ, faith healing, the baptism of the Holy Spirit, and sanctification. However, the group believed in an immediate, and not gradual, conversion and sanctification following the acceptance of Christ and baptism of the Holy Spirit. While living in Cincinnati, Seymour suffered from smallpox, causing blindness in his left eye. He felt a calling on his life, and in 1902, he was ordained as a minister in the Church of God. He was thankful to still be alive after the attack of smallpox and still have a chance to serve God. For the next three years, he traveled as an evangelist throughout different states, then settled in Houston, Texas, in 1905, where his family had moved to.

That summer, he served as the temporary replacement pastor for Lucy Farrow, a holiness minister and niece of black abolitionist Frederick Douglass. Through Farrow, Seymour met Charles F. Parham, briefly attended his Bible school, and learned about glossolalia, tongues, and baptism in the Holy Spirit. God used Charles F. Parham to impart to William J. Seymour what he needed to later

The Tale of Two Cities

have an enormous impact on the development of Pentecostalism in the United States and throughout the world.

Neely Terry, an African American woman who attended a small holiness church pastored by Julia Hutchins in Los Angeles, made a trip to visit family in Houston late in 1905. While in Houston, she visited Seymour's church, where he preached about the baptism of the Holy Spirit with the evidence of speaking in tongues. And though William Seymour had not yet experienced this personally, Neely Terry was very impressed by his humble demeanor and message. Once home in California, Terry suggested to Pastor Hutchins that Seymour be invited to speak at the church. Seymour received an invitation to speak at Pastor Hutchins's church in February 1906. After praying about it, he accepted the invitation, and Charles F. Parham sent him off with his blessings and an offering.

Seymour arrived in Los Angeles on February 22, 1906, and within two days, was preaching at Julia Hutchins's church at the corner of Ninth Street and Santa Fe Avenue. During his first sermon, he preached that the baptism in the Holy Spirit would inevitably be followed by the sign and evidence while speaking in tongues, glossolalia. Hutchins and the elders of the church initially rejected Seymour's teaching primarily because he had yet to experience the very thing that he was preaching about. Also, the Holiness movement did not receive his teaching at that time because they felt that it was possible to be baptized in the Holy Spirit without having the evidence or gift of tongues. Pastor Hutchins promptly padlocked the door to the church, so when Seymour returned on March 4, he was locked out and could not get in.

Although later Hutchins agreed with and believed Seymour's doctrine and teaching, initially Seymour had a very discouraging and rough start to his arrival in Los Angeles. One of the members of Pastor Hutchins's Holiness Church, Mr. Edward S. Lee, took compassion on Seymour and brought him into his home, where they began to hold Bible studies and prayer meetings. Seymour and his small group of new followers soon relocated to the home of Richard and Ruth Asberry at 214 N Bonnie Brae Street. White families from local Holiness churches began to attend as well. The group would get together regularly and pray to receive the baptism of the Holy Spirit.

On April 9, 1906, after five weeks of Seymour's preaching and prayer and three days into an intended ten-day fast, Edward S. Lee spoke in tongues for the first time. At the next meeting, Seymour shared Lee's testimony and preached a sermon on Acts 2:4, and soon, six others began to speak in tongues as well, including Jenny Moore, who would later become Seymour's wife. A few days later, on April 12, 1906, Seymour spoke in tongues for the first time after praying all night. Acts 2:1–4 (NIV) states,

> When the day of Pentecost came, they were all together in one place. Suddenly a sound like the blowing of a violent wind came from heaven and filled the whole house where they were sitting. They saw

The Tale of Two Cities

> what seemed to be tongues of fire that separated and came to rest on each of them.
> All of them were filled with the Holy Spirit and began to speak in other tongues as
> the Spirit enabled them.

News of the Bonnie Brae Street gathering spread throughout the neighborhoods and city and began to quickly attract a broad and diverse spectrum of all kinds of people of every race, income level, and denominational background. It was a perfect example of diversity as various speakers would preach to the crowds of curious and interested onlookers from the front porch of the Asberry home. Even Pastor Hutchins and the Holiness Church showed up, and they were also all baptized in the Holy Spirit and spoke in tongues. Soon, the crowds became very large and were full of people speaking in tongues, shouting, singing, and praying. They quickly outgrew the location, and the front porch even collapsed under the weight of all the people, but no one was hurt. It was Easter season, and the whole city was stirred as people came from everywhere, but they had to find a new, larger location (Seymour, William Joseph, 2018).

312 Azusa Street, Los Angeles, California

Anyone who came to the Azusa Street Mission had to humble themselves. And really, why would anyone want to go to this tumbled-down shack sided with weathered whitewashed clapboards and dirt floors located in the worst part of town? The answer was

The Rise and Fall of the American Empire

God. Yes, this initial group of people, especially William Seymour, were incredibly dedicated in their prayer and seeking of God, but it truly seemed like God had chosen this time and place to meet the people and pour out His spirit. And why not? It states in the final book of the Bible, Revelation, that heaven will consist of people from every language group, race, and nation from all over the earth.

California, and specifically Los Angeles, was the perfect place to launch a revival that would spread throughout the city, the state, the nation, and out across the globe. It might have been mostly African American, White, and Latino attendees initially, but then the Armenians, Russians, Swedes, Germans, Italians, Chinese, Japanese, Native Americans, and many other ethnic groups began to come and show up. Why? Because God was there, and He was touching the people in new and remarkable ways. People were getting filled with the Holy Spirit, healed and saved, and most importantly, people were reordering their lives. Whoever truly experienced Azusa Street and the power of God was marked for life and changed forever with new and higher priorities. They held their first meeting at the Azusa Street Mission on April 14, 1906, and everyone pitched in to clean it up, repair it, and get it ready. And if the small city of Los Angeles didn't already have the awareness and fear of God beginning to move through it, the great earthquake of San Francisco happened just four days after the first Azusa meeting on April 18, 1906.

The news, the stories, and aftershocks rolled through the city

The Tale of Two Cities

of Los Angeles, and the churches and the Christians interceded for the mercy of God upon Los Angeles. About that time, 125,000 copies of a tract called "The Earthquake Tract" went out, provoking people to think about God and the message of the tract. All the while, the meetings at the Azusa Street Mission continued to grow quickly into the hundreds and on to as many as 1,500 each day. The first secular news reports about Azusa hit the newsstands on the morning of April 18, the same day as the earthquake. It didn't matter if the reports were good or bad; you could not keep the people away.

A massive spiritual awakening and a new Pentecost had come to Azusa Street, and God had opened the portals of heaven and once again sent great power. The building at 312 Azusa Street had formerly been an African Methodist Episcopal Church and an assortment of other uses. The last thing that the building had been used for prior to the Azusa Street Mission was a horse stable on the bottom floor. God's ways can certainly confound the wise. How could a great move of God be birthed in a stable? How could the baby Jesus Himself be birthed in a stable in Bethlehem?

From April 1906 through 1909, the crowds came, and the meetings were almost twenty-four hours a day nonstop. The presence and spirit of God brought about unity and cohesion among people of all races and backgrounds, who worshipped together well ahead of the beginning of the civil rights movement. Seymour called for unity and love with an agreement in God and to put aside denominational differences. When Charles F. Parham came to the Azusa

The Rise and Fall of the American Empire

Mission to preach, he said that it made God sick to his stomach to see black and white and all races worshiping together. But the truth was that it made Parham sick to his stomach, not God; it was Parham's problem. Even though Charles F. Parham was a founder and played a very important role in the Pentecostal movement, from that time on, it diminished, while humble William Seymour's role continued to rise. None of the leadership or people at the Azusa Street Mission wanted Parham to come back and preach anymore. Although Azusa was ahead of its time, most churches went back to segregation within a brief period after this.

Much can be learned from the Azusa Street Mission on many levels. The people were hungry for God and fervent in prayer. They had a reverence and fear of God and were committed to holiness and evangelism. They were not high-minded and prideful but would patiently wait on God. The leadership did not limit God but allowed Him to move as He would. The power and presence of God were undeniable, and the people flowed in the gifts of the Spirit. There were tongues and interpretation, singing in the spirit and prophecy, salvations, healings, deliverance, and miracles. There were crutches, canes, and braces along the walls left by people who were healed and no longer needed them. There were also notable and unusual manifestations of the Spirit.

One night, in particular, the fire department had been called after many neighbors reported that they saw a fire on the roof. When the fire department could not find a fire, the mission leadership said that it was the fire of God on the roof, like the burning bush

The Tale of Two Cities

Moses saw. When people heard that they were speaking in tongues like the apostles did on the day of Pentecost, they kept coming in droves to the mission. About 700 to 800 maximum could fit inside, and there would be hundreds more outside by the windows and entrance, and they would come and go twenty-four hours a day.

The leadership also started to print a publication called *The Apostolic Faith*, and it grew to a circulation of about 50,000, informing the readers of the events and news of the Azusa Street Mission. Ironically, this publication became one of the very things that led to the diminishment and demise of the mission. Upstairs on the second floor, twelve of the mission leaders and staff lived, including William Seymour and his wife. Seymour and his wife, Jenny Evans Moore, had met, fell in love, and married in 1906, around the time that he had first arrived in Los Angeles. One of the staff members, another woman, became offended with them for getting married and stated that it was a time for spiritual matters and not a time to get married. It is very possible that she was jealous that Seymour took to Jenny Evans and not her. Whatever her motivation was, she took the names and addresses of the 50,000 *Apostolic Faith* circulation list with her and left town. The Azusa Street Mission was never able to get them back, and many of those people were financially supporting the mission.

Once the Azusa Street Mission had given birth to its historic purpose and died, its spiritual children lived on. It had served its purpose and accomplished its destiny. Numerous lives were marked, changed, and never to be the same again. Missionar-

The Rise and Fall of the American Empire

ies were sent out from Azusa to over fifty nations of the earth to spread the message of Jesus and the empowerment of the Spirit. Leaders and churches were born and strengthened. Whole denominations like the Assemblies of God, the Apostolic, and Foursquare were also birthed. The worldwide Pentecostal and Charismatic movements were born and can be traced to Azusa. There are even approximately 150 million Catholics who are now part of the Catholic Charismatic revival (Cauchi, n.d.). The total number of Pentecostal and Charismatic Christians worldwide is now above 600 million. Thousands of pastors and leaders from all over the world visited the Azusa Street Mission and experienced this divine outpouring. They took back home the fire of God to kindle the Pentecostal flames in their nations (Melton, 2023) (Blumhofer, 2006) (Robert, 2017) ("History of the Catholic Charismatic Movement," n.d.).

CHAPTER 17

The Roaring Twenties

After America had gone through the horrors of World War I and the Spanish flu pandemic, it then drew a collective sigh of relief and just wanted to get back to normal. But many of the young men who were returning from the war had been so shell-shocked and traumatized that they felt a deep detachment from civilian life. They were called "the lost generation," and there was also a group of writers who picked up on this sentiment and mirrored it in their books. And many people sought various forms of entertainment to get their minds off the day-to-day routines. And some people called the roaring twenties the crazy years when many were pushing the boundaries of culture.

It was a period of economic prosperity, especially for those who continued to migrate from the country to relocate into the cities and urban areas. This economic growth accelerated consumer demand and introduced significant new trends in lifestyle and culture. The media, funded by the new mass market advertising industry, is driving consumer demand and is focused on celebrities, especially movie stars and sports heroes.

Before World War I, cars were a luxury for most Americans. But then the Ford Motor Company began to mass-produce them, and they became more affordable to the average person. By 1929, there were about 27 million cars in the United States, and the auto industry had jump-started other industries such as steel production, highway and road construction, motels, service stations, car dealerships, and new housing outside the urban centers. In a short time, the automobile had become an indispensable part of American culture.

The film industry led to the rise of Hollywood movie stars and celebrity influence. The films started out silent, but many new improvements were made, including sound and, later, color. The cinema boomed, producing a new form of entertainment that virtually ended old vaudeville theatricals. Watching a film was cheap and accessible; crowds poured into new downtown movie palaces and neighborhood theaters. The first all-talking full-length feature film was *Lights of New York*, released by Warner Brothers in 1928. The film industry introduced America to an array of different stars during Hollywood's Golden Era. New genres of music, including jazz, inspired many new dances that accompanied the songs. Even Mickey Mouse was first introduced in the 1928 film *Steamboat Willie* by Walt Disney Animation Studios. Television began to also develop in the 1920s, but the American public did not see any television shows until the 1940s.

Radio became the first mass broadcasting medium. Radios were expensive, but their mode of entertainment was revolutionary. Radio advertising became a platform for mass marketing. Radio programming was as varied as television became in the twenty-first century. In 1925, electrical recording, one of the greater advances in sound recording, became available with commercial-

The Roaring Twenties

ly issued gramophone records.

Electrification of the homes and cities of America slowed during the war but began to gain momentum in the 1920s. Industries switched from coal power to electricity. Telephones also became more common as lines continued to be strung across the continent. More of the new homes were getting indoor plumbing, made possible by modern sewer systems. New novel electrical gadgets and appliances were added to homes.

The skyscraper wars began in New York City and Chicago in the 1920s. With the increased population density and demand for office space, the race to go higher and higher was on. In 1920, the highest building in Chicago was the Wrigley and the highest in New York City was the Woolworth. Then, many others were built, including the Bank of Manhattan Trust and the Chrysler Building.

Art Deco first developed in France and then attracted international attention. Both the Chrysler Building and the Empire State Building were Art Deco icons. Construction on the world's tallest building of that time, the Empire State Building, began on March 17, 1930. The design for the Empire State Building was changed fifteen times until it was ensured to be the world's tallest. The Empire State Building held the record for the world's tallest building for forty years until 1971 (Cunningham, 2023) (Lindop, 2010).

Abraham Lincoln believed that God was the author of all human history but that He used people to write that history. God is also going to use you to help write the final chapter of human history. So, let's take a step back and rise above the cities and countryside of 1920s America and look at what was going on through both the eyes of God and of evil ("Lincoln Quotes," n.d.).

The Bible states that God does not change. See Malachi 3:6 and James 1:17. Our theology, understanding, and trust in God should not vary depending on circumstances, how we feel, what we see going on in the world, or even the pain and tragedies of our own lives. God is good, and He never changes. Yet we live in a broken, fallen world filled with sin, sickness, and disease, and evil is very active. There is a God-shaped vacuum inside everyone, and we can try for a lifetime to fill it with many things, but only God can fill this void. Every human heart is in search of significance and meaning, and only through a personal relationship with God will people find this.

As we build these monuments of man, what will matter and truly last for eternity? *The Titanic* could never possibly go down, right? Not even the hand of God could sink it. The Empire State Building will last forever, and New York's Twin Towers shall always stand, right? Christians have often been particularly ineffective at communicating the truth, and the devil is a well-practiced liar. It is the comparison of the eternal perspective and the temporal focus. For example, money without a mission and purpose can lead to materialism. Oftentimes, men are building their temporal kingdoms and empires while neglecting the eternal kingdom. Sensuality and sexuality without biblical boundaries weaken and

The Roaring Twenties

destroy the family unit and, eventually, a civilization.

Brilliant Harvard professor Carle C. Zimmerman began to study and write about these correlations as early as the 1920s and 1930s. He wrote that one of the first steps to destroy a civilization was to weaken and destroy the family unit, otherwise termed the nuclear family (Zimmerman, 2007). One excellent evil strategy is "the frog in the kettle." Keep turning up the heat slowly and keep introducing lies incrementally so they don't notice until they are being boiled alive. A stronghold is a network of lies that the devil builds inside a person or society that argues against the truth of God. And so, a spider web of lies is woven to entangle the sophisticated with complexities, entirely missing the simplicity of a loving God and the good news message. Is this the beginning of the "me, myself, and I" generation that defiantly declares, "Leave me alone; let me do what I want to do. Let me go to hell since it can't possibly be true anyway. I refuse to believe in God or follow Jesus."

Thomas Andrew Dorsey

Thomas Andrew Dorsey was born on July 1, 1899, in Villa Rica, Georgia. There were many great singers, songwriters, and composers of jazz, blues, and different genres during this time, but Dorsey was special. He was a key figure in the creation and popularization of gospel music throughout churches in America, which, in turn, influenced music and parts of society at large. Many of the first generation of twentieth-century gospel singers trained and worked with Dorsey, including James Cleveland, Sallie Martin,

The Rise and Fall of the American Empire

Roberta Martin, and the soulful anointed Mahalia Jackson.

Thomas Dorsey was born of Thomas Madison Dorsey, a minister and farmer, and Etta Plant Spencer. The Dorseys sharecropped on a small farm while the elder Dorsey, a graduate of Atlanta Bible College, traveled to nearby churches to preach. Music and the church were at the center of young Thomas's life, and he was exposed to a variety of musical styles at an early age. The Dorseys may have been poor, but they owned an expensive organ, and his mother, Etta, played it during his father's church services. His uncle was also a traveling musician who played a part in the early development of country blues. Also, slave spirituals, church sharp note singing, and conservative Protestant hymns all made a deep impression on young Thomas Dorsey.

Seeking a better life, the Dorseys moved to Atlanta but encountered other difficulties in the move and transition. Thomas dropped out of school after the fourth grade at age twelve. After wandering into the nearby 81 Theater and watching the Vaudeville Acts and Blues musicians, Dorsey aspired to join the 81 Theater's band. While he worked at the theater selling concessions, he befriended musicians who mentored him and trained him musically, all the while practicing long hours at home on his family's organ. As a teenager, he began to work with bands around Atlanta, playing barrel houses and rent parties.

Barely twenty years old, Thomas Dorsey relocated to Chicago in 1919, seeking opportunities in music. He quickly realized that

The Roaring Twenties

up-tempo jazz was more popular in 1919 Chicago, but later, as the Great Migration occurred from South to North, blues also gained recognition and popularity because that was a significant part of the music in the South. Dorsey began to compose songs, eventually copywriting approximately 3,000. He became one of the first musicians to copyright blues music. Thomas Dorsey did not seem to be particularly interested in writing church music, that is, until 1921, when he saw W. M. Nix perform "I Do, Don't You?" at the National Baptist Convention.

Upon hearing W. M. Nix sing, Dorsey was overcome, later recalling that his "heart was inspired to become a great gospel singer and worker in the Kingdom of the Lord and move people just like W. M. Nix did that Sunday morning." The experience prompted him to copyright his first religious song in 1922, "If I Don't Get There," a composition in the style of Charles Tindley, whom Dorsey idolized. He continued to work in blues music as well to make a living.

As more of Dorsey's compositions were recorded by Chicago's top artists, his reputation grew, and he was also hired by the Chicago Music Publishing Company and as a music arranger for Paramount Records. While working for Gertrude "Ma" Rainey from 1923 through 1926 as pianist and leader of the Wildcats Jazz Band, Dorsey composed and arranged her music in the blues style he was accustomed to, as well as vaudeville and jazz. In 1925, Thomas Dorsey married Nettie Harper, and she joined Dorsey on tour as "Ma" Rainey's wardrobe assistant.

The Rise and Fall of the American Empire

"Ma" Rainey was enormously popular and had a very rigorous touring schedule, but beginning in 1926, Dorsey was dealing with an ongoing deep depression that lasted for two years and considered suicide. Dorsey later recalled a big turning point in his life where he vowed to serve God and concentrate all his efforts on gospel music. He tells the story of how he attended church in 1928 with his sister-in-law, and while the minister was praying for him, he could literally feel the minister pulling a spirit, like a serpent, out of his body and out of his mouth. He related that he no longer felt depressed or suicidal after that deliverance. Then, after the death of a close friend of his, Dorsey was inspired to write his first gospel song with a blues influence: "If You See My Savior." The devil could see the calling on Thomas Dorsey's life and his potential greatness and tried to destroy him. But God had a plan for Thomas to fulfill, and as he gave God his "yes, Lord," that destiny began to increasingly be fulfilled.

There has always been debate in the Christian churches through the years about what is the best music for the church to represent God in worship and in other areas. In the 1920s, in Dorsey's era, many of the churches had ornate, sophisticated liturgical compositions by classical European composers, such as Handel's "Messiah" (1742). and Mozart's "Hallelujah" (1773). Personal expressions such as clapping, foot stomping, hand raising, and improvising with lyrics, rhythm, and melody were actively suppressed as being unrefined, vulgar, and degrading to the music and to the church. To say that there was pushback to gospel blues

tionally (Rosenberg, 2019).

The Harlem Renaissance

The Harlem Renaissance was an intellectual and cultural revival of African American music, dance, art, fashion, literature, theater, politics, and academia centered in Harlem, Manhattan, New York City, New York, rolling through the roaring twenties and into the 1930s. The movement also included the new African American cultural expressions across the urban areas of the Northeast and Midwest United States affected by a renewed militancy and the general struggle for civil rights, combined with the Great Migration of African American workers fleeing the racist conditions of the South, with Harlem often being the destination (Hutchinson, 2023).

And really, all of America in the 1920s was filled with a newfound optimism. The Wright brothers had amazingly put an airplane into the air, and the planes were only getting better and faster. There was money, investment, and refined engineering, and soon there were airlines connecting the cities. It seemed like anything was possible. As early as May 20, 1927, Charles A. Lindbergh successfully flew his single-engine plane, named the *Spirit of Saint Louis*, all the way across the Atlantic nonstop to Paris, France. There was a litany of things that Lindbergh had to deal with in the flight, but fatigue was at the top of the list. Numerous pilots had already died attempting what Lindbergh did. Because of his busy schedule and the stress, Lindbergh was not able to sleep the night prior to leaving. He ended up being awake for about fifty-five hours straight, flying without crashing. But the reality is that he dozed off many times in flight, sometimes for just a moment and sometimes longer (Charles Lindbergh, 2020).

The United States had also just recently finished building the Panama Canal in 1914, showing to the world what it could do by this engineering marvel. It was, at that time, the most expensive and extensive construction project in the history of the world ("Panama Canal," 2022).

America had greatly helped to obtain victory in World War I, yet when the courageous hard-punching battle unit, the Harlem Hell fighters, returned home, they were still met with prejudice by many Americans.

Many Americans felt like they were on top of the world in the roaring twenties as Babe Ruth continued to hit home runs and as many people were getting rich in industry and in the stock market. But there was a dark, black, bleak storm on the horizon for America in 1929. People were overconfident that the market would continue to grow, leading many to buy on margin or credit. Buying on margin meant purchasing shares with mostly borrowed money. Many were overconfident about the market and felt comfortable taking on loans, and banks were very relaxed in issuing them. The Great Stock Market Crash of 1929 largely occurred at the end of October. By mid-November, the stock market had lost nearly half of its value ("Stock Market Crash of 1929," 2010).

The Roaring Twenties

Times Square. New York about 1930.

CHAPTER 18

The Great American Depression

The Great American Depression was the worst economic downturn in the history of the industrialized world, lasting from the stock market crash of 1929 to 1939. It also affected world economies and played a role in the rise of fascism in Germany and Europe. When the US stock market crashed, it triggered a crisis in the international economy, which was linked via the gold standard.

Throughout the 1920s, the US economy had expanded very rapidly, and the nation's total wealth more than doubled. The stock market, centered in New York City on Wall Street, was the scene of reckless speculation where everyone from multi-millionaires to average daily citizens poured their savings into stocks. As a result, the stock market underwent rapid expansion, reaching its peak in August 1929. By then, production had already declined, and unemployment had risen, leaving stock prices much higher than their actual value. Also, wages at that time were low, consumer debt was growing, and the agricultural sector of the economy was struggling due to drought and falling food prices, and banks had an excess of large loans that could not be liquidated.

On October 24, 1929, as anxious investors began selling over-priced shares en masse, the stock market crash that many had feared had begun. Thirteen million shares were traded that day, which became known as Black Thursday. Another wave of panic hit Wall Street investors the following week when some 16 million shares were traded on Black Tuesday. Millions of shares ended up being worthless, and those investors who had bought stocks on the margin or with money they had borrowed were wiped out completely. Within ten weeks, the Stock Exchange had lost about 50 percent of its value. As consumer confidence vanished in the wake of the stock market crash, the reduction in spending and investment led factories and other businesses to slow down production and begin firing their workers. As stocks continue to fall, businesses increasingly fail, and unemployment rises rapidly. By 1932, about one out of every four workers was unemployed. For those who were fortunate enough to have a job, wages fell, and buying power decreased. Prior to the 1920s, most Americans had the pay cash mentality, and then through the 1920s, more average American citizens were using credit for purchases. Then, after the stock market crash, more Americans purchased with credit and increasingly fell into debt, seeing repossessions and foreclosures climb steadily. The economic woes of the US spread internationally because of the global adherence to the gold standard, which joined currencies and countries around the world to a fixed exchange.

Despite promises from the president that things would turn around and get better, matters continue to worsen, and millions were out of work and struggling to survive. The country's industrial production had dropped to half. Despite the federal government's efforts to come up with various solutions throughout the

The Great American Depression

1930s, it wasn't until the end of the decade, when World War II had begun, and the mighty gears of industry began to turn at full speed, that the recovery truly began.

And it wasn't just the families in the cities and urban areas trying to survive, with rising numbers of homeless relying on soup kitchens and breadlines. However, the farmers and folks in rural areas were also hit very hard by several factors. Sometimes, farmers couldn't afford to harvest their crops to get them to the starving people who desperately needed them, so they left the unharvested crops rotting in the fields. Also, the price being paid to farmers for the crops had been severely cut. Then, there was the "dust bowl" phenomenon that had occurred all the way from South Dakota to Texas starting in 1930. Severe droughts in the southern Plains, a farmed top layer of soil, high winds, and nightmarish dust killed crops, livestock, and people, inspiring a mass "grapes of wrath" migration of people from farmland to cities in search of survival and work ("Dust Bowl," 2009). There were four waves of banking panic that began in the fall of 1930. Large numbers of depositors lost confidence in the solvency of their banks and began to demand their money immediately, forcing banks to liquidate loans to supplement their insufficient cash reserves on hand. Bank runs hit the United States again in the spring of 1931 and the fall of 1932, and by early 1933, thousands of US banks had closed their doors. Hoover's administration tried to support failing banks with government loans in hopes that they would, in turn, loan to businesses that would hire back employees. By 1932, most American citizens

The Rise and Fall of the American Empire

lost confidence in Herbert Hoover's ability to manage or solve the nation's ongoing crisis, and they voted overwhelmingly for Franklin D. Roosevelt in the presidential election. Despite health issues and later the inability to walk, Roosevelt was a strong and steadying leader for the American public and was repeatedly reelected to the presidency until he died in office near the end of World War II (Franklin D. Roosevelt, 2020).

By Inauguration Day, March 4, 1933, every US state had ordered all remaining banks to close at the end of the fourth wave of banking panics, and the US Treasury didn't have enough cash to pay all government workers. FDR's calm demeanor and optimism did well towards restoring public confidence and steadying the nation's nerves with a series of radio broadcasts called "Fireside Chats." During Roosevelt's first one hundred days in office, his administration passed legislation that aimed to stabilize industrial and agricultural production, create jobs, and stimulate recovery. Additionally, FDR sought to reform the financial system, creating the Federal Deposit Insurance Corporation to protect depositors' accounts and the Securities and Exchange Commission, designed to regulate the stock market and prevent abuses of the kind that led to the crash of 1929.

When FDR began his first term as president, he passed an unprecedented amount of legislation to cope with the crisis of the Great Depression. Perhaps the thing that FDR was successful at was walking that long, arduous road to recovery with the American people and inspiring hope in the bleakest of times. Eleanor

The Great American Depression

continued to push God out of America, and a hideous darkness and chaos has entered in to take its place. We have had an overall absence of good and strong leadership steering the nation. It is possible that there are verifiable entities actively working to weaken, destroy, and overthrow the United States of America to continue to further a global agenda.

The American economy is currently saddled with a $34 trillion and growing national debt weighing down all efforts to move forward and make progress. We have had an incremental weakening and disintegration of the American nuclear family, step-by-step destroying the core strength of our civilization. The most recent COVID pandemic continued to weaken the nation in numerous ways, causing fear, instability, economic strain, and mental health issues as well. Organized crime and narcotics syndicates have caused an epidemic of death, drugs, and addiction, destroying America's youth and populace in general.

Human trafficking also ties into pornography and many other insidious spheres. Our nation, over the last several generations, has been subjected to a torrent of poisonous, deceptive alternative spiritualities. We have systematically killed and aborted over 50 million unborn children in the last fifty years alone, effectively erasing any solution, answer, or contribution to the world or society that they could have had. And like raw sewage, we have had a steady stream of ungodly messages, imagery, and ideologies poured out for our youth to drink through music and media. We have the pervasive teaching of humanism in our universities and colleges, and it is a miracle if a young person graduates with their faith intact or any left at all.

Many of our major cities have become war zones of crime, hopelessness, and the homeless. We also have an ongoing stream of illegal immigration crossing our borders, some of which are of criminal elements or terrorists. These are just some of the examples of the causes of decline, but there are many more. So, is it possible that we could see a second Great American Depression occur? Given the perfect storm, including economic collapse, war, and nuclear war, it could be worse.

Nobody knows exactly when Jesus will return, and the Lord controls the rise and fall of nations. I believe that there is a window of time to choose which ship to board, *the Titanic* ("*Titanic*," 2023) or Noah's ark. *The Titanic* is a type of trusting in the world, and the New Testament ark of Noah ("Noah's Ark," 2019) is a type of trusting in the unsinkable salvation of God through faith in Jesus.

CHAPTER 19

Aimee Semple McPherson

We see, throughout the Bible, real stories about real people. Sometimes, they made little mistakes, and sometimes, they made some big ones. We learn about the characters and individuals in the Bible, but we also learn about the redemptive love, goodness, and character of God. He sees us at our lowest points and at our worst and still loves us, wants us, and continues to work in our lives. Who is the biblical character that you would like to meet and talk to in heaven, and what might you ask them? All the believers and Christians who have gone before us were just like you and me, including Aimee Semple McPherson. They were subject to the same temptations, subject to humanity and the world, and did not always float around in prayer and walk on water.

Benny Hinn threw out startling statistics and figures on how many ministers fell or who have fallen, and it is very sobering ("About Pastor Benny Hinn," n.d.). Who in the world wants to answer the call of God and face the possibility in the future that your ministry, marriage, and life could become a disaster and a target of tabloid fever? Yes, answer the call, but get rock solid in God and forever be alert because you are being watched closely by everyone, including the enemy. Yes, God can restore fallen ministers, but the enemy loves to put fallen ministers on the front page and cry out, "Look at these circus clowns. Do you really want to follow Christianity?" Now, of course, those who have understanding and who are mature in their faith follow God and not people and put these types of things in perspective. God is perfect, His Word is eternal, and His plan is perfect, but He uses imperfect people, including Aimee Semple McPherson. So, with that in mind, let's look at the remarkable life of Aimee Semple McPherson.

Aimee Elizabeth Kennedy was born October 9, 1890, in the quiet rural community of Salford, Ontario, Canada. In her time and generation, she was the most famous evangelist in the world, surpassing Billy Sunday and other predecessors. Sister Aimee was also credited with the founding of the Foursquare Church, whose roots, along with the Assemblies of God churches, could be traced back to the Azusa Revival and outpouring in Los Angeles. The Foursquare Church believed in salvation, the baptism of the Holy Spirit, and the imminent return of Christ. Sister Aimee conducted healing services with thousands in attendance with good results. Sister Aimee utilized broadcast radio and other media, along with Angelus Temple Church, to point thousands of people to salvation in Jesus. Sister Aimee held the view that the United States was a nation founded and sustained by divine Providence and inspiration. She was very influential in the church, the Pentecostal movement, and later charismatic Christianity.

Aimee Elizabeth was born to James Morgan and Mildred Ona Kennedy in the late nineteenth century in Ontario, Canada. She had an early exposure to the teachings of the Bible through her mother, Mildred, who worked with the poor in Salvation Army soup kitchens. As a child, she would play "Salvation Army" with

Aimee Semple McPherson

classmates and preach sermons to dolls. At the turn of the century, teenager Sister Aimee strayed from Salvation Army teaching and began to read novels, watch movies, and go to dances. Then, in high school, she was taught the theory of evolution but began to question how that could possibly agree with the Bible. She wrote to a Canadian newspaper, questioning the taxpayer-funded teaching of evolution in the schools, and had people from all over the nation respond to her letter. Throughout her lifetime, she was a staunch anti-evolutionist.

While attending a revival in 1907, Aimee Elizabeth met Robert James Semple, a Pentecostal missionary from Ireland. At this meeting, Sister Aimee became enthralled by Semple and his message. She soon dedicated her life to Jesus and began courting Robert Semple. After a short time, they were married in a Salvation Army ceremony in August 1908. They moved to Chicago together and joined William Durham, Full Gospel Assembly. As she continued to study the Bible with her husband, Robert, while at Full Gospel Assembly, William Durham instructed Sister Aimee in the nine gifts of the Holy Spirit.

Both Sister Aimee and her new husband, Robert, agreed to go on a mission trip to China together, but both contracted malaria soon after arriving. Robert Semple also contracted dysentery and did not recover, dying in Hong Kong. Aimee Semple did recover and had a child, Roberta Star Semple, before returning to the United States. She continued to recuperate in New York City and then joined her mother, Mildred, who worked with the Salvation Army.

The Rise and Fall of the American Empire

While in New York, she met Harold Stewart McPherson, and they wed in 1912. After moving to Providence, Rhode Island, Aimee Semple McPherson had her second child, Rolf Potter Kennedy McPherson, in 1913.

She thought her days of evangelism and mission work were over, but still, a calling persisted. She struggled initially with emotional distress and then later with serious illness until she obeyed the calling to preach. Aimee McPherson did not believe that her husband, Harold McPherson, would agree with her at all, so she left with the kids to go preach without him. A few weeks later, she sent him a note and asked him if he would like to join her in the evangelistic work. Harold went after her to bring her home but relented after seeing her in action preaching. He then joined her in evangelism, setting up tents for revival meetings and preaching. But despite his initial enthusiasm, Harold got tired of being on the road and returned to Rhode Island by himself. In 1918, Harold McPherson filed for separation; then, a divorce was finalized in 1921. Aimee Semple McPherson had reached a fork in the road, and she felt that there was no other choice but the gospel road. However, Harold McPherson decided that he was not going with her.

In the early days of her ministry training, prior to leaving for China, Sister Aimee had a great mentor and help in William Durham and the Full Gospel Assembly in Chicago. She also became more familiar with the operation of the gifts of the Spirit and seemed to be particularly gifted in interpreting Glossolalia: translating the words and messages of people speaking in tongues.

Aimee Semple McPherson

During her ministry, she utilized most of the gifts of the Spirit, especially the gift of healing. In 1913, Sister Aimee began evangelizing, holding tent revivals across the country. She soon amassed a large following, oftentimes needing to relocate to bigger buildings to accommodate the ever-increasing crowds. People loved her infectious attitude and optimism, and the power and anointing of God flowed through her and the ministry. And as important as healing and the other gifts and operation of the Spirit were, she would try to maintain order in her meetings and place souls and salvations at the top of the list.

In 1916 and then again in 1918, Sister Aimee went on tours of the southern United States, sometimes even preaching, standing on the back seat of her convertible, the Gospel car, with a megaphone drawing crowds. In 1917, she started a magazine, *Bridal Call*, where she drew an analogy between Christ and His church as a marriage and encouraged women to step up and take active roles in the church. This magazine and her high profile continued to transform Pentecostalism into a main component of the American church. It was in Baltimore when Sister Aimee began to conduct evangelistic services at the Lyric Opera House, and the newspapers began writing many articles about her and the ministry. During these events, the crowds could barely be kept under control, and this time, it became a pivotal point in her career.

She moved to Los Angeles in 1918, and her continued rise in the public eye and the favor of God in her life enabled her to build the Angelus Temple, which had the largest congregation in the world at that time. According to church records, Angelus Temple received 40 million visitors within the first seven years (Semple McPherson, n.d.). When Sister Aimee had first arrived in Los Angeles, her mother, Mildred Kennedy, rented the 3,500-seat Philharmonic Auditorium, and people waited for hours to enter the crowded venue. Sister Aimee was ordained by the Assemblies of God in 1919, but despite her affinities with Pentecostals, her beliefs were interdenominational. She believed that Jesus was Lord over the whole church and not just one denomination. Los Angeles was the perfect place for the ministry to be located and have a local, national, and even international impact. Los Angeles itself, by that time, had become increasingly diverse and international, with people having moved there from all over the globe. Also, the area had become a very popular vacation destination, with a steady stream of visitors from everywhere. For several years, Sister Aimee traveled and raised money for Angelus Temple, but not wanting to incur debt, she found a construction company willing to work with her with a small down payment. They ended up raising more money than expected, building a larger church than originally envisioned, and paying for it all cash by the dedication on January 1, 1923.

Sister Aimee always had a heart for ministry and for people and would always look for ways to win souls for Jesus and make a difference in the city. She had a very strong personality that enabled her to do what she did, but perhaps she could have been a little better at listening to her mother's and daughter's advice. She

Aimee Semple McPherson

began to get the notion that she could utilize Hollywood and celebrity influence to broaden her evangelistic outreach. In the long run, that had mixed results. Sister Aimee had always had very sound conservative foundational theological beliefs. But she began to dress differently, with more sophistication and a touch of Hollywood celebrity. This, along with other issues, created strain with her mother, daughter, and some ministry staff and may very well have contributed to added stresses in her ministry and life, leading to an early demise.

Sister Aimee was never short on ideas on how to bless the community and always looked for opportunities to do so. She developed Angelus Temple to be an organization to provide for physical and spiritual needs. The temple began to collect donations for a humanitarian Relief Fund, and there were always needs. When men were released from prison, the Angelus men's ministry helped them to find jobs. The women's ministry sewed and made clothes for babies and children of poor mothers. After an earthquake in Santa Barbara in 1925, the church responded to help with food and blankets and in any way that they could. Angelus Temple had a free clinic to treat children and the elderly, staffed by doctors and nurses. They helped pay families utility bills in emergency situations so their power would not be shut off. Drawing on her experience working for the Salvation Army in her youth, Angelus Temple opened a commissary in 1927. As the Great Depression set in, the church tirelessly helped the community with a soup kitchen, free clinic, charity, food, clothing, and blankets. Church records show an estimated 1.5 million meals were served during the Depression. When the government shut down the free school lunch program, Sister Aimee had Angelus take it over, keeping the children fed. All were welcome and ministered to at Angelus Temple, including migrants.

Sister Aimee became the master of the illustrated sermon, having a small group of artists, electricians, decorators, and carpenters who built a different set for each service and sermon idea that she had. They had an orchestra and large choirs, and their church held as many as twenty-two services a week. Sister Aimee condemned most theater and film as the devil's workshop but incorporated cinematic methods to present biblical messages in a fresh and energetic way. You would most certainly not fall asleep in a 1920s Angelus Temple church service. Sister Aimee preached a conservative gospel but utilized radio, stage, cinema, and every modern means possible.

When Sister Aimee went back out on the road periodically between 1919 and 1922 for revival events, she broke all existing attendance records of any kind, political, theater, et cetera. One such event was held in a boxing arena, and she walked around with a sign that read "Knock Out the Devil." In San Diego, the National Guard had to be called in to help control one of her revival crowds of 30,000 people. Another reason that so many people came to her revivals and services was that she prayed for the sick. She had faith for this, even as a young woman, and prayed for many thousands of people in her ministry. Throughout the years, Angelus

Temple would continue to have weekly and monthly services with healing prayer for the sick.

Another great accomplishment of Sister Aimee was helping found the Foursquare Church, which now has about 8 million members. She also helped unify all of Pentecostalism in general to become part of mainstream Christianity. Aimee Semple McPherson died at the young age of fifty-three, September 27, 1944, in Oakland, California. Once again, thousands gathered, but this time to mourn the farm girl from Ontario who rose to be the greatest evangelist of her generation ("Aimee Simple McPherson: Four-square Phenomenon," n.d.) (Aimee Semple McPherson, 2022) ("Aimee Semple McPherson's Biography," n.d.). Sister Aimee's son, Rolf K McPherson, became the president and leader of the Foursquare Church for the next forty-four years. Angelus Temple has just held its one-hundred-year anniversary in 2023. Founder and CEO of the Dream Center Los Angeles, Matthew Barnett, and his wife, Caroline, currently serve as lead pastors of the historic Angelus Temple. Matthew Barnett arrived in Los Angeles in 1994, hoping to just stay for a few months until his father, Tommy Barnett, could find a pastor to lead the church. Almost thirty years have gone by now, and he is a much older, wiser man who has learned much about patience and grace, leading an inner-city Ministry in Los Angeles (Klett, 2020).

CHAPTER 20

Kathryn Kuhlman

Kathryn Johanna Kuhlman was born on May 9, 1907, in Johnson County, near Concordia, Missouri, to German-American parents Joseph Adolph Kuhlman and Emma Walkenhorst. Her father, Joseph, had a 160-acre property outside of Concordia but, after selling it, moved into town.

In 1972, towards the end of her life, Kathryn Kuhlman spoke to a crowd of students at Oral Roberts University, many of whom would go on into ministry. With Oral Roberts himself sitting mid-stage right behind her, she poured out her heart and wisdom to these young future ministers, imparting wisdom of a life lived, serving, and following God. She was like an old, tired warrior pacing back and forth in front of the new recruits in boot camp, trying to drive home the reality of the sacrifice that went on behind the scenes in her life and ministry. You see the seven-course meal served at the banquet, but it took a lifetime to prepare and serve it. You see the crowds at the events and the television shows, and you hear about the countless thousands healed. And you watch the dramatic figure named Kathryn Kuhlman in the middle of it all, and you think, *How cool.* But you don't know, and you don't realize the price that she paid. It cost her everything (Kuhlman, 2020). Just like George Whitefield, she was always a hard worker and drove herself tirelessly, even with health issues, all the way to the end of her life and ministry, aged sixty-eight, February 20, 1976.

The Rise and Fall of the American Empire

God has been restoring to the church, at the end of this dispensation, all the aspects and dimensions of the Spirit, including the healing ministry. And though there have been many great ministers and ministries in this sphere, perhaps of all of them, Kathryn Kuhlman was the one used by God who stood out in the miraculous. Many are called, but not everyone responds and answers the call. Kathryn Kuhlman developed, throughout her life, a remarkable sensitivity to the Holy Spirit, a deep understanding of the nature and character of God, and a very close walk with Him. She recalls her first experience with the Holy Spirit at age fourteen and being born-again at her mother's Methodist Church. She said jokingly that she wasn't sure if anyone had ever been saved in that church, before or since, but she was. She did not know anything about the Holy Spirit, but as they came to the last song, while she was holding the hymnal, she felt the spirit of God and began to shake and tremble. She had to set the hymnal down in the pew and respond. She felt an overwhelming awareness of her spiritual condition and then did the only thing that she knew to do. She got up and went to the chair where she had seen people praying for and receiving ministry, and then she sat down and wept. No one really led her to the Lord, but she clearly counted that to be the time and moment when she was saved and born again.

Her first exposure to ministry began as a teenager, assisting her older sister Myrtle and brother-in-law in Idaho and other areas of the Great Northwest. Her sister Myrtle had married a traveling evangelist, Everett Benjamin Parrott, after meeting him at Moody

Kathryn Kuhlman

Bible Institute in Chicago. Myrtle probably needed help with several things, including the children, and asked the Kuhlman parents to allow young Kathryn to join them on the ministry trail, which they reluctantly did. It was 1924, and seventeen-year-old Kathryn never really went back to Concordia after that time.

Although the life of a traveling evangelist was very difficult, and there seemed to also be some additional stresses in Everett and Myrtle's marriage, the hands-on education was invaluable for Kathryn. Everett Parrott operated in many of the gifts of the Spirit, including healing, and young Kathryn saw, for the first time, that people fall under the power of the Holy Spirit. Something resonated deep within Kathryn Kuhlman, and she knew that this was who she was and this was what she was supposed to do. There may have been several people, ministers, and convergences of circumstances that helped birth the healing ministry of Kathryn Kuhlman, including Aimee Semple McPherson, Reverend Mother Amanda H. Williams, and especially the early years assisting Everett Benjamin Parrott. Parrott's mantle and anointing fell on Kathryn. And though Parrott eventually left the evangelism trail at that time, and Myrtle soon followed, remarkably, Kathryn Kuhlman continued and developed as an evangelist and minister. She described herself as a one-girl army.

Sometimes, the way people are hardwired enables them to do what they do and to fulfill a God-given purpose and destiny. There were some very humble stories in the beginning of her ministry, like the time she was preaching, but the farmer didn't have any

The Rise and Fall of the American Empire

more room in the house, so he cleaned out the Turkey house for her to stay in. Or when she did get a room in a house in winter, there was no heat, and she would hide under three blankets with her head poking out to study the Bible. She was remarkably determined and began to blossom and grow into a very good minister. And in those early days, she taught what she knew, and that was a salvation message delivered in a manner that connected with the people. It was in Denver, Colorado, that Kathryn Kuhlman developed a church that grew to 2,000 members, with many of the prominent traveling evangelists and ministers stopping there on their circuits to preach.

A tragedy occurred in the winter of 1934 when Kathryn's beloved father, Joseph, whom she adored, was struck by a car and died. She drove for hours and miles through ice and snow but did not make it in time to see him alive, as he died prior to her arrival. She was heartbroken and even angry with the teenager who had struck her father, Joseph, with the car. She stated that somewhere around the time of the funeral, God gave her a grace to forgive the young man who had struck her father with the car. Kathryn's mother, Emma, had a beautiful salvation experience sometime later, but Kathryn privately wondered about her father and whether he made it to heaven. Sadly, he had never seen his daughter preach over the last ten years, as there was a big distance, and they were both busy with life. Joseph Kuhlman had attended the local Baptist Church in Concordia, Missouri, and he knew about Jesus well, but the unknown question to Kathryn was whether her father knew

Kathryn Kuhlman

and trusted Jesus in a saving relationship.

And just when Kathryn Kuhlman was getting some momentum and being established as a minister, the big mistake came: the derailment of her ministry and the wilderness years. Yes, God is the God of a second chance, and he can take our failures and brokenness and make something beautiful out of it. But the process is not always easy. In life, we all want to be loved and to love someone, and whom we choose to marry is one of the most important decisions that we will ever make. Especially for someone who is called by God. Is this person going to encourage, support, and help my calling and destiny? During the time that Kathryn Kuhlman had the large 2,000-member Denver Revival Tabernacle in Colorado, many ministers and evangelists came through town and preached there, including Burroughs Waltrip, an evangelist from Texas. He probably initially presented himself to Kathryn as a single man, but that was not accurate. He may have wanted a divorce from his wife and was moving in that direction, but he was a married man with kids.

Kathryn was completely smitten by the man and became entangled emotionally with someone who really didn't care about what was best for her but what he wanted. The handsome evangelist had already dumped his wife and kids and moved to Mason City, Iowa, where he started a revival ministry called Radio Chapel, as that was one of the biggest and growing mediums of communication of that time. Kathryn and pianist Helen Gulliford helped Waltrip raise funds for Radio Chapel. As Kathryn became romantically involved with Waltrip, it hindered her ability to find the will of God in the matter.

From the time that she was young, she had struggled with a degree of low self-esteem and may have reasoned that she would not find someone else to love her. Whatever her private thoughts were on the matter, against the advice of friends and family, she and Burroughs Waltrip were wed in a secret ceremony on October 18, 1938. It is even recorded that she fainted prior to the ceremony. When they were first married, Waltrip would do all the preaching and would not allow Kathryn to preach. People later recalled that they would see Kathryn Kuhlman crying and weeping in those events, with her head down, thinking that she was under the power of the Holy Spirit, but likely, it was the effects of regret. Although she was miserable in the marriage and had no peace, she tried to do different things with her time, including attending Aimee Semple McPherson's Life Bible School for a period. It was during this time in Los Angeles that she had her dead-end day. That day, she brokenly walked by herself to the end of a dead-end street. She felt that her very life had come to a dead end. She cried out to God and said, "All I have is my love for you. I have nothing, but if you still want this nothing, I give it to you." There was no question in her heart and mind about what she had to do. She went home, packed her bags, left Waltrip, and returned to following and serving God, no matter what the future would hold. The year was 1944, but it would take until 1948 before the divorce was finalized. Kathryn had worked so hard at establishing a ministry when

Kathryn Kuhlman

she was younger, and she was determined to get back and build it again, and she did so for the remainder of her life.

The first place Kuhlman went after her separation from Waltrip was Franklin, Pennsylvania, where she held a series of meetings. But the rumors that continued to follow her, about her and Waltrip, did not make it easy to reestablish her preaching ministry. There were many obstacles that she continued to overcome and press through, one being the prevailing attitude at that time that there should not be women preachers, much less a divorcee. A turning point occurred in 1946 when Kuhlman was invited by Matthew J. Maloney, the owner of the Gospel Tabernacle in Franklin, Pennsylvania, to return there to conduct a series of meetings. The meetings went very well, and then Kuhlman also began to preach radio broadcasts on station WKRZ and nearby Oil City, Pennsylvania. Things were looking up, and within a few months, her program had also been added to the schedule of WPGH, a Pittsburgh station.

By 1948, Kuhlman began holding meetings in neighboring cities, including Pittsburgh. God used everything that Kathryn had gone through, including the wilderness years, to transform her into what she was. She had gone through just about every town nook and cranny preaching salvation in Idaho as a teenager and young woman. She had diligently built up the ministry in Colorado, including the Denver Revival Tabernacle, learning invaluable preaching and ministry skills from Phil Kerr and all those who preached on divine healing and the Holy Spirit who had come through there. She was influenced by Aimee Semple McPherson

The Rise and Fall of the American Empire

and other healing evangelists, briefly attending Sister Aimee's Bible college. She learned death of self, picking up her cross, walking and talking with Jesus, and allowing Him to continue to transform her. Perhaps God even used the lingering agony of her father's early death, and not knowing fully if he made heaven, to inspire Kathryn Kuhlman to lead countless thousands to salvation. She had begun to learn to pay and pray the price in following Jesus, and it wasn't cheap; it cost her everything.

In the previous phase of her career, Kuhlman was strictly an evangelist and limited her preaching to a salvation message. While in Franklin, she occasionally preached on healing and would call people to the front, not only for salvation but also to be healed. Not fully understanding the occasional healings, Kuhlman began investigating these manifestations of God's power more thoroughly. In 1947, she preached her first series on the Holy Spirit. During the first meeting, a woman was healed of a tumor while listening to Kuhlman preach. Later, during the series, a man also received a notable healing and miracle. These events marked the beginning of Kathryn Kuhlman's healing ministry.

The first time Kuhlman preached in Pittsburgh was in 1943, when she held a six-week preaching series. At that time, she met Maggie Hartner, who later became her secretary and close friend. Hartner continued to urge Kathryn to move her ministry to Pittsburgh, which she finally did following a series of events, including the roof collapsing at the Faith Temple location after a heavy snowstorm. It was now the late 1950s, and she set up her office

Kathryn Kuhlman

in the Carlton house and began to hold regular meetings at Pittsburgh's Carnegie Hall, where she continued until 1971.

Things went well as the success of the ministry grew, yet the feathers of competition had been ruffled, with many pastors accusing her of stealing away their church members. One preacher in particular, Dallas Billington of Ohio, charged her with impropriety for being a woman who preached and claimed that miracles no longer happened since the days of the apostles. Billington also enjoyed waving around in front of people that she had been divorced.

In 1965, Kuhlman extended her ministry to California with a meeting in Pasadena. Soon after, she began holding meetings in the Shrine Auditorium in Los Angeles, which she continued until 1975. Sometimes, God uses particular people in specific ways. I think of Reverend Kenneth E. Hagin and how God used him to teach faith to the body of Christ. Reverend Hagin also taught something I found very interesting, which was the transference of mantles. A mantle passed from Elijah to Elisha. Many great and anointed individuals received an anointing and a mantle from the individual that they were under, learning from, and being instructed by. For example, Richard Roberts was probably the main recipient of the Oral Roberts anointing. Reverend Kenneth E. Hagin stated that he believed that the main mantle that came upon Kathryn Kuhlman was from Everett Benjamin Parrott, Kathryn's sister Myrtle's husband.

183

The Rise and Fall of the American Empire

Parrott had many notable miracles during his ministry. So how did God use Kathryn Kuhlman, and what was the main purpose of her ministry? Perhaps it was the beginning of the restoration of the miraculous in this dispensation, prior to the return of Jesus. The Kathryn Kuhlman Foundation estimated the number of healings and miracles that occurred during her ministry, recorded, and reported to be at least 2 million, most of which occurred in the last ten to fifteen years of her life. Reverend Kenneth E. Hagin said that it was very important for individuals who had received a miracle or healing to know the Word of God, learn it, and be strong in it and strong in faith so they do not lose their healing.

In one incident, Hagin observed Everett Parrott pray for a man in Tucson, Arizona, who was as stiff as a board, and this man was completely healed. Sometime later, Hagin saw and talked to this same man, and he had lost his healing; Hagin had to explain to him what had happened, walk him through it, and pray for him again patiently to get it back (K. E. Hagin, *The Healing Anointing*, 1997). Kathryn Kuhlman had countless people come forward and testify of the miracles that they had received from God. Perhaps the greatest symbol of Kathryn Kuhlman's ministry was an empty wheelchair. There were numerous occasions where people were healed at her services without her even touching them or, in some cases, without even saying a word.

There was one man in particular who testified of the miraculous. He had been a captain in the Houston police force and later went on to be the head of the Reverend Billy Graham's security force. He was a big-time skeptic of the miraculous and frankness of Kathryn Kuhlman. Later in his life, he became very sick and ill to the point where he had pretty much resigned to dying and began to put his house in order. Whatever his motivation was, to possibly see if something could happen, he attended a Kathryn Kuhlman service. He was completely miraculously healed and stated that he felt the power of God come on him, and the most utter fatigue and exhaustion left him, and life and energy entered him! (Kuhlman, 2020)

Many individuals and ministers, including Benny Hinn, were greatly impacted by Kathryn Kuhlman's ministry. He relates that as a young man, when Kuhlman was still alive, he would attend her services and watch everything that was going on like a sponge soaking it in. And in one service, he states that the Holy Spirit came upon him in a powerful and remarkable way, forever marking him and changing his life.

Pastor and Evangelist Benny Hinn was originally born in Israel and has had an amazing ministry for fifty years. He has a very deep and profound knowledge and understanding of the Word of God and is a great Bible teacher. He just recently finished another phase of his education, having gone to Hebrew language school to deepen his already insightful understanding of Scripture ("About Pastor Benny Hinn," n.d.). Healing Evangelist Mario Murillo was also greatly impacted by Kathryn Kuhlman's ministry, relating the amazing stories of her time at the Shrine Auditorium in Los Angeles, where countless thousands of miracles took place.

The Rise and Fall of the American Empire

Mario Murillo is a strong, fierce, fiery minister (Murillo, 2021) cut in the mold of a David Wilkerson or John Osteen. A remnant of these culture-shaking change agents is left. Men like John Hagee and his son in Texas, "the sons of thunder," Matthew and Luke Barnett, Pastor Michael Maiden, and others. Doctor Maiden has had a Churchillian bulldog determination and tenacity in a nearly fifty-year ministry. He has had a remarkable never-give-up, never-quit mentality and has encouraged others to let God finish writing the end of their stories.

Although there will always be skeptics and naysayers, Kathryn Kuhlman would state that the miracles of healing need no defense. And she was always just as happy as the people who got miracles each time. Countless thousands of people testified of the miracles that they had received through the years at her services. She was like Oral Roberts in that she would point people to God and say in different ways and words, "Don't look at me, but keep your eyes on God; keep focused on the Holy Spirit." Kathryn Kuhlman's fame and celebrity continued to rise not only because of the healing miracles but also because she was very high profile in the media. She had two television programs in the 1960s and 1970s, including *I Believe in Miracles*, which brought her into the American living rooms and conscience.

Kathryn Kuhlman cared about people, human suffering, and their eternal souls. She desired that everyone would be healed at her services, yet some left still in pain. Throughout her years of ministry, she also introduced countless thousands to the greatest

Kathryn Kuhlman

miracle of all: salvation. Once in a service, Kathryn stated that she herself was not immune to sickness. She had been diagnosed in 1955 with a heart condition by medical professionals. Throughout the years, she had kept a very busy schedule that only got busier and more intense as time went on.

During the last couple of years of her life, the pain in her chest intensified to the point where it was almost unbearable. And instead of slowing down, she only pushed herself harder with travel and meetings and services. She probably reasoned to herself that she would not die until her race was over. She finished her race on February 20, 1976, at Hillcrest Medical Center, Tulsa, Oklahoma. The attending medical personnel stated that a bright light hovered over her body at her passing, and other nurses and personnel stated that a fragrant smell of roses permeated the hospital at her passing ("I Am God's Witness," 2022).

You might ask, "Why didn't Kathryn get a miracle in her heart?" Well, I believe that she did. I draw a comparison to the great basketball player Pete "Pistol Pete" Maravich. At his death, they discovered a major problem in his heart where he could have died at any time, much younger. I saw him on Christian television, relating how he had an experience with God and became born again, and he died shortly after that. God kept Pistol Pete Maravich alive until he was saved, gave his testimony to thousands, and finished his course. God supernaturally kept Kathryn Kuhlman alive, despite her heart condition and her relentless schedule, until she had finished her course and race (Foust, 2009).

Kathryn Kuhlman authored fifty-one different books, including *I Believe in Miracles*, *Nothing Is Impossible with God*, and *A Glimpse into Glory*. Numerous authors wrote books about her, including Jamie Buckingham's *Daughter of Destiny*. In 1957, The Kathryn Kuhlman Foundation was established to fund mission projects around the world, as well as other ministry works. There were many beautiful songs sung on the day of Kathryn Kuhlman's funeral, and just as she would have wanted, they pointed the people to God (Selvidge, 1999) ("Kathryn Kuhlman's Biography," n.d.).

Winston Churchill

CHAPTER 21

America Enters World War II

In the 1930s, the Great Depression in America had been like a war, a battle for survival by Americans, both in the cities and in the rural communities. And ironically, it would be the beginning of another war that ultimately brought the United States to full economic recovery. FDR had introduced a vast array of legislation and ideas to get the country back on track, some of which worked well and others not so well. When FDR saw Germany and Adolf Hitler amassing a giant war machine in the late 1930s, he and America began to respond in kind. Winston Churchill had been sounding the alarm for years, warning of the impending German threat. He had observed Germany's bitter defeat in World War I and the lingering smoldering desire for vengeance by many, especially the rising Adolf Hitler.

Churchill had not only read Hitler's *Mein Kampf* but had been observing Germany steadily amassing the largest war machine the world had ever seen. He repeatedly tried to warn England and all of Europe that you cannot reason with Adolf Hitler, but you must stop him (*Mein Kampf*, 2023). Churchill even stated privately that he could literally see the evil inside Hitler through his eyes (W. R. Manchester, 2012). The United States tried very hard to stay out of World War II until it was no longer possible. Up until the time that the Japanese attacked Pearl Harbor and the United States entered the war, FDR had already instinctively ramped up the gears of American industry to help the Allied war effort. It was at that time in the late 1930s, when America began to accelerate efforts in the factories and industry that the economy began to fully recover from the effects of the Great Depression.

I want to mention that the Bible talks about spiritual warfare and draws a parallel between the natural and the spiritual. It talks about a battle between light and darkness, good and evil, and speaks of the devil as the adversary of mankind. The Bible talks about the necessity of Christians to have the mindset of a soldier, enduring hardship with an eternal perspective and not getting caught up or entangled in the world or civilian affairs. It talks about an unseen spiritual dimension where holy angels and evil spirits war. The Bible talks about the need to be strong in our faith, strong in knowing the Word of God, and clothed in the armor of God.

Prior to being deployed on D-Day and in many other theaters of war and battles, there were many religious services, church services, and prayers going up, as many young soldiers were uncertain if they would even make it back alive. The average age of an American soldier starting World War II was barely twenty years old. In the late 1930s, many young, unemployed American men voluntarily enlisted in the different branches of the military just to be able to have a job and two meals a day.

World War II Begins

When Germany invaded Poland in 1939, that marked the beginning of World War II and a long global conflict involving thirty

concentration camps to be worked to death in service of Germany's deteriorating war effort. When World War II was finally over, more Jews immigrated to the United States and Israel. Israel was once again established as a nation on May 14, 1948. How Holocaust survivors rebuilt their lives was complex and individual. Some would return to their hometowns and villages only to find that there was no longer anyone there, and they had to find somewhere else to go to start again ("The Holocaust," 2023).

The Battle of Britain

From July 10 to October 31, 1940, Germany's Luftwaffe air force bombed London and England during the blitz to destroy the RAF prior to invading. While the Royal Air Force and Navy responded with their own assaults and bombings and with help from new defense systems and radar, Britain was able to regroup and eventually win the battle. During this time, Winston Churchill lived underground in a fortified bunker but was notorious for rushing up onto the rooftops during air raids to see what was going on. All the while, he continued to plead with FDR for help, and while he obtained munitions and resources, America continued to stay out of the war ("Battle of Britain," 2022). One of the reasons was that FDR did not believe America was yet ready for a total war effort. So, he had the factories and industry kick it into another gear of accelerated preparation while young, unemployed Americans continued to enlist.

The Battle of Crete

On May 20, 1941, German paratroopers invaded the Greek island of Crete, marking history's first mostly airborne attack. Day one of the campaign resulted in heavy losses for the Germans, but fearing that there could be an additional sea assault, Allied forces soon withdrew and evacuated in defeat. Although the Germans took the island of Crete, primarily due to the heavy losses, Hitler declared that the day of the parachutist was over, and it became Germany's last parachutist airborne attack. Churchill continued to press FDR for help, relating Britain's dire circumstances. The role of the Russians on the Eastern Front also continued to escalate and intensify (Gilbert, 2023).

The Siege of Leningrad

In the last hundred years, the world has increasingly become interconnected and international, and more so now. What happens in one part of the world has a ripple effect throughout the rest of the world. As the siege of Leningrad wore on, Joseph Stalin continued to press Winston Churchill to put up a Western Front to alleviate the fierce, unrelenting pressures of the Eastern Front. Churchill had flown to Russia for another round of talks with Joseph Stalin, who once again taunted him, asking him why he was afraid of the Germans and why he wouldn't put up the Western Front.

The British army was stretched thin, and they had been doing everything they could to stave off German advances in Africa, the Mediterranean, at home, and elsewhere. But it simply was not enough. Stalin insisted on a western front if his army was to survive. Churchill had his head lowered as he walked back to his room at the Kremlin after a night of drinking and talking to Stalin and his war counsel. Suddenly, in frustration, he jammed his lit cigar into the gold-leafed wall, knowing Stalin was right. He would once again talk to Franklin Roosevelt regarding America's much-needed entry into the war. That night in the Kremlin war room, it was as much a vodka drink-a-thon as a conference. Before the night was over, at least one of Stalin's generals was passed out under the table (W. R. Manchester, 2012).

Whether Hitler had planned it all along or if he decided Russia and their ideologies could never fit into his grand vision of a new German world, he turned on Russia and began to attack. It gave the battered English army time to regroup, and Churchill continued to lobby FDR. Hitler felt that the German army could quickly advance and roll over the Russians on the Eastern front like they had so successfully done to many other European countries. This one decision, along with the hand of Providence, eventually led to the defeat of the Axis powers in World War II. Hitler had riled the Russian bear, and he underestimated them.

Joseph Stalin was every bit as ruthless and brutal as Adolf Hitler (Hingley, 2023). He was said to have a machine gunner behind his penal troops in case anyone tried to retreat (Vnutrennikh, n.d.). During the brutal siege of Leningrad itself, which lasted nearly 900 days, from September 1941 to January 1944, Stalin did little to alleviate the suffering of the Russian people trapped in the city.

Leningrad had become encircled by the German troops from the south, the Finnish forces from the north, and the Azuls, a division of Spanish volunteers.

Of the 2.5 million inhabitants of Leningrad on the eve of the conflict, only 600,000 were still alive in the city when it was finally liberated by the Red Army on January 27, 1944. Around 1 million had been evacuated before and during the siege. It is estimated that 800,000 people in Leningrad died during the siege, mostly from cold and hunger. One small Russian girl named Tanya Savicheva kept a diary of her family's experience of being trapped in Leningrad during the war. There was relentless bombing of the city, with all food and supplies cut off. Most of the electrical grid was knocked out, as temperatures dropped to negative twenty degrees centigrade and even as low as negative forty degrees centigrade as the starving family huddled together to stay warm in the winter of 1941. Dogs and cats disappeared from the city as the starving people tried to survive. In her diary, little Tanya Savicheva recorded the death of every family member until only she was left ("The Diary of Tanya Savicheva," 2007).

Winston Churchill also said that Hitler had forgotten that Russia had a winter. Many German soldiers did not have sufficient clothing when they were deployed and suffered frostbite or worse. The German tanks were like rolling ice boxes, sometimes colder inside than out. Germany had sent their finest troops to the Eastern Front, hoping for a relatively quick victory, but the Red Army was relentless. The German army would knock out one red division, but then another one would move up and take its position. Some of the fiercest fighting of World War II was at the Eastern Front. The German forces were close to taking Leningrad in August-September 1941 but failed to break the defense. The Red Army finally moved into Leningrad in January 1944 to liberate the city (Andrews, 2016).

The Battle of Moscow

Following Germany's Operation Barbarossa, which was the invasion of the Soviet Union, the Axis launched the campaign to capture the capital city of Moscow before winter set in. A little late, though, as the German army launched the campaign on October 2, 1941, and it was already getting cold in Moscow. In preparation, the Red Army fortified the city and brought in reinforcements. After a series of gains and losses on both sides during harsh weather, the Germans were eventually beaten back and forced to retreat on January 7, 1942 (Swift, 2023).

Pearl Harbor

The Sleeping Giant Awakens

Why in the world would the tiny island nation of Japan launch a surprise attack on the United States naval base at Pearl Harbor, Hawaii, on December 7, 1941, killing 2,400 Americans and destroying twenty-one ships and 300 aircraft? Stepping back into the 1800s, Japan had been an isolated island nation in Asia with a largely agricultural economy. But then the Meiji Restoration began around 1868, lasting till 1912, transforming Japan into an industrial power.

They reinstalled the emperor as the head of state and increasingly became militaristic and nationalistic. At the turn of the century, they began to flex their muscles and aggressively fought the first Sino-Japanese War and the Russo-Japanese War, which they won. They began to establish themselves as an imperial superpower and were even allies of the United States during World War I. However, because Japan was very reliant and dependent on international trade, with its diminishment due to the onset of the Great Depression, it became significantly weakened.

Japan and its emperor decided that instead of allowing the nation's economy to collapse, they would invade Manchuria, China, to plunder them and their natural resources. The public opinion of Japan in America continued to grow worse, especially after they attacked Nanjing and American citizens were killed in the attack. The United States was largely an ally of China at that time and renounced Japan, but it was not keen on entering into another war.

Tensions continued to rise in the late 1930s when the United States established economic sanctions against Japan, which stifled their economy. Japan's response was to invade French Indochina in 1940 to assert its nationalism. The United States responded by instituting a trade embargo on Japan, effectively crippling their economy. Ninety percent of Japan's oil came in from other countries, and if they were not able to get oil, their militaristic expansion also came to a standstill. They were as mad as hornets at the

America Enters World War II

United States and went ahead and allied with Germany and Italy in World War II, also because of their shared desires of conquest and nationalism. Perhaps they were also emboldened by their new alliance with Germany; they decided to attack Pearl Harbor and continue to expand their occupation of Southeast Asia. So, the attack on Pearl Harbor was a surprise, but tensions had been building for years.

It seemed like a win at first, but then the emperor of Japan realized that he had awakened a sleeping giant. The next day, December 8, 1941, the United States declared war on Japan, and by the following week, Germany had declared war on the United States of America. The mindset of America and FDR shifted to total war, and within six months, the US military struck back against Japan with a big victory at the Battle of Midway. FDR had felt for some time that the United States was simply not ready for a total war effort, but there were no choices or alternatives now.

Privately, Winston Churchill was greatly relieved that the Americans had entered the war, and he could see their vast potential. FDR had already begun spinning the wheels of the war effort for the last several years, not only by assisting the British but also by beginning to build up American military strength and put Americans back to work in the factories. Now, there was a sense of urgency, with the priority being Japan, and yet Stalin continued to desperately call for a Western Front to alleviate the crushing pressures of the Eastern Front (Pruitt, "Why Did Japan Attack Pearl Harbor?" 2020).

The Rise and Fall of the American Empire

War in the Pacific Some of the 90th Bombardment Group

CHAPTER 22

War in the Pacific

To the Japanese people, Emperor Hirohito, 1901 to 1989, emperor of heaven, was not really a man at all; he was divinity, the living embodiment of the Japanese people. He was the larger-than-life figure who rose at age fifteen to assume the chrysanthemum throne. Emperor Hirohito was perhaps one of the most enigmatic figures of the twentieth century. Like Hitler, the people viewed Hirohito as a God, and if he was a God, he could not make a mistake.

History was easy on Emperor Hirohito, stating that he was essentially a pawn of the militarists who had gained control of the government shortly after he had taken the throne ("Hirohito's Biography," 2021). But General Douglas MacArthur, who needed to run a smooth occupation once the war was over, in remaking Japan along an American model, made it very clear to Hirohito: "Renounce your divinity, help me, and I'll keep you from being tried as a war criminal" (Groom, 2015). And perhaps that was part of the mindset of the Japanese military that inspired them to be one of the fiercest fighting forces the world had ever seen. They simply felt that they could not be defeated. But just like the looks on the faces of the once so proud but now defeated German forces at war's end, reality can be telling.

The Pacific War, sometimes called the Asia Pacific War, was the theater of World War II that was fought in the Pacific Ocean,

Eastern Asia, the Indian Ocean, and Oceana. It was an enormous area geographically, including the vast Pacific Ocean theater, the Southwest Pacific theater, the Second Sino-Japanese War, and the Soviet Japanese War. There were even battles fought as far north as the Aleutian Islands, as Japanese forces had invaded and occupied them. The whole conflagration lasted three years, eight months, three weeks, and five days until the Japanese surrendered, not counting Japan's first invasion of Manchuria prior to Pearl Harbor (Toll, 2015). The Japanese simply would not surrender or stop fighting until the United States dropped two atomic bombs, one on Hiroshima and the other on Nagasaki on the island of Japan.

Japan had first invaded Manchuria in 1931 without declaring war, and further hostilities had been in progress since July 7, 1937, with the Republic of China ("Invasion of Manchuria," n.d.). Most historians marked the beginning of the Pacific War as December 7, 1941, when Japan simultaneously attacked American military bases in Hawaii, Wake Island, Guam, the Philippines, and also the invasion of Thailand. Also, the British colonies of Malaya, Singapore, and Hong Kong were invaded (Little, 2022). The Japanese accomplished incredible success in the initial phase of their campaign but began to get driven back by US forces, one island at a time. The Allies adopted a Europe-first stance with priority given to defeating Nazi Germany but still managed to bring to bear the vast industrial might of the United States.

The Japanese had great difficulty replacing their losses in ships and aircraft while determined American factories and shipyards produced ever-increasing numbers of both with a sense of urgency. Fighting included some of the largest naval battles in history and massive Allied air raids over Tokyo and Japan. Thirty different countries took sides during World War II, and many different nations helped the United States in the Asia-Pacific theater. America's major allies in the area were China, the British Empire, and the Philippine Commonwealth. Colonial forces from India contributed, and Burma, Malaya, Fiji, Tonga, Australia, New Zealand, Canada, and even Mexico helped (Toll, 2015).

The Japanese Imperial General Headquarters began planning for war with the Western powers in April 1941 ("Pre-War Japanese Military Preparation 1941," 2006). Japan increased its naval budget and put large formations of the army and its attached Air Force under Navy command. Japanese planning was for a limited war where Japan would seize key objectives and then establish a defensive perimeter to defeat Allied counterattacks, which in turn would lead to a negotiated peace. Japanese military planners' expectation of success rested on the United Kingdom and the Soviet Union being unable to effectively respond to a Japanese attack because they would both be too busy fighting Germany. The Japanese leadership was aware that a total military victory against the US in a traditional sense was impossible. They were hoping that after their initial victories, they could continue to have their way in Asia and that the US would be content to sign a peace treaty after being hammered by Japan.

The Rise and Fall of the American Empire

As previously mentioned, it was not just Pearl Harbor on the island of Hawaii that was attacked in the first wave, but also the Philippines, Guam, Wake Island, Malay, Singapore, and Hong Kong. Concurrently, Japanese forces invaded southern and eastern Thailand, where they held out briefly and then were pressured to sign an armistice and ally with Japan. The Japanese had gambled that the Americans, faced with such sudden and massive losses, would agree to a negotiated settlement. This gamble did not pay off.

The United States military took an inventory and State of the Union and realized that despite the losses, they could and would regroup quickly. Three American aircraft carriers were at sea during Pearl Harbor and were spared, vital naval infrastructure was all intact, a strategic submarine base was unscathed, and signals intelligence units were all intact. These attacks ignited waves of outrage across America, causing many men to enlist, and the factories and shipyards were operating full speed ahead. All Pearl Harbor did was awaken a sleeping giant and unite Americans in a common cause. Any opposition to war vanished after the attack ("Pearl Harbor," 2022).

On December 8, 1941, the United Kingdom, the United States, Canada, and the Netherlands declared war on Japan, followed by China and Australia the next day. Four days after Pearl Harbor, Germany and Italy declared war on the United States, drawing the country into a two-theater war. This ultimately became the very thing that led to Germany's defeat, a Western and Eastern Front in

War in the Pacific

Europe simultaneously.

Japan had the momentum finishing out 1941 and heading into 1942, as it would take time for America and its allies to regroup. Many US allies were already stretched thin due to months of ongoing battles in Europe, North Africa, and at home, offering only token assistance. In January of 1942, Japan invaded British Burma, the Dutch East Indies, New Guinea, and the Solomon Islands and captured Manila, Kuala Lumpur, and Rabaul. After being driven out of Malaya, Allied forces in Singapore attempted to resist the Japanese in the Battle of Singapore but were forced to surrender to the Japanese on February 15, 1942, with 130,000 Indian, British, Australian, and Dutch soldiers becoming prisoners of war. The cruelty of man can be astonishing, but in the theater of war, it is at its worst. The Japanese instituted, at one point against the Chinese in retaliation, the "three alls policy." Kill all, burn all, loot all. Germany's murderous cruelty to the Jews left the lasting horrific legacy of the Holocaust. And of the 130,000 POWs captured in the Battle of Singapore, of those that survived, they were treated harshly, tortured, and had the most meager allotment of food and water ("The Fall of Singapore," 2023).

The pace of Japanese conquest was rapid as both Bali and Timor fell in February. The continued and rapid collapse of Allied resistance left American, British, Australian, and Dutch areas split in two. A dejected British commander, Wavell, resigned and returned to his post in India. Japanese aircraft had all but eliminated Allied air power in Southeast Asia, then began to bomb Darwin on

February 19, which was a further psychological blow.

At the Battle of the Java Sea in late February and early March, the Imperial Japanese Navy inflicted a resounding defeat on the main Allied naval forces, and subsequently, the Dutch East Indies campaign ended with the surrender of Allied forces on Java and Sumatra ("Java Sea," 2019). In March and April, a powerful Imperial Japanese naval carrier force launched a raid into the Indian Ocean. British Royal Navy bases in Ceylon were attacked, and the aircraft carrier HMS *Hermes* and other Allied ships were sunk. The Royal Navy withdrew to the western part of the Indian Ocean, which enabled Japan to begin to assault Burma and India. The Japanese army captured Moulmein and Toungoo in Burma after severe fighting between January and April 1942. At one point, the Japanese 33rd Division had entirely encircled 7,000 British soldiers but were rescued by the Chinese 38th Division. Japan continued to exploit the disunity in China between the Chinese nationalists and Communists, enabling them to press ahead in their offensives.

The Philippines

On December 8, 1941, the Japanese also struck airfields in Luzon. They caught most of the planes on the ground, destroying 103. Two days later, they devastated the Cavite naval yard. By December 13, Japanese attacks on the Philippines wrecked every major airfield, annihilating American air power in the area. Very few forces remained in the Philippines, and FDR ordered General

War in the Pacific

Douglas MacArthur to evacuate to Australia. Only General Wainwright and his forces remained, aided by the Filipino army. The Japanese overran the defenders at Bataan on a final offensive on April 9, 1942, and Bataan fell. The Japanese forced the remaining prisoners of war, who had survived, to take the grueling sixty-six-mile Bataan death march. Later in the decade, three Japanese generals were executed for the war crimes committed during this cruel march. If any Filipino or American soldier showed fatigue, they were struck in the head with a rifle butt. If they collapsed or fell, they were shot and left for dead ("Bataan Death March," 2022). The remaining forces on Corregidor surrendered to Japanese forces after intensive aerial and artillery bombardment on May 9, 1942.

Australia had been shocked by the speedy and crushing collapse of British Malaya and the fall of Singapore, in which around 15,000 Australian soldiers became prisoners of war. Prime Minister John Curtin predicted the battle for Australia would soon follow. The Japanese had established a major base in New Guinea, beginning with the capture of Rabaul on January 23, 1942. On February 19, 1942, Darwin suffered a devastating air raid, and over the following nineteen months, Australia was attacked from the air almost one hundred times. President Franklin Roosevelt ordered MacArthur to formulate a Pacific defense plan with Australia in March 1942. Curtain agreed to place Australian forces under the command of MacArthur, who became supreme commander of Southwest Pacific (John Curtin, 2023). MacArthur moved his headquarters to Melbourne in March of 1942, and American troops began massing in Australia. Japanese submarines launched a surprise attack on Sydney in May and then again on June 8, 1942.

On March 10, 1942, American carrier aircraft successfully attacked invasion forces launched by Japan's second operational phase, inflicting significant losses. In April 1942, sixteen bombers took off from the USS *Hornet*, 600 miles from Tokyo, Japan, in the Doolittle Raid. The raid inflicted minor damage on the Japanese homeland but was a huge psychological boost for the Americans, exposing the vulnerability of the Japanese homeland from American carrier force assault ("Doolittle Leads Air Raid on Tokyo," 2021).

Admiral Yamamoto proposed the destruction of the US Navy by occupying Midway Atoll ("Isoroku Yamamoto, Japan's Mastermind of the Pearl Harbor Attack, Is Born," 2021). But there was just enough pushing and pulling in the higher Japanese ranks to remove the Japanese margin of superiority in the Midway attack. Forces were sent by the Japanese to occupy the Aleutian Islands, and another full carrier division was allocated to the Port Moresby operation. The attack on Port Moresby was code-named MO Operation by the Japanese and would unfold in different stages, starting with the occupation of Tulagi on May 3, which was successful.

The next stage of the MO Operation was a sweep of the Coral Sea by sixty ships led by two carriers to eradicate the Americans.

War in the Pacific

The element of surprise by the Imperial Japanese Navy was lost due to the success of Allied codebreakers (Pruitt, "How Code-breakers Helped Secure US Victory in the Battle of Midway," 2023). On May 4, aircraft from the carrier Yorktown struck the invasion force. Allied forces were determined to stop the fall at Port Moresby as they felt it was too critical. The USS *Lexington* joined *Yorktown* in the Coral Sea. On May 8, the opposing carrier forces finally found each other, and fierce combat ensued. Aircraft from the two Japanese carriers succeeded in sinking the carrier *Lexington* and damaging *Yorktown*.

In return, the Americans damaged *Shokaku* and inflicted heavy losses upon *Zuikaku*, leading to the Japanese cancellation of the MO operation and abandonment of attempts to isolate Australia. Although they sank the *Lexington*, the battle was a disaster for the Japanese as all three carriers that had gone to the Coral Sea would now be unavailable for the operation against Midway. The Japanese Navy still had *Soryu*, *Kaga*, *Akagi*, and *Hiryu* and believed that the Americans would only have two carriers for Midway, but the *Yorktown* was successfully repaired in three days, enabling it to sortie for Midway as well.

Midway

The Battle of Midway was a key turning point in the War of the Pacific. By the end of this battle, the Americans could feel the shift and the tide turn. The carrier *Yorktown* had been badly damaged in the battle of the Coral Sea and limped back for repairs. Initial estimates had the repair at ninety days, but high command ordered it to be done in three days, with further repairs of holes and damage being done en route while it sortied for Midway. US intelligence codebreakers had further determined in May that the Japanese planned to attack Midway. Admiral Yamamoto hoped that the attack on Midway would lure the Americans into a trap, yet his complex plan had no provision for intervention by the American fleet before the Japanese had expected them. The Japanese also did not properly execute surveillance preemptively on the American fleet nor set up submarine scouting lines on time. They were also unaware that American intelligence was deciphering significant amounts of their messaging.

The first attack on Midway occurred roughly twelve hours after Pearl Harbor when the Japanese destroyers Sazanami and Ushio bombarded the power plant and seaplane hangar on Sand Island. The strategic importance of Midway could not be underestimated. If the islands could be seized by Japan, then the American military presence in Hawaii, 1,100 miles to the southeast, would be threatened. Furthermore, the supply lines of the United States and Australia could be threatened and severed, thereby crippling the Allied war effort and opening the Southwest Pacific to conquest.

Despite a strategic setback at the Battle of the Coral Sea, the Japanese, under the command of Admiral Yamamoto, continued with plans to seize the Midway Islands and bases in the Aleutians. On May 4, 1942, Vice Admiral Nagumo set out for Midway with four heavy carriers, *Akagi*, *Hiryu*, *Kaga*, and *Soryu*, and was also

War in the Pacific

supplemented by two light aircraft carriers. They also had two seaplane carriers, seven battleships, fifteen cruisers, forty-two destroyers, ten submarines, and various support and escort vessels. Their orders were to engage and destroy the American fleet and invade Midway.

Fortunately for the Americans, their codebreakers had determined Japanese intentions, and it gave them time to prepare. Admiral Chester Nimitz had to focus on what he did have and not on what he did not have and utilize everything and all forces to their maximum potential. The Battle of Midway would go down in history as one of the greatest naval battles in the history of the world. Admiral Nimitz had heavy carriers *Hornet* and *Enterprise*, and after lightning-fast repairs, *Yorktown* rolled out to join them, boosting morale (Chester W. Nimitz, 2017). The Americans had eight cruisers, eighteen destroyers, nineteen submarines, and about 115 land-based Navy, Marine, and Army planes from Midway and Hawaii. Vice Admiral William "Bull" Halsey became incapacitated and missed the battle completely.

Initial contact was made the morning of June 3 when an American reconnaissance plane was fired upon by Japanese deck gunners from the lead elements of the invasion fleet. Shortly after that, another pilot stated that he had located the main body of the Japanese fleet, but again, this sighting was only a small portion of the lead element and not the main force. Just past noon, a force of *B-17* bombers was dispatched from Midway but proved ineffective against moving naval targets.

211

Just past 9:00 PM, before the *B-17*s had returned, a quartet of *Consolidated Catalina* seaplanes were launched from Midway. This group intercepted a Japanese surface force at about 1:15 a.m. on June 4 and carried out a torpedo attack and strafing run with limited success. As the *Catalinas* made their way back to Midway, they were notified by radio that the islands were under attack by Japanese aircraft. At least the *Catalinas* sunk the tanker *Akebono Maru* on their run. At 5:45 a.m. on June 4, 1942, an American *Catalina* pilot radioed that many Japanese planes were sighted and heading for Midway, and within minutes, two Japanese carriers were sighted. In just fifteen minutes, nearly every one of Midway's planes was airborne and on combat patrol.

The American pilots fought bravely but were outnumbered four to one and lost half of their numbers that morning. At about 6:30 AM, with the island's fighter screen largely neutralized, the aerial bombardment of Midway began and lasted thirty minutes, causing extensive damage. Midway's runways were unharmed because the Japanese intended to use them themselves once the invasion had been completed.

While Midway was being hammered by the Japanese bombing assault, land-based planes were converging on the Japanese fleet. Just after 7:00 AM, four *B-26 Marauders* began a torpedo attack run on the *Akagi*, closely followed by six Navy *Avenger* torpedo bombers. Unfortunately, most of these planes were shot down, and the US Mark 13 torpedoes were ineffective.

War in the Pacific

At about this time, Vice Admiral Nagumo and the Japanese were feeling confident, and Nagumo gave the order for the fueled and ready planes on the *Kaga* and *Akagi* to switch out torpedoes for bombs and strike Midway again to finish it off. At 7:28 AM, one of Nagumo's scouts spotted ten American surface ships, drastically altering the assault dynamic. At 7:45 AM, Vice Admiral Nagumo ordered those planes that had not yet switched over to prepare to attack the American naval fleet. So, at that time, the flight and hangar decks of the Japanese carriers were now covered with fueled and armed aircraft as well as unsecured ordinance. Basically, they were now like giant bombs just waiting to be ignited.

Nearly an hour after the initial American strike at the Japanese carrier force, Midway launched sixteen *Douglas Dauntless* dive bombers against the *Soryu*, but they were unsuccessful and lost half their planes in the run. Roughly fifteen minutes later, Army Air *B-17s* tried some high-altitude bombing on the Japanese fleet, but it also did not work. At approximately 8:20 AM, the last of Midway's planes, eleven US Marine Corps *Vindicator* dive bombers, targeted the battleship *Haruna* but were unsuccessful. As the *Vindicators* were being chased away, the planes from the Midway attack were returning to the Japanese carriers and were low on fuel. The American carrier force was divided into two groups: Task Force 16, which included the *Enterprise* and the *Hornet* under Rear Admiral Raymond Spruance, and Task Force 17, which included the *Yorktown* under Rear Admiral Frank Jack Fletcher.

The Rise and Fall of the American Empire

History records Spruance as one of the finest American naval commanders of the war. Hoping to catch the Japanese carriers by surprise before they could launch a second attack on Midway, Spruance gambled by launching his planes at 7:00 a.m. from a distance. At 8:38 a.m., having recovered his scouts and believing that his fleet had been discovered, Rear Admiral Fletcher began launching planes from *Yorktown*. At 9:20 a.m., fifteen *Devastator* bombers attacked the *Soryu*, and every single one of them was shot down. At 10:20 a.m., *Devastator* squadrons from the *Hornet* and *Enterprise* met similar results.

Low on fuel and lacking any additional information about the location of the Japanese fleet, Lieutenant Commander Wade McCluskey decided to turn northwest to keep looking instead of returning to the *Enterprise*'s squadron of *Douglas Dauntless* dive bombers, then spotted the destroyer *Arashi*, which led them to the rest of the fleet. At 10:22 a.m., they moved into position to attack the *Kaga* and *Akagi*, diving out of the sun! Just as the torpedo attack concluded, the *Dauntless* scored multiple devastating bomb hits on both the *Kaga* and *Akagi*.

Almost simultaneously, seventeen *Dauntless* that had accompanied the *Yorktown* dove on the *Soryu*. Within minutes, the three enormous Japanese carriers were in flames, and the war in the Pacific began to shift in the American's favor. The fourth Japanese carrier would also soon be given a deadly blow. More than twelve *Dauntless* crews went down, but they had inflicted enormous damage on the Japanese fleet.

War in the Pacific

At about 10:50 AM, as the other three Japanese carriers burned, Rear Admiral Tamon Yamaguchi ordered an attack force into the air from the surviving *Hiryu* to chase the American strike force back to the *Yorktown*. Just after noon, they carried out a dive-bombing attack that left the American carrier dead in the water. Just past 2:30 PM, a second wave of planes struck *Yorktown* again, and Captain Buckmaster gave the order to abandon ship. The mighty *Yorktown* once again battled to the end, but the following day, a Japanese submarine snuck up on the old carrier and finished it off. By this time, American scouts had located the *Hiryu*, and a mixed force of *Dauntless* from the *Yorktown* and *Enterprise* took to the skies at 3:30 p.m. and were soon joined by additional dive bombers from the *Hornet*.

Just before 4:00 p.m., Admiral Fletcher turned over operational control to Vice Admiral Spruance since Task Force 17 had ceased to be a functioning battle group. The first wave of bombers descended on the *Hiryu* at 5:00 p.m. and reduced the Japanese carrier to a flaming fireball; the next wave of bombers tried to hit the *Hiryu* support battle group but had limited success. The next day, Spruance sent sixty bombers to chase the Japanese fleet but was unsuccessful. But then the following day, June 6, he tried again and was able to sink the cruiser *Mikuma* and seriously damaged the destroyers *Asashio* and *Arashio*. But that day, June 4, he felt that it was the best decision to direct Task Force 16 out of the area and head east since their main objective was accomplished and the Japanese battle force was already heading back (M. D. Hull, 2006).

The Rise and Fall of the American Empire

Admiral Yamamoto had hoped to stop the American forces in short order and with a midway victory, as he knew that the accelerating American war machine was only going to get stronger. A short while later, American intelligence identified that Admiral Yamamoto was on a mission in a plane, and they were able to locate it and successfully shoot it down, further knocking Japanese morale. Japanese casualties were enormous at Midway as they lost 3,000 sailors and airmen to 317 Americans. Three hundred twenty Japanese airplanes went down compared to 150 American planes. They also lost four heavy aircraft carriers and one cruiser to one American aircraft carrier and one destroyer. Japanese Admiral Yamaguchi chose to go down with his ship, and Rear Admiral Tomeo Kaku did the same. Because the Japanese fleet left the action area in relative haste, many of their sailors and pilots were left behind in the waters.

Japanese land forces continued to advance in the Solomon Islands and New Guinea. In early September of 1942, Japanese marines attacked a strategic Royal Australian Air Force Base at Milne Bay, near the eastern tip of New Guinea. They were beaten back by the Allied forces, which was the first defeat of the war for Japanese forces on land. Allied forces became aware through coast watchers of a Japanese airfield under construction at Guadalcanal.

On August 7, 1942, 16,000 US Marines landed on Guadalcanal and Tulagi in the Solomons. The night of August 8 to 9 was a terrible night for the US Navy. Vice Admiral Gunichi Mikawa, commander of the newly formed Eighth Fleet at Rabaul, quick-

War in the Pacific

ly sailed to engage the Allied force off the coast of Guadalcanal, sinking four Allied heavy cruisers. The victory was mitigated only by the failure of the Japanese to attack the vulnerable transports. An unusual dynamic developed on Guadalcanal.

Japanese and Allied forces occupied different parts of the island at the same time over the next six months while both sides poured resources into an escalating battle of attrition. Guadalcanal became the scene of numerous and ongoing naval, air, and land battles throughout 1942 and into 1943. US Naval Admiral John S. McCain Sr. hoped to use the American numerical advantage at Guadalcanal to progressively drain Japanese manpower. In the six-month war of attrition at Guadalcanal, the Japanese lost because they failed to commit enough forces in sufficient time (Bland, 2020).

The Japanese evacuated and withdrew from Guadalcanal in February of 1943, but not before sinking the USS *Wasp* and USS *Hornet* and inflicting heavy damage on the USS *Saratoga*. The mighty *Hornet* and her crew made it through Midway but went down at Guadalcanal. Ultimately, nearly 20,000 Japanese died on Guadalcanal compared to 7,000 Americans.

American industry continued to feverishly build new armaments, planes, cruisers, and carriers, and yet Joseph Stalin continued to press for a Western Front against the Germans in Europe. The American military continued with grit and determination in the war of the Pacific against the fierce Japanese who would never give up, that is, until they were hit with two cataclysmic knockout punches. In the southwestern Pacific, the Allies seized the strategic initiative for the first time during the war and, in June 1943, launched Operation Cartwheel, a series of amphibious invasions, to recapture the Solomon Islands and New Guinea and ultimately isolate the major Japanese forward base at Rabaul. These landings prepared the way for the Nimitz Island hopping campaign towards Japan.

In November 1943, US Marines sustained high casualties when they overwhelmed the 4,500-strong Garrison at Tarawa. This helped the allies to improve the techniques of amphibious landings, implementing changes such as thorough preemptive bombings and bombardment, more careful planning regarding tides and landing schedules, and better coordination. Operations on the Gilbert Islands were followed in late January and mid-February 1944 by further less costly landings on the Marshall Islands.

On November 22, 1943, US President Franklin D. Roosevelt, British Prime Minister Winston Churchill, and ROC Generalissimo Chiang Kai-shek met in Cairo, Egypt, to discuss a strategy to defeat Japan (Chiang Kai-shek, 2023) ("Pacific War," 2023) (Welt Documentary, 2021). Remarkably, Japan honored its neutrality treaty with the Soviet Union and ignored American freighters shipping military supplies from San Francisco to Vladivostok, much to the consternation of its German ally.

Even though submarines made up a small portion of the US

Navy, less than 2 percent, they played a very important and strategic role in the victory of the War of the Pacific. Submarines strangled Japan by sinking its merchant fleet, intercepting many troop transports, and cutting off nearly all the oil imports essential to weapons production and military operations. By early 1945, Japanese oil supplies were so low that its fleet was virtually stranded. American submarines accounted for 56 percent of Japanese merchantmen sunk and 28 percent of Japanese warships destroyed. Furthermore, they played important reconnaissance roles and rescued hundreds of downed pilots.

Only by 1944 did the US Navy begin to use its submarines to maximum effect, with the installation of effective shipboard radar, new effective commanders, and fixing the faults of the torpedoes. American submarines destroyed about 1,200 merchant ships and 200 Japanese warships. Yet to be on a submarine crew in the War of the Pacific was one of the most dangerous jobs, as 22 percent never returned from the ocean (Vergun, 2020).

In 1944, Japan mobilized over 500,000 men and launched a massive operation across China under the code name Ichi-Go, with the goal of connecting Japanese-controlled territory in China and French Indochina and capturing air bases in southeastern China where American bombers were based. Though Japan lost almost 100,000 men, they gained much ground, yet the operation overall failed to provide Japan with any significant strategic gains. A great majority of Chinese forces were able to retreat out of combat areas, regroup, and turn right back around and attack.

CHAPTER 23

D-Day: The Normandy Invasion

The big three heads of state arrived at the Tehran Conference on December 1, 1943. They needed to finalize the key decision of moving ahead with an offensive against Germany to once and for all stop Hitler. Joseph Stalin had been demanding a Western Front for a long time as the Russian army had been engaged in total war with Germany on the Eastern Fronts, grinding and battling it out. Winston Churchill and the Allies had already attempted a soft belly attack against Germany via North Africa, the Mediterranean, and Italy, but it really didn't work and was stopped short in Naples ("Allied Invasion of Sicily," 2023).

Franklin D. Roosevelt simply did not feel that the US was ready for a massive total war operation, but he also felt that it was time to stop Adolf Hitler. Hitler had always known that the Americans would come since they had entered the war, but they had been battling it out with Japan in the Pacific. FDR handpicked General Dwight D. Eisenhower to plan and lead the huge operation and also brought in General Omar Bradley as part of the high command and planning. Field Marshal Bernard Montgomery, who had pitted strategies against Rommel in North Africa, was picked by Churchill to lead the British. Hitler had promoted Rommel to field marshall, and he and Gerd von Rundstedt oversaw German operations in the West (Groom, 2015) (Görlitz, 2023).

The Normandy landings of Operation Overlord were code-named Operation Neptune (Nasuti, 2019). This enormous and epic operation was the largest seaborne invasion in the history of the world. The planners had to go over every possible detail, scenario, and circumstance that could be encountered, and then there was still the element of the unknown. They also chose a window of time when there would be a full moon, hoping the tide and the weather would be more favorable for the landings. But they were delayed by a fierce storm that arose, testing everyone's patience and focus. There was also another enormous storm that struck the coast of France from June 19 to 22 that hammered operations.

The war planners had to think of every conceivable detail to ready men and machines for what would be encountered on D-Day. Hitler, in preparation for the invasion, had constructed the Atlantic Wall, a 4,000-mile-long fortification that extended from Norway to Spain ("The Atlantic Wall: Eleven Key Facts about the Nazi Defenses at Normandy," 2014). In addition to the Atlantic wall, Field Marshal Rommel had made every effort to fortify and bolster defenses along the coast and beaches of France, especially trying to fill in gaps between towns. He added stakes, tripods, and barbed wire to delay and impede the Allies' advance. "The Desert Fox" also increased the number of mines and added additional booby traps and obstacles. He added many new fortifications, including machine gun encasements. He also began flooding the fields along the coast of France to add another hindrance and deterrence to the Allied advance.

D-Day: The Normandy Invasion

Allied planners began strategizing in every possible way. The French resistance supplied the Allies with hundreds of aerial photos of the coast of France to be able to identify airfields, bases, aircraft, roads, train tracks, and infrastructures. The French resistance was assigned four operations beginning two to four weeks prior to D-Day. They had a fifteen-day operation to sabotage the rail system, and they had Plan Bleu, which focused on destroying electrical facilities. They also orchestrated strategic attacks to slow the Axis' advance to the coasts of Normandy. They also had Plan Violet, which consisted of cutting underground telephone and printer cables. For various reasons, General Charles de Gaulle had been kept out of the loop for as long as possible but was brought in to coordinate with the French and the French resistance after the Overlord was launched (Pickles, 2023) (Trueman, 2015).

Allied intelligence began an incremental onslaught of disinformation to continue to throw off the Germans as to the whereabouts of the actual landings. They even set up fake, inflatable decoy airplanes and landing strips. The Allies rigorously tested mine-sweeping machines and the new Willys Jeeps. The training of the men was so intense and grueling that hundreds lost their lives in the months of preparation leading up to D-Day ("Allies Prepare for D-Day," 2023). They also constructed massive Phoenixes and docks to help with the landing invasion. War planners chose Normandy for the landings, not because it was the closest but because it was less well-defended than other areas. The Allies determined to establish five main beachheads spread out over a large enough area to have room for the landings. Their code names were Utah, Omaha, Gold, Juno, and Sword, each with their own assignments, yet coordinating together to penetrate the coast and begin the liberation of France and Europe (Greenspan, "Landing at Normandy: The Five Beaches of D-Day," 2014).

After one false start and the weather began to clear, on the morning of June 6, 1944, the largest armada in the history of the world set out for the coast of France. It was an awe-inspiring sight as 7,000 ships and vessels escorted by 20,000 fighters and bombers began to cross the English Channel. There were 195,700 naval personnel and 156,000 soldiers, with another huge contingent preparing to come behind them. There would be well over 800,000 Allied soldiers who would arrive at the coast of Normandy by the end of June, fighting for the liberation of Europe.

First, the French resistance went into action in the weeks preceding D-Day. Also, around June 3, a contingent of Royal Navy X-craft submarines had deployed to the coast of France, hiding until it was time to guide in the first Allied craft at Juno and Sword beaches. Also, prior to the armada's arrival, the Allied bombers and gunners absolutely hammered the coast of Normandy to soften it up. Then, the naval destroyers moved into position to unleash a massive artillery assault on the Atlantic wall. After the smoke cleared, 24,000 paratroopers were dropped behind enemy lines with the mission to attack and cause chaos against German forces to slow them down and take some heat off Allied landing forces.

D-Day: The Normandy Invasion

Eisenhower did not take a breath or relax until June was over, as there was so much on the line, and as keenly confident and prepared as they were, there were no guarantees ("Dwight D. Eisenhower's Biography," 2021). There was an unusual mood among the soldiers and naval personnel as they crossed the channel, many of them realizing that it could be their last day alive. Some of them just wanted to get off the sardine-packed ships full of men, diesel fumes, and sea sickness. That previous Sunday, June 4, most of the soldiers attended church and services, especially the devoutly Christian Canadian troops, and everyone everywhere prayed for God's help, protection, and the liberation of Europe.

At the light of dawn, under a relentless hail of fire, the first soldiers embarked on the beaches of Normandy. Things were so rough and went so badly, especially at Omaha, that the high command considered calling the whole thing off. But they couldn't. They could not stop now. They just needed a little time and momentum. Slowly but surely, they began to break through and take ground and take out machine-gun positions. The sacrifice and the number of men who laid down their lives on that first day alone was staggering. There were 10,500 Allied soldiers killed on D-Day and nearly as many Germans.

As the invasion force continued to pour onto the five main beaches, men and machines began to break through the formidable Atlantic Wall. Complicating matters, strong winds blew landing craft east of their intended positions, especially at Utah and Omaha. Montgomery had insisted that they widen the target landing area on Normandy to a fifty-mile stretch to ensure adequate room for the five landing groups. Casualties were highest at Omaha, with its high cliffs and machine gun encasements in place. The men had to cross 300 yards of beach, and even if they were wounded, they had to keep running and fighting, or they would be cut to pieces by the German gunners. Planners wisely had all vehicles and tanks backed in at England so they would come out forward, ready to fire in France. They also had specially designed tanks to take out the machine gun emplacements. At Gold, Juno, and Sword, several fortified towns were cleared in house-to-house fighting.

The Allies failed to achieve any major objectives on the first day. Only Juno and Gold beaches had been linked, with all five beachheads being connected by June 12. However, they did gain an important foothold on the first day, which they expanded on over the next weeks and months. Carentan, Saint Lo, and Bayeux remained in German hands, and Caen, a major objective, was not captured until July 21. From that time on, General Eisenhower began to increasingly look to General Bradley, and Field Marshall Montgomery perhaps held a diminished role in the operation (Omar N. Bradley, 2022). There were thirty-nine divisions committed to the Battle of Normandy, of which twenty-two were American, twelve were British, three Canadian, one Polish, and one French, totaling over a million troops. The push to Paris was anything but a victory march, but it was rather a total war grind, one hedgerow and acreage at a time.

D-Day: The Normandy Invasion

In the east, Joseph Stalin was relieved by the push of a Western Front as his troops had already taken Stalingrad and were holding their ground against elite German forces. And although Germany still had at its disposal fifty divisions in France and the Low Countries, in early 1944, the German Western Front was significantly diminished by personnel and material transfers to the Eastern Front. It would eventually result in Hitler's undoing, as he had picked a fight with the whole world. He was stretched thin with troops in North Africa, the Mediterranean, Italy, Russia, France, Germany, and throughout Europe.

Field Marshal Rommel had well believed that the invasion force would indeed come in at Normandy, and he did not make it easy for Operation Neptune, as he had increased fortifications along Normandy. He would have done significantly more if he had had his way, but he was overruled by Rundstedt, Geyer, and other senior commanders. Rommel had also wanted to bring in Panzer formations to the coast of Normandy, but Rundstedt ordered them to hold them back until the location of the invasion was identified.

The Allies had specially designed DD amphibious tanks and other modified landing craft to provide close support fire; however, some did not arrive in advance of the infantry or never made it out of the water. They also made full use of the *Churchill Crocodiles* as they proceeded inland; the flame-throwing tanks spared nothing in their paths.

The Utah beach landings began at six thirty and were conducted by the fourth and eighth infantry. Their landing crafts were pushed to the South by strong currents, and they found themselves about 2,000 yards from their intended landing zone, which perhaps turned out to be better. The pre-coastal bombing by IX Bomber Command had done a good job in this area, reducing the strongholds to only one remaining. Also, the strong currents had washed ashore many of the underground water obstacles that had been placed by the Germans. Brigadier General Theodore Roosevelt Jr., the first senior officer ashore, made the decision to start the war from right there and ordered further landings to be rerouted to that location. General Roosevelt was one of many heroes that day who risked life and limb, going beyond the parameters of duty to protect his men and ensure the success of the invasion force (M. D. Hull, 2023).

The initial assault battalions were quickly followed by twenty-eight DD amphibious tanks and several waves of engineer and demolition teams to remove beach obstacles and clear the area directly behind the beach of obstacles and mines. Gaps were blown in the sea wall to allow quicker access for troops and tanks. Combat teams began to exit the beach around nine, with some infantry choosing to wade through the flooded fields rather than traveling single file on the road. Two main German fortifications were taken and destroyed by noon. The fourth infantry may not have met every objective on the first day, but they were able to land 21,000 troops with minimal casualties.

Pointe Du Hoc, a prominent headland situated between Utah

and Omaha, was assigned to 200 men of the Second Ranger Battalion, commanded by Lieutenant Colonel James Ruder. Their incredible task was to scale one-hundred-foot cliffs with grappling hooks, ropes, and ladders to destroy the coastal gun battery located at the top. The cliffs were defended by the German 352nd Infantry Division and also, unbelievably, by French collaborators firing from above. Allied destroyers USS *Satterlee* and HMS *Talybont* provided fire support. The rangers suffered very high casualties but accomplished their goal of destroying the Coastal Gun Battery (Randall, 2019).

Unfortunately, for fear of hitting the landing craft, US bombers delayed releasing their loads, and as a result, most of the beach obstacles at Omaha remained undamaged when the men came ashore. Also, Omaha was the most heavily defended beach with the entire 352nd Infantry Division present, rather than the expected single regiment. Again, the strong ocean currents forced many LCVP landing craft east of their intended position or caused them to be delayed. With many of the landing craft running aground on sandbars, heavily laden soldiers had to wade one hundred meters in water up to their necks under fire. They also dropped two companies of DD amphibious tank units 5,000 yards from shore, but it exceeded their capacities, as most never made it out of the water. The ones that did make it to the beach, even if they were disabled, at least provided covering fire until their ammunition ran out.

Casualties were enormous, with the men being subjected to enemy fire from the cliffs above (Roos, "How Many Were Killed on D-Day?" 2019). Problems due to obstacles in clearing Omaha Beach led to the commander calling a halt to further landings at about eight fifty. A group of destroyers arrived about this time to provide fire cover and support so landings could resume. Exit from the beach was only possible by five heavily defended gullies, and by late morning, barely 600 men had reached the higher ground. By noon, as the artillery fire took its toll and the Germans began to run out of ammunition, the Americans were able to clear some lanes on the beaches. They also started clearing the gullies of enemy defenses so that vehicles could move off the beach. The tenuous beachhead was expanded over the following days, and the D-Day objectives for Omaha were accomplished but at a very high cost.

At Gold Beach, direct hits by the cruisers HMS *Ajax* and *Argonaut*, at six twenty, knocked out three of the four guns at the Longues-Sur-Mer battery, helping diminish resistance for the Allied landing. And yet high winds and strong currents once again made conditions difficult for the landing craft at Gold. Also, the placement of DD amphibious tanks was not ideal. The invasion force stormed the beach at seven thirty but was still met by stiff resistance. Aerial attacks had failed to knock out the Le Hamel Strong Point, which had its embrasure facing east to provide enfilade fire along the beach, and it had a very thick concrete wall on the seaward side. Its 75 mm gun continued to inflict heavy damage until 4:00 p.m., when, at that time, an armored Royal Engineers tank fired a direct hit large petard charge into its rear entrance.

A second casemated emplacement at La Riviere containing an 88 mm gun was neutralized and taken out by another tank at seven thirty. It was not until the following day they were able to force the surrender of the Longues-Sur-Mer Battery and its Garrison. Meanwhile, infantry began clearing the heavily fortified houses along the shore and then continued to advance on targets further inland. The 47th Royal Marine Commandos moved toward the small port at Port-en-Bessin and were able to capture it the following day after an epic battle. Company Sergeant Major Stanley Hollis received the Victoria Cross for successfully charging two pillboxes at Mont Fleury High Point ("Stan Hollis and the D-Day Victoria Cross," n.d.). On the western flank, the First Battalion, Royal Hampshire Regiment, captured Arromanches and successfully connected with Canadian forces at Juno. Bayeux was not captured on the first day due to unrelenting resistance from the 352nd German Infantry Division. The Allies were able to make a good foothold at Gold Beach but at a very high cost.

At Juno, the pre-landing bombardment was ineffective, as it had mostly missed the German defenses (Keegan, 2023). The landing was also delayed due to rough, choppy seas, and the men arrived ahead of their supporting armor, suffering many casualties while disembarking. Several exits from the beach were created, but only with ingenuity and problem-solving. At Mike Beach on the western flank, a large crater was filled using an abandoned AVRE tank and several rolls of fascine, which were then covered by a temporary bridge. The beach and nearby streets were clogged

The Rise and Fall of the American Empire

with traffic for most of the day, making it difficult to move inland.

Major German strongholds with 75 mm guns, machine gun nests, concrete fortifications, barbed wire, and mines were located at Courseulles-Sur-Mer, Saint Aubin-Sur-Mer, and Bernieres-Sur-Mer. The towns had to be cleared in house-to-house fighting. Soldiers on their way to Beny-Sur-Mer, three miles away, had to swing around behind machine gun emplacements and take them out before they could proceed. Elements of the Ninth Canadian Infantry Brigade advanced to within sight of Carpiquet Airfield late afternoon, but their supporting armor ran low on ammunition, so they dug in for the night. The fighting in the area intensified, so they were unable to take the airfield till the following month. By nightfall, Juno and Gold were contiguous and connected, spanning an area twelve miles wide and seven miles deep. Casualties approached 1,000 on the first day of fighting at Juno.

Just like the other main beaches, Sword was hit with high winds, strong currents, and a tide that was coming in quicker than expected. The beach was also heavily mined and held many barriers and obstacles. However, at least twenty-one of the twenty-five first-wave DD tanks were successful in getting safely ashore to provide cover for the disembarking infantry. Members of Number 4 Commando moved off the congested beach through Ouistreham to attack from the rear, a German gun battery on the shore. It took a couple of days to fully take out this concrete emplacement.

French forces, under Commander Philippe Kieffer, were the

D-Day: The Normandy Invasion

first French forces to arrive at Normandy, attacked and cleared the heavily fortified strongpoint at Riva Bella ("Philippe Kieffer's Biography," n.d.). The Second Battalion, King's Shropshire Light Infantry, advanced to the outskirts of Caen but had to withdraw due to lack of armor support ("D-Day Veterans," 2004). At 4:00 p.m., the Twenty-first Panzer Division mounted a fierce counter-attack between Sword and Juno, nearly making it to the channel, but were beaten back by the British Third Division, so the Twenty-first Panzers withdrew to assist in the area between Caen and Bayeux. Estimates of casualties at Sword approached 1,000. The D-Day landings at Normandy constituted the largest seaborne invasion in the history of the world.

The supreme commander of the Allies, Eisenhower, was not sure if Overlord would be successful or not. They had made every conceivable preparation and plan but were never entirely sure what the massive German war machine might have in reserve. But Overlord did work, and it was indeed a tremendous Allied success. And yet, the war for the liberation of Europe would rage and go on for almost one more year. In Chapter 24, we will look at the surrender of Germany and the terrifying conclusion to the war with Japan. We will also take a closer look at the hard-charging General George Patton and his leadership.

CHAPTER 24

The Surrender of Germany and Japan

The invasion of Normandy, which began on June 6, 1944, was successful, but it would be almost a year till the surrender of Germany on May 7, 1945. The road to Paris and the Rhine may have begun to open, but it resembled more of a total war grind than a victory march. The massive German war machine would mount numerous counterattacks against the Allies, including the epic "Battle of the Bulge." Never once did the notion of defeat enter the minds of the German army, but the high command knew better. The Russians had broken through the Eastern Front and began steadily advancing towards Berlin.

As the Allies had moved into position to take Paris, Hitler had already moved many of his elite troops to the Eastern Front in a vain attempt to stop the relentless Russians. The Allies still had to press through fifty German divisions in the advance to Paris, yet many of the German soldiers on the Western Front were aging or very young. In many instances, a group of German soldiers would be captured, with some being "small fryes." They would pull their helmets off and look at them and realize that they were looking at a boy who might have barely been a teenager. The German Luftwaffe had also become significantly weakened and diminished through many campaigns and attrition. Those who were close to Hitler began to see a shaking in his hands and body, and doctors would administer an array of various pills and liquids to him for

The Rise and Fall of the American Empire

depression, anxiety, and who knows what else.

General George Smith Patton was selected by Eisenhower and Bradley to lead the Third US Army across Europe to crush the Nazi war machine. The aggressive, hard-driving, cussing Patton had been in North Africa since late 1942 and told the troops there, "We shall attack and attack until we are exhausted, and then we shall attack again." It was this formidable aggression and unrelenting discipline that pushed Rommel back in North Africa and would do it once again on the Western Front of Europe (*The West Point History of World War II: Volume 1*, 2015).

General Patton was born in 1885 in San Gabriel, California. His family, which was originally from Virginia, had a long military heritage, including service in the Civil War. Patton decided early on that he wanted to carry on the tradition and graduated from the US Military Academy at West Point in 1909. Patton was also a great athlete and represented the United States in the Stockholm Olympics in 1912. Competing in the grueling modern pentathlon, he was up against the best athletes in the world, running, swimming, fencing, riding, and shooting, and finished fifth overall in the event.

Patton had his first real military battle in 1915, leading cavalry troops against Mexican forces led by the legendary Pancho Villa. He also served as an aide de camp to General John J. Pershing, Commander of American forces in Mexico, and accompanied General Pershing on his 1916 expedition against Pancho Villa.

The Surrender of Germany and Japan

When the United States entered World War I in 1917, Patton went along with General Pershing to Europe, where he became the first officer assigned to the newly established US Tank Corps. He soon earned a reputation for his leadership, skill, and knowledge of tank warfare.

Through the 1920s and 1930s, Patton served positions in tank and cavalry units at various posts, rising through the ranks to colonel by 1940 and the onset of World War II. Soon after the Japanese attack on Pearl Harbor, Patton was given command of the First and Second Armored Divisions, then headed for North Africa. In late 1942, Patton led American forces to the war's first major victory against the German forces in the Battle of El Guettar in March 1943. A month later, Patton turned over his command in North Africa to General Omar Bradley to prepare the US Seventh Army for its planned invasion of Sicily, which was very successful.

Oftentimes, people have a God-given purpose and destiny that they were born to fulfill, and George Patton was no exception. Just like FDR, Churchill, and Eisenhower, Patton was the man for the hour. Adolf Hitler was a forerunner to the Antichrist, as nearly 50 million people died because of his initiating World War II. Now, it was time to stop him. General George Patton was a man who was born to fight, born to battle, and this was his time. All the years of honing his military skills and genius would be used in the next year. Patton often had to make decisions based on limited information, and he knew how to avoid paralysis by analysis, making quick, effective decisions while moving forward. One of his quotes was: "A good plan violently executed now is better than a perfect plan next week" (Groom, 2015) (Lovelace, 2023).

After the Allies successfully executed Operation Neptune and gained the necessary foothold at Normandy, Patton led the Third US Army, breaking through German defenses and clearing a path across northern France. The Third US Army consisted of the Eighth, Twelfth, Fifteenth, and Twentieth Army Corps, which successfully advanced across France, later crossing the Rhine and moving into heartland Germany and Austria. When the Allies invaded France on D-Day, they fully intended to bypass Paris to continue advancing and not be slowed down. Engaging in a protracted urban battle would risk destruction of the city, slow the advance, and many other logistical issues. From a military standpoint, liberating Paris offered no advantage to the Allies, but the French in Paris saw it differently. With the taste of imminent victory, it stirred up strikes, resistance, rebellion, and attacks on Wehrmacht patrols. General Charles de Gaulle, who arrived on the continent on August 20, warned that a determined German effort would surely defeat the French rebels. Eisenhower realized that they had to intervene, so on August 22, he ordered General Omar Bradley, commander of the Twelfth US Army Group, to seize the city. Paris was successfully liberated by Free French forces under General Philippe Leclerc on August 25, 1944, under the coordination of Eisenhower and overseen by General Bradley (History. com Editors, 2020).

The Twentieth Corps remained under Patton throughout his

The Surrender of Germany and Japan

march. After the town of Avranches was taken on July 31, his army blasted forward with immense speed until September 24, when the Third Army was forced to stop near Moselle to resupply the troops. There were many fierce German counterattacks, but the greatest of all was the Battle of the Bulge, which began on December 16, 1944. In early December 1944, the weather along the Western Front through the Ardennes, Belgium, Luxembourg, and Germany began to turn bitter cold.

The thinly spread lines along the ghost front had become over-confident and began to daydream about returning home. It was called the Ghost Front because there was absolutely nothing going on. But little did they know that Hitler had been planning another blitzkrieg counter-offensive for months. Never mind that Von Rundstedt and Walter Model had their misgivings about the viability of the offensive from the beginning, as Hitler would not listen and was pushing ahead. The fuhrer was hoping to split the Allied forces, encircle and destroy, forcing a peace agreement with the Allies that favored Germany.

Hitler's other gamble was that he hoped the Russian Red Army would hold off their planned winter offensive on the Eastern Front until the objectives of the Battle of the Bulge were largely met. One of those objectives was also to halt further utilization of the Belgian port of Antwerp, which hindered Allied resupply. How was it that Allied intelligence failed to recognize that there were 449,000 German soldiers, 557 tanks, and 667 tank destroyers and assault guns amassing and moving in their direction the second week of December? There were also 1,496 AFVs, 4,224 anti-tank and artillery pieces, sixteen infantry divisions, eight armored divisions, and three armored brigades ("Battle of the Bulge," 2020).

In addition to ground forces, the Luftwaffe also bore down on the Allies. The Germans achieved a total surprise attack on the morning of December 16, 1944, due to a combination of Allied overconfidence, preoccupation with Allied offensive plans, and poor aerial reconnaissance due to bad weather. Also, prior to the Normandy invasion, the French resistance's aerial reconnaissance and assistance had been invaluable but were no longer there. At this phase of the operation, American forces bore the brunt of the attack. First, the Germans attacked a weakly defended section of the Allied line, taking advantage of heavily overcast weather conditions that grounded the Allied superior air forces.

Fierce American resistance on the northern shoulder of the offensive around Elsenborn Ridge and in the South around Bastogne blocked German access to key roads to the northwest and West that they counted on for success. Columns of armor and infantry that were supposed to advance along parallel routes found themselves on the same roads. This congestion and terrain that favored the defenders threw the German advance behind schedule and allowed the Allies to reinforce the thinly placed troops. The mighty German army was flexing its bulging muscles in the last great battle of Western Europe but would soon begin to run out of gas in more than one way.

The Surrender of Germany and Japan

In the Battle of the Bulge, General George Patton encountered forms of warfare that he had never seen before. He was at his best when he was charging, destroying, and taking ground. Yet there were times that he encountered huge groups of underground German fortifications where he had to slow down and figure out how to take out hundreds of heavily armed soldiers underground.

Supreme Allied Commander Eisenhower called an emergency War Council with Field Marshal Montgomery and General George Patton to discuss reinforcing the strategic and critical point at Bastogne, being held by the Tenth Armored Tiger Division, the fierce 101st Airborne Division, and the African American 969th Artillery Battalion. Eisenhower basically told them that he needed one of them to go to Bastogne to reinforce the position. Field Marshal Montgomery stated it would take him two weeks to move his army there, and General Patton said it would take him two days. The choice was simple for Eisenhower; in the ice and snow, it would probably take Patton twice as long as his projected time frame of two days. But that was better than Montgomery's projection of two weeks.

The men at Bastogne were holding their positions with fierce determination against repeated advances from gritty German forces. Some historians believe that in the epic Battle of the Bulge, Bastogne was the hardest fought and the most notable battle of them all. And some may ask, who were the true heroes of Bastogne? And I believe that the best answer is that they all were. Perhaps the 101st Airborne Division stood out the most because they

241

had been ordered into defending this position, and it was clearly outside of the parameters of their usual assignments. They had a ranger, elite training mentality with tremendous tenacity and resolve. So, they adapted the best that they were able in harsh winter elements, running out of food and ammunition, closed within a ring of German forces.

Most of the medical personnel and supplies were lost, and many of the wounded could only last so long in the freezing temperatures. Oftentimes, when the ground was frozen solid, a foxhole had to be dynamited out because it was impossible to dig. At one point in the Battle of Bastogne, the Germans sent in an order to General Anthony McAuliffe to surrender or be destroyed. He sent back a typed message with the word "*nuts*" highlighted. The Germans asked for a translation, and so they finally understood what it basically meant: "I don't think so!" (Sterne, 2020) They then were hammered by a ten-day siege, which included four straight nights of bombing by the Luftwaffe, temperatures hovering at twenty degrees Fahrenheit with snow up to their knees, while most of them simply did not have proper winter gear. And still, they held on, valiantly firing what munitions and artillery they had left, stopping each German assault. One member of the 969th admitted that if they had charged from multiple directions, we could not have held out.

Improved weather conditions over Bastogne, Belgium, from around December 24 permitted Allied air attacks on German forces and supply lines, which sealed the failure of the German of-

The Surrender of Germany and Japan

fensive there. They were also able to air-drop more munitions to the soldiers at Bastogne, which boosted morale. Also, at the same time, in a one-hundred-mile race to Bastogne, Patton's US Third Army lead elements broke through German forces to ensure that the brutal siege of Bastogne was over.

The remaining survivors at Bastogne fondly renamed themselves "The Battered Bastards of Bastogne" and even placed it on a large placard. But they would never forget their fallen comrades who laid down their lives for the liberation of Europe and the continued freedom of all Americans. Young people today need to understand the price of freedom and honor and appreciate those who paid that price (Dean, 2021).

The most powerful punch that the Nazis could throw was halted, and the walls were beginning to close in on Hitler and the invincible Third Reich that wanted to reign for 1,000 years. By the end of the Battle of the Bulge, German strength had been irredeemably impaired. And to make matters worse, the Red Army had broken through in the East and was marching towards Berlin. The Americans had 75,000 casualties in the Battle of the Bulge, but the numbers were far higher for the Germans. The German high command had been unraveling for some time now. There had been an assassination attempt on Hitler as early as July 20, 1944, and many high-ranking officers, including Field Marshal Rommel, died as a result ("Assassination Plot against Hitler Fails," 2020).

The stress of the war had taken its toll on many, and Winston Churchill's wife, Clementine, was sure the war would kill him. But Churchill lived longer than most, into his nineties, all the way to 1965 (W. R. Manchester, 2012). The great American leader Franklin D. Roosevelt, who had led the nation through the Great Depression and most of World War II, died on April 12, 1945. He had been strong in spirit, courage, mind, and character, but his body had become increasingly weakened (Mead, 2020). The diabolical and cruel Adolf Hitler, who had dreamed of a 1,000-year Reich, committed suicide in his bunker on April 30, 1945 ("Adolf Hitler's Biography," 2021).

The Russian Red Army would successfully enter Berlin a few days later and plant the Russian flag in the Berlin Reichstag. On May 7, 1945, the German army surrendered, and the war was over in Europe ("Germany Surrenders Unconditionally to the Allies at Reims," 2021). And after the most glorious year of his life, charging across Europe, General George Patton hoped to go to the Pacific to help finish off the Japanese army. But unfortunately, he had gotten into trouble with the Supreme Allied Commander Eisenhower again, and he was ordered to retire, which he dreaded. In an unusual twist of irony, on December 9, 1945, while riding in the back of his limousine in Mannheim, Germany, Patton's driver plowed into a left-turning army truck heading into a depot. He died twelve days later, on December 21, 1945, and would never see retirement ("How Did Patton Die? Here's a Summary of the Events," n.d.).

Patton was such an intriguing figure that he was the subject of numerous books and movies. Joseph Stalin died in 1953 and had played a huge role in the defeat of Nazi Germany. Supreme Allied Commander Eisenhower would go on to be the thirty-fourth president of the United States, but first, he had to coordinate with the War Council on defeating Japan, as they would not lay down their arms. The steady, reliable General Omar Bradley died on April 8, 1981, and would go down in history as one of the last great five-star generals. He held a rising role in the culmination of the war in Europe, as Eisenhower increasingly looked to his leadership.

After the death of the great American leader Franklin D. Roosevelt on April 12, 1945, Harry S. Truman was sworn in as the thirty-third president of the United States of America, which office he held until January 20, 1953.

Harry S. Truman was born in Lamar, Missouri, on May 8, 1884. His father, John Truman, was a farmer and a livestock dealer. When Harry was six years old, his parents, John and Martha, moved to Independence, Missouri, so he could attend the Presbyterian church Sunday school and learn about God and the Bible. Truman entered World War I in 1917 as an ordinary family farmer who had also worked in clerical jobs that did not require the ability to motivate and direct others. However, during the war, which was a transformative experience for him, he gained leadership experience and a record of success that greatly enhanced and supported his postwar political career. Truman was honorably discharged from the army as a captain on May 6, 1919.

The Rise and Fall of the American Empire

In 1920, he was appointed a major in the Officers Reserve Corps. He became a lieutenant colonel in 1925 and a colonel in 1932. After promotion to colonel, Truman advanced to command of the same regiment that he had been part of. Truman was awarded a World War I Victory Medal with two battle clasps and a Defensive Sector Clasp. He was also the recipient of two Armed Forces Reserve medals. After World War I, Truman returned to Independence, Missouri, where he married Bess Wallace, and the couple had one child, Mary Margaret. After serving as a county judge, Harry S. Truman was elected United States Senator from Missouri in 1934.

Truman was elected vice president of the United States on the Roosevelt ticket on January 20, 1945. Truman had been vice president for eighty-two days when President Roosevelt suddenly died in office on April 12, 1945. Truman had been presiding over the Senate that day when he was urgently summoned to the West Wing of the White House, where he was sworn in as president at 7:09 p.m. by Chief Justice Harlan F. Stone. Ironically, although Truman generally did not like reporters, he asked them to pray for him on his first full day in office. He opened up and was very candid with them. He said, "Boys, if you ever pray, pray for me now. I don't know if you fellas ever had a load of hay fall on you, but when they told me yesterday I would be sworn in, I felt like the moon, the stars, and all the planets had fallen on me" (Glass, 2018).

President Roosevelt had never discussed the Manhattan Project with Vice President Truman. Secretary of War Henry Stimson

The Surrender of Germany and Japan

mentioned it to him the evening of April 12, after he was sworn in as president, but then Stimson gave him the details and a fuller briefing on April 25 ("Harry S. Truman's Biography," 2021).

The Manhattan Project was an unprecedented top-secret World War II government program in which the United States had hundreds and thousands of both civilian and military personnel working at Los Alamos, Hanford, and Oakridge sites, developing the world's first atomic weapons. They were trying to get it done before German scientists and engineers did, as they had already made great advancements in rocket development and other areas ("Manhattan Project," 2023).

No one individual can be credited with producing the first atomic bombs, but physicist J. Robert Oppenheimer and Army Lieutenant General Leslie Groves played major roles in its development. Testing different methods, on July 16, 1945, they attempted the implosion method at the Trinity Site, which was successful. President Harry Truman had just arrived in Potsdam, Germany, to meet with Joseph Stalin and Winston Churchill to negotiate terms for the end of World War II.

Truman mentioned to Stalin that the United States was testing a top-secret weapon, but Joseph Stalin had already known about it, even prior to Truman, through Russian intelligence. President Truman was informed on July 16, 1945, while he was in Potsdam, that the Trinity test was successful. As the Manhattan Project moved closer to the use of the first atomic bomb, ethical questions arose in the minds of some who understood the project's intent. Truman sat alone in the Oval Office with his head down on the desk, praying intently. In his last briefing by the military high command, he was informed that Japan would not quit, that they did not know how to stop fighting. The Trinity test had ushered in the nuclear age with the world's first man-made nuclear explosion. The decision was made to drop them on Japan.

The first atomic bomb, named Little Boy, was dropped on Hiroshima from the *Enola Gay*, a B-29 bomber, at 8:15 a.m. on August 6, 1945. Then, the Soviet Union shocked policymakers in Japan by declaring war on Japan on August 8, 1945. Then, on August 9, 1945, the United States dropped a second bomb, a plutonium-fueled weapon named Fat Man, on Nagasaki from a B-29 bomber named *Boxcar* at 11:02 a.m. on August 9, 1945. The combination of the two atomic bombs and the declaration of war by the Soviet Union finally pushed Emperor Hirohito to announce Japan's surrender on September 2, 1945, officially ending the most deadly and destructive war in human history ("Bombing of Hiroshima and Nagasaki," 2023).

Could there be a World War III in our time and generation? As of this writing, Israel has just come under attack by Hamas, and Israel has declared war, with threats on every side. Islam has clearly laid out a plan for global conquest, including the United States. There are now about 12,512 nuclear warheads in the world, with Russia, the United States, and China holding the majority. Yet, in the hands of North Korea, Iran, or other unstable entities, it creates a very dangerous dynamic. China has also made no secret about its intentions to invade and take Taiwan. Russia and Vladimir Putin have very recently met with China and Xi Jinping, getting cozy and conducting coordinated military drills over the Ural mountain range.

War in Korea

Since the beginning of the twentieth century, Korea had been a part of the Japanese Empire, and after World War II, it fell to the Soviets and the Americans to decide what should be done with their enemies' imperial possessions. In August 1945, two young aides at the State Department divided the Korean Peninsula in half along the thirty-eighth parallel. The Russians occupied the Communist North, and the Americans occupied democratic South Korea. On June 25, 1950, 75,000 soldiers from the North Korean People's Army poured across the thirty-eighth parallel, invading South Korea, which became the first military action of the Cold War.

President Truman told the war-weary American public, "If we let Korea down, the Soviets will keep right on going and swallow up one place after another" (Offner, 2000). The war on the Korean Peninsula became a symbol of the battle between East and West, good and evil, and against communism itself. America reluctantly entered the war under the leadership of Truman.

After back-and-forth fighting across the thirty-eighth parallel, casualties mounted to five million soldiers and civilians as American officers worked anxiously to fashion an armistice with the North Koreans, as they feared that the war could spread to Russia, China, and World War III. Finally, the Korean War came to an end in July 1953. It became known as the "Forgotten War," although there was an enormous number of casualties. The American media and public had become war-weary and no longer wanted to cover it or talk about it ("Pearce Rotondi," 2023). The steady and reliable American leader, Harry S. Truman, died on December 26, 1972 ("Harry S. Truman's Biography," 2021).

CHAPTER 25

Faith, Healing, and Salvation

The Lives and Stories of Kenneth Hagin, Oral Roberts, and Billy Graham

We can gain a better understanding of what is going on in the spirit realm by observing what is going on in the natural world. When all hell is breaking loose on the earth, as in the time of World War II, we are more clearly able to see the chaotic push of evil on the earth. This chapter, "Faith, Healing, and Salvation," is about three generals, Kenneth E. Hagin, Oral Roberts, and Billy Graham, and how God worked through them to impact and change the world. All three men were contemporaries of the same generation and were born about the same time. We will start with the life of Kenneth Hagin first.

Faith

Kenneth Erwin Hagin was born on August 20, 1917, in McKinney, Texas, and was called by God to teach the church faith. He operated in most of the gifts of the Spirit in his nearly seventy years of ministry. He had a deep and profound knowledge and understanding of Scripture and yet would impart his wisdom in a relaxed, comfortable, fatherly way to all people. With his years of walking with the Lord, he would discuss the supernatural as if it were quite natural. He would rattle off one amazing story after another about miracles, healings, moves, and revelations of God. And anyone who listened to him for any length of time would be edified and grow in faith.

He had a friendly, down-home demeanor that made all who listened to him very comfortable. He would tell countless stories about extraordinary events that imparted faith to the listener. Kenneth Hagin also had an amazing memory where he could recall specific dates, times, and details of events in his life.

Kenneth had a sister and two brothers, but sadly, his father abandoned the family when he was just six years old. And under the stress of trying to go on by herself and take care of the children, Kenneth's mother had an emotional breakdown. Fortunately, Kenneth's grandparents loved him, took him in, and raised him. He was also taken to a church as a child, where he was baptized and began to learn about the Bible. However, it is possible that his father's abandonment of the family played a role in his inability and unwillingness to trust God and commit his life to Jesus in his early years. Kenneth Hagin had been diagnosed with a deformed heart and rare blood disease that caused him to be very sickly and unable to run and play with the other children.

Kenneth Hagin relates the terrifying story of April 22, 1933, when, at age fifteen, he died and left his body three different times, descending into the depths of hell, where each time a hideous creature attempted to drag him to the gates, where once inside, no one can return. And each time a booming voice spoke and shook the

Faith, Healing, and Salvation

place, the creature released him, and he would ascend back up the shaft to his house, his bedroom, and reenter his body. I would like to stop here for just a moment and say that whether you believe or don't believe Kenneth Hagin's testimony about going to hell, the Bible is very clear that it is a real place.

There are many references to heaven and hell and the afterlife, so let's look at one. Jesus stated in Luke 12:4–5 (NIV), "I tell you, my friends, do not be afraid of those who kill the body, and after that can do no more. But I will show you whom you should fear: Fear him who, after your body has been killed, has authority to throw you into hell. Yes, I tell you, I fear him."

The first two times that Kenneth descended into hell, he thought that he might be hallucinating. But then, the third time, he realized that it was quite real and began to cry out to God for help. He said, "I should not be here. I should not be going this way. I was baptized. I went to church." Then, he began to scream out to God as loud as he could: "God, save me! Save me in Jesus's name. Save Me!" Again, a booming voice spoke, and the place began to shake, and the hideous creature who was dragging him to the gates of hell released him. Once again, he began to ascend back up the dark shaft very fast, back to his house, back to his bed, and back into his body through his mouth ("I Went to Hell: Kenneth E. Hagin's Testimony," 2021).

I also met a very big truck driver from Albuquerque who told me a very similar story. He said that one night, he overdosed on cocaine and started to quickly descend this immensely dark shaft. He began to see flickering fingers of light as he neared the end, which he realized were flames. Once he got there, a suction began to pull him, and then a very large, hideous creature grabbed him and began to drag him to the gates of no return. He remembered what his grandmother said: "When in trouble, call on Jesus." He began to scream, "Jesus, save me! Jesus, help me!" The large, hideous spirit released him just prior to putting him behind the gates of hell. He went up the dark shaft, rapidly ascending, and returned to his house, his bed, and back into his body. Opening his eyes, he realized that he, too, had just escaped the eternal torments of hell and was saved and given another chance.

From April 22, 1933, to August 8, 1934, Kenneth Hagin remained bedfast, paralyzed, and sickly. For sixteen months, after his descent into hell three times and his salvation experience, his heart still was not beating right, and he was sickly. But God began to personally mentor him and teach him things that he would, in turn, teach the church for the next seventy years. Kenneth began to hear a still, small voice witnessing to him, "You can be healed; you don't have to die at this early age." So, Kenneth, not yet understanding the voice or leading of God, began to ask family and friends what they thought about this. And so, he had a parade of "Job's comforters" come to him and, like good Baptists, told him, "No, you can't be healed; since the time of the apostles, healing has been done away with." And yet, occasionally, one of his comforters would say, "Well, you know, God is all-powerful, and it's

Faith, Healing, and Salvation

possible He could heal someone, but it probably won't be you." And yet that thought persisted with Kenneth Hagin: *You can be healed.* One day, in his bedroom, lying paralyzed on his bed, Kenneth blurted out to God, "If I could be healed, how?" The still, small voice spoke to him, "It's all in the book." So, with no one to teach or mentor him, Kenneth Hagin began to voraciously study and read the Bible and pray.

Many scriptures and places in the Bible began to minister to him, but especially Mark 11:23–24. And when he read that, he excitedly exclaimed, "That's it. That's it!" Mark 11:23–24 (NIV) reads as follows:

> "Truly I tell you, if anyone says to this mountain, 'Go, throw yourself into the sea,' and does not doubt in their heart, but believes that what they say will happen, it will be done for them. Therefore I tell you, whatever you ask for in prayer, believe that you have received it, and it will be yours."

There was one night when Kenneth Hagin felt like he was dying, just barely hanging on by a thread, so he quoted Mark 11:23–24 all night long. Within time, he said that he began to see it, more than just memorizing it; it got down into his spirit; he knew it, he believed and received it, and it was his.

The Rise and Fall of the American Empire

No one had taught Kenneth how to pray or raise his hands or say "hallelujah," but he began to thank God and praise Him for his healing. Kenneth was still learning to hear the voice of the Holy Spirit, and he heard, "Now you believe you're healed; well, get up then." He made the effort on August 8, 1934, at 10:30 AM. He made an effort to stand, and the power of God went through his body and came out of his feet. He stood there strong and straight and began to walk around his room that day and the following day. He did not tell anyone what happened because he did not want anyone to discourage him like before. But after two days, he asked his mom to set out his clothes so he could join the family. At breakfast the following day, she tried to talk him out of it for forty minutes, but he finally convinced her: "Just set out my clothes; I can do it; I have been walking around the room for two days."

The next morning, he set off completely dressed, all eighty-nine lbs. of him to the dining room to join the family for breakfast. His mother knew that he was coming, but his grandfather looked up at him walking in and commented, "Is the dead raised? Is Lazarus raised up?" And Kenneth responded, "Yes, God has raised me up." His grandfather would generally not speak while he ate, and such was the case this time as well. Everyone sat quietly and ate breakfast, but there was one big difference: Kenneth was there, sitting with them at the table.

The next big lesson Kenneth had to learn was to discern the difference between the voice of God and of the devil. His heart was beating right, his paralysis was gone, and he could walk, but

Faith, Healing, and Salvation

he still felt weak, so he laid down to take a nap after breakfast. Sometimes, the devil knows who someone is before they do. He had very early on tried to take this future general out before he could step into his purpose and destiny.

When Kenneth woke up from his nap, an unusual voice began speaking to him with a declaration, quoting Scripture and trying to sound very authoritative, and told him to get ready, that he would die that day. At first, he thought that it was the voice of God. He would not eat that day and thought that he was going to die. Then a still, small voice spoke to him, like a witness floating up in his spirit, and said, "With long life, will I satisfy you and show you my salvation." Then Kenneth blurted out, "Who said that?" Then a stronger voice, which seemed audible, said, "Psalm 91." So, he got his Bible and read Psalm 91, and hope began to spring up in his heart.

After he studied more Scripture and Bible references, he realized the hope that sprung up in his heart was the Holy Spirit, and the voice that was trying to lie to him and tell him that he was going to die was the devil. So, Kenneth promptly kicked the devil out of his bedroom and learned another deep and valuable lesson that day. Throughout his years of ministry, he was good about getting people's faith to rise about healing and living and not accept dying prematurely ("K. E. Hagin: Full Testimony of How Kenneth E. Hagin Received His Miraculous Healing on His Deathbed," 2021).

The Rise and Fall of the American Empire

Kenneth Erwin Hagin was one of those individuals who grew and matured quickly as a believer and as a Christian. He may have had some mentors and learned from others, but it would seem his direct teacher was the Holy Spirit, and he had a remarkable desire to know and study the word of God. His first understanding of Christianity theologically was through the lens of the Baptist Church. But even before he had preached his first sermon, as the young teenage pastor of the small Community Baptist Church in Roland, Texas, he already believed in healing and the infilling of the Spirit, even when he was yet to have it himself.

As a teenager, his mother encouraged him to go see a ministry that had come into town, where they were teaching healing and the gifts of the Spirit. He eventually was exposed to the baptism of the Holy Spirit with the evidence of speaking in tongues and the gifts of the Spirit. Throughout his seventy years of ministry, Kenneth Hagin had a remarkable understanding of flowing with the Spirit and operated in almost all nine gifts of the Spirit. Like what happened years later to John Osteen, the Baptists, when they felt that Kenneth Hagin had gone too far, gave him the left foot of fellowship ("The Legacy of Hope Began," n.d.). In 1936, young Kenneth founded his first nondenominational church. In 1937, he became an Assemblies of God minister for twelve years, with the last church he pastored being in Van, Texas.

On November 25, 1938, he married Oretha Rooker, with whom he had two children, Kenneth Jr. and Patricia. Years later, Kenneth Hagin Jr. took over Rhema Bible College and Kenneth

Faith, Healing, and Salvation

Hagin Ministries. Kenneth Hagin Sr. related the story of how, one day, he was focusing on praying in the Spirit. And then, each time he stopped, an evil spirit would try to lie to him and say that he was not accomplishing anything and was wasting his time. So, in response to that, Kenneth Hagin continued to pray in glossolalia (tongues) for five hours and forty-five minutes. And at the end of that period, the Holy Spirit spoke to him and said, "After the end of World War II, there would be a revival of the healing ministry," which absolutely came to pass (K. Hagin, 1997).

From about 1947 to 1958, Kenneth Hagin joined Oral Roberts, Gordon Lindsay, T. L. Osborne, and a group of one hundred other evangelists in the Voice of Healing Revival. In 1949, Jesus appeared to Kenneth Hagin and instructed him to leave the pastorate, be an evangelist and Bible teacher, and teach His people faith.

Kenneth Hagin was a gifted minister who drew from his walk with the Lord and his rich life experiences. In 1974, Kenneth Hagin founded Rhema Bible Training College, which has trained over 80,000 graduates who reside and minister in fifty-two different countries. Rhema has a 110-acre campus in Broken Arrow, Oklahoma, and specializes in seven different areas of ministry. Rhema has also established many other training centers in other countries throughout the world. Rhema Bible Training College and Kenneth Hagin Ministries and Evangelistic Association continue to be led by his son, Kenneth Hagin Jr. Kenneth Hagin wrote more than forty-two different books, including *The Believer's Authority* in 1985. And though Kenneth Erwin Hagin lowered his head for the final time on Friday morning, September 19, 2003, his influence lives on in thousands of ministers trained and a multitude of people ministered to ("Biography of Kenneth E. Hagin," 2016) (Olsen, 2003).

Healing

Granville Oral Roberts

Oral Roberts was born on January 24, 1918, in Pontotoc County near Ada, Oklahoma, the fifth and youngest child of the Reverend Ellis Melvin Roberts and Claudius Priscilla Irwin. At the height of his ministry, Oral Roberts was one of the most well-known evangelists in the world, spearheading the healing revival that began after the end of World War II and went on through much of the second half of the twentieth century.

His early childhood began in a very humble rural Oklahoma setting in the 1920s. Three months before his birth, Oral's mother was called to pray for a neighbor's child who was seriously ill. As she was crossing the field, she stooped to climb through a fence, sensing the presence of God in the wind; she made a vow to God. That if God would heal the child that she was about to pray for, and also if the child that she would soon have was a boy, she would dedicate her son to Almighty God for the ministry (Voight, n.d.). Well, God healed the child she prayed for that very same night, and when her son Oral was born, she dedicated him to God and prayed that God would call him into the ministry.

Faith, Healing, and Salvation

In the 1930s, the Depression hit Oklahoma hard, and his father's plight was that of a small-town Pentecostal preacher. Many of Reverend Roberts's congregants were with little or no work, with very few options to make money. And so, the Roberts household, like many, struggled to survive. To make matters worse, most of the Christians in the area ridiculed Pentecostalism, and young Oral bore the brunt of most of the persecution. Not only was he a Pentecostal preacher's son, but he was also a stutterer with the name Oral, which most of the students found quite amusing. At age fifteen, after several years of struggling to find acceptance in this environment, he ran away from home. Oral had a dream of becoming an attorney and going into politics, but his mother continued to remind him of the vow she had made. In many ways, Oral did pretty well for himself, working his way through school and even excelling in basketball. At this point in his life, he had yet to commit his life to Jesus and was more concerned about being a teenager and playing sports.

In 1935, at the age of seventeen, Oral Roberts returned home, but he was dying. His basketball coach carried Oral into the house; his lungs were hemorrhaging, and he was spitting up blood. He had contracted tuberculosis, a disease that had plagued the Indians in Oklahoma for many years. His grandfather and other relatives had died of tuberculosis. This was prior to the time when they began to discover drugs to treat tuberculosis, as most did not recover. All that young Oral had to look forward to was being admitted into the state sanitarium in Talihina to wait to die.

He lay in bed in his parents' home for many months, becoming increasingly frail and weakened. Then, one day, his sister Jewel came into his room and said, "Oral, God is going to heal you." He answered, "Is He, Jewel?" He had yet to become a Christian and knew little about God's healing power, but her words gave him hope. Sometime later, his brother Elmer came into the room and told Oral that he was going to take him to the healing revival in Ada, where an evangelist was praying for the sick. On the way to the revival, lying on a mattress in the back of the car, Oral heard a still, small voice speak to him, "Son, I am going to heal you, and you are to take the message of My healing power to your generation."

That night, Oral was the last one to be prayed for, and he felt the healing power of God go through him, and he could breathe deep and freely again. At the same time, God also healed his stammer and stutter, and he stood up and exhorted for some time what Jesus had done for him. Oral Roberts became a living testimony of the love and healing power of God. Although it took some time to regain his strength, he began to preach, and he preached his first small sermon just two months after his healing in 1935.

Soon after, young Oral Roberts was ordained in the Pentecostal Holiness Church and later on in the United Methodist Church as well. He had a tremendous hunger to know the Scripture and matured very quickly in the things of God, and soon became a pastor, which he did for the next twelve years. In 1936, while attending a camp meeting in Sulphur, Oklahoma, he took his place

Faith, Healing, and Salvation

in the orchestra, looked over at the young woman on his right, and asked, "Do I look all right? Is my hair combed?" She responded, "Oh, yes, you look very nice." Later that night, Evelyn dreamily wrote in her diary: "I sat by my future husband tonight." So, that was the beginning of the courtship of Oral and Evelyn Roberts. And, you know, someone is serious when they want you to meet their parents.

One fine day, Oral loaded his beautiful new blue Chevrolet coupe with his mother aboard for the 600-mile trip to Texas to meet Evelyn. Miss Evelyn was a teacher, and all the children were giggling and excited to see her with her boyfriend. On the last day of his time in Texas with her, they went fishing together, but the only thing that they caught was each other. On the way back from fishing, he stopped to propose to her. The first time that he did it, he used the most incredible descriptive, poetic prose. And Evelyn said, "Listen here, boy, if you're trying to propose to me, talk in the English language." So, he did it all over again, and she said yes; then, they sealed it with a kiss.

Oral Roberts continued to pastor and hold evangelistic meetings, and Evelyn continued to teach school in Texas. And on Christmas Day in 1938, Oral and Evelyn were married. The twelve years from 1935 to 1947 were the wilderness years for Oral Roberts and his ministry. One part of Oral couldn't help but feel like he had "missed it." But maybe he didn't. Perhaps God was continuing to develop his character, prepare him, ready him, and transform him into the person that he needed to be before stepping onto a huge national platform. So, during the twelve years prior to his launch into a healing evangelist ministry, he pastored churches, taught in Bible school, wrote books and articles, and evangelized.

In 1947, while pastoring in Enid, Oklahoma, and attending Phillips University, he began to experience an ever-increasing divine frustration. He was miserable because he felt like something was missing from his ministry. One day, he received a call from a desperate person who wanted prayer for a man who had had a terrible accident. A very large, heavy object had fallen on his foot and crushed it, and when he arrived, he saw the man rolling around on the floor in agony, hollering and screaming. Without really thinking about it, he got down on the floor and prayed for him, praying that Jesus would heal his foot. The man stopped yelling and took off his boot, looked at Oral, and said, "What did you do?" Oral said, "I didn't do anything; I just touched your foot and asked Jesus to heal it." The man got up, stomped down on his foot a couple of times, took a short walk, and then looked at Oral in complete amazement. And Oral looked back at him with just as much amazement. His other friend who was there asked him, "Can you do this all the time? If you could, you would bring a revival to all mankind" (Voight, n.d.) (R. Roberts, "The Story of Oral Roberts's Ministry—How It Began," 2020).

And then Oral Roberts began to have a recurring dream. In this recurring dream, Oral would see the multiplied millions of humanities pass by him, and God opened his eyes to see them as they truly were. Most people were broken and afflicted in some way. So many hurt, lost, sick, and dying people, diseased people, and sad children, and the utter brokenness of humanity was completely overwhelming. Sometimes, he would wake up outside of his bedroom, sleepwalking and even crying, and Evelyn would ask him, "Oral, what are you doing?" So, he told her about the recurring dream and the burden that it brought. So, she asked him, "So, what are you going to do about it?" One of the things Oral Roberts did was begin to earnestly seek God concerning his ministry. God began to speak to Oral and direct him. One of the things that God instructed him to do was to read through the four Gospels and the book of Acts while in the humble position of being on his knees. One of the things that happened to Oral was that he began to see Jesus in a new light, a compassionate Savior who healed broken people.

Another word and instruction Oral received was: "Don't be like other men; be like Jesus" (R. Roberts, "The Story of Oral Roberts's Ministry—How It Began," 2020). Another thing that Oral did was wait on the Lord in prayer. He would lie on the floor for hours and ask God to give him a healing anointing, and one day, he felt like the flow of electricity went through his body, and he was then confident that God had given him a healing anointing. Also, later in his ministry, he related how Jesus gave him, specifically, a gift of healing through his right hand.

It was about now that Oral Roberts decided to put out a fleece before the Lord to test and see if this was the leading of the Lord. He rented an auditorium in Enid, where he held a healing service. Within the fleece that he had put before the Lord, he asked for three things. One that 1,000 people would attend the healing service, which seemed impossible to him because he was currently preaching to around 200 every Sunday. He also asked that the $160 that it required to rent the building for a Sunday afternoon be raised, and the third one was that someone would be healed in the service to validate the healing ministry. He announced and advertised the healing service, but he also got a job at a men's clothing store at the same time. He decided that if God did not confirm his call, he was going to leave the ministry and start selling clothes (Voight, n.d.).

On the day of the healing service, everyone was milling around after the initial teaching, waiting to go into the healing meeting. When he walked into the building, the custodian said, "Preacher, I hear that you want at least 1,000 people. Well, there are 1,200 seated in the auditorium." Then, when they took up the offering, it totaled $163.03, which was able to meet the expense for the rental of the large auditorium. Then while Oral Roberts was preaching, he jumped off the platform, and at that moment, a German mother cried out that her crippled hand had been healed. She showed everyone and exclaimed that God had opened her hand, and because of that incredible miracle, seven men accepted Jesus as their Lord and Savior. This marked the birth of Oral Roberts's healing ministry (R. Roberts, "The Story of Oral Roberts's Ministry—How It Began," 2020). Oral Roberts wrote in his book *The Call* that the Lord had taken him from abject poverty, a runaway on his death-

Faith, Healing, and Salvation

bed, to being miraculously healed in the making of his ministry.

Not long after, Oral was in Tulsa, while Reverend Steve Pringle had a large tent set up on the north side of the city. Reverend Pringle invited Oral Roberts to preach at the tent meetings, and one night, a man from across the street fired a weapon at him, and the bullet whizzed past his ear, nearly taking him out before this general could even get started. This story became a headline all over the country, and from that time forward, the name Oral Roberts was nationally known. On top of that, the tent revival meeting went on for weeks, and they had many miraculous healings. Oral's ministry began to get thousands of letters and a huge response, and one of his friends looked at his office and the pile of letters and said, "You really need to get organized."

It was about this time that Oral, Evelyn, and those close to him decided to move to Tulsa. And in November of 1947, he launched the *Healing Waters* magazine, which also included testimonials of people who had been healed. Also, in 1948, he incorporated the Healing Waters organization. With his ministry headquartered in Tulsa, he began to assemble a staff and ministry team, including Robert DeWeese. In the first year alone, as the letters continued to pour in, they mailed back and out 90,000 copies of the *Healing Waters* magazine, 15,000 books, 30,000 prayer clothes, and 25,000 letters (Voight, n.d.).

And just as the Lord had spoken to Kenneth Hagin, after the end of World War II, a healing revival would arise in America, and

267

The Rise and Fall of the American Empire

Oral Roberts was at the forefront of this revival (K. E. Hagin, n.d.). He was also one of the leading individuals who brought Pentecostalism and the gifts of the Spirit into mainstream America. Billy Graham became a lifelong friend of Orals and had great respect for him and his ministry. One account held that Billy Graham had taken his grandmother to a Roberts crusade, and she was healed at the meeting ("Voices of Oklahoma," 2018). When Oral Roberts preached and taught, he would draw on the deep reservoir of biblical and experiential knowledge that he had. He would tell people, "What God did for me, He can do for you." He believed that the Word of God gave people the ability to believe right and correctly.

Oral Roberts also taught that God had the desire to save, heal, make whole, and bless all humanity and that all we must do is call on Him in faith. Oral, having grown up in the Depression, hated poverty, and he did not believe that it was a blessing. He believed that Christians should not only stretch their faith to believe for their need met but to have an abundance to be able to help others in need and be able to support churches, ministries, outreaches, and other godly works. In behind-the-scenes interviews about Oral, people would describe him as a very humble person who genuinely cared about people.

In 1948, Oral Roberts began his first crusade in Durham, North Carolina, with a large tent that seated 3,000 people. When that tent was destroyed by a storm in Amarillo, Texas, in 1950, he responded by getting a bigger one that seated 7,500 people. In 1953, he purchased his final tent, which sat an enormous crowd of 12,500

Faith, Healing, and Salvation

people. For twenty years, he held tent crusades throughout America and traveled to fifty-four different countries, seeing thousands saved, blessed, and healed (R. Roberts, "The Story of OralRoberts's Ministry—How It Began," 2020). He was a very strong man who was built like a fullback, but sometimes, it could be a very grueling schedule.

In an interview, Oral shared the story of a determined woman who grabbed him after a crusade in the parking lot demanding prayer. He told her that he was exhausted and so tired that he was leaving. But she hung onto his coat until he prayed for her, and she was healed (O. Roberts, 1952). Kathryn Kuhlman got to the point where she had a group of people encircle her when she left the building so that would not happen. But Oral Roberts was good about realizing that the people were coming to see God, to be healed by God, to be touched by God, not him. He would always say, "I can't heal anybody; God does the healing" (R. Roberts, "The Story of Oral Roberts's Ministry—How It Began," 2020).

He began his television ministry in 1954 and always had a keen understanding of the ability of the media to further extend the hand of the evangelist. People would also testify that they were ministered to and healed while watching an Oral Roberts crusade on TV. In 1955, the first tent crusade was televised, and from 1955 to the final tent crusade in 1967, the ministry was on television. The television ministry took a break but resumed in 1969, televising primetime specials and having the legendary Mahalia Jackson as his first guest star. Oral Roberts also extensively utilized the medium of radio and, additionally, wrote more than 120 books, including *Expect a Miracle* (Voight, n.d.).

As always, the wife is the backbone of any great man, and Evelyn was a tremendous support to him, raising their four children and always encouraging him with the work of the Oral Roberts Evangelistic Association ("Biography of Oral Roberts," 2016). After many years of healing crusades, Oral Roberts expanded his evangelism to higher education. It was a simple yet brilliant idea. He realized that he was only one man, yet if hundreds and thousands of young people received an education at a great Christian university, they would potentially spread their faith and influence not only into churches and ministry but into every sphere of endeavor that they went into.

Oral Roberts University broke ground in 1961 with the vision for a full Liberal Arts University and a theological seminary composed of a spirit-filled faculty recruited from the best schools in the nation. Oral Roberts University was chartered by the state of Oklahoma in 1963 and then held its first classes in 1965 with an enrollment of 303 students. By the time of its dedication on April 2, 1967, the university had eight completed buildings situated on a 420-acre campus. The keynote speaker at ORU's official dedication was the Reverend Billy Graham. Rapid growth occurred at ORU in the 1970s, and enrollment was 1,000 students by 1971. They were also accredited by the North Central Association of Colleges and Secondary Schools.

Faith, Healing, and Salvation

The Mabee Center, housing performing arts and an indoor sports arena, was completed in 1972. Other buildings constructed included residence halls, a worship center, a graduate center, and 196 student apartments. ORU added a school of nursing in 1975 and medicine and dentistry in 1978. By 1983, graduate degrees were offered, and the campus held twenty-two buildings on more than 500 acres. Also, by 1983, the City of Faith Medical and Research Center was constructed, combining the vision of faith and medical science. The massive 2,200,000 square foot city of Faith consisted of three high rises, one with sixty stories and the other two having thirty stories and twenty stories, holding a clinic, hospital, and research facility. Due to an economic downturn and other factors, the City of Faith closed in 1989 and was eventually sold to other entities.

ORU has continued; as of 2022, undergraduate enrollment stands at 4,402 students. The vision Oral Roberts had for education came to pass, sending hundreds and thousands out to have an influence in every area (Wilson, 2010) (Ruffle, 2023).

There are many notable ORU alumni who are making an impact and a difference in ministry and different spheres; for example, one bright light in Hollywood, media, and entertainment is Kym Bankier Douglas (MediaNews Group, 2021).

Richard Roberts has carried on most of the leadership for the Oral Roberts Evangelistic Association for the last sixty years ("About Richard Roberts Ministries," n.d.). Just prior to his death,

Oral Roberts had a dream and vision that he told to his son, Richard, and Kenneth Copeland. The essence of the vision is that the return of Jesus is getting very close and that the Lord would call an army of evangelists to help bring in the final harvest in a condensed period of time: as many as would respond to that call (R. Roberts, "Wake Up—A Prophetic Message by Oral Roberts," 2023).

The visionary, the evangelist, the great Granville Oral Roberts died on December 15, 2009, in Newport Beach, California, and was preceded in death by Evelyn in 2005 (Schneider, 2009).

Salvation

The Reverend Billy Graham

The man whom many called America's pastor, William Franklin Graham, was born on November 7, 1918, in Charlotte, North Carolina. Billy Graham communicated the gospel message via indoor and outdoor crusades, radio, television, books, and the Internet to more multiplied thousands than any evangelist in the history of the world. His children, including Franklin Graham, have continued to carry on the great work and ministry of the Billy Graham Evangelistic Association until the present (F. T. Graham, 2018).

One of the consistent themes and messages throughout his ministry was the decline of current culture and the spiritual condition of America. In 1962, Billy Graham issued a dire prophetic warning to America. He stated, essentially, that if we do not, individually and collectively as a nation, turn back to following

Faith, Healing, and Salvation

Christ, mighty America is headed for a fall, just like the Roman Empire, which collapsed from within. And how is America doing now, sixty-two years later, after the warning of the Reverend Billy Graham? (B. Graham, *America at the Crossroads*, 2020). Rick Renner, who pastors churches in both Russia and Ukraine, stated in a recent interview with Perry Stone, "We are witnessing the fall of Western civilization" (Renner, 2020).

Billy Graham grew up in rural North Carolina, the son of a prosperous dairy farmer. In 1934, young Billy attended a revival meeting led by the evangelist Mordecai Ham and had a conversion experience, making the decision to follow Christ. As a teenager, he was already tall and popular, with piercing blue eyes and blonde hair that darkened as he got older. In 1936, he left his family's dairy farm in North Carolina to attend Bob Jones College but stayed for only a semester because of the rigidity and strict fundamentalism. He transferred to Florida Bible Institute (now Trinity College) and graduated in 1940 as an ordained Southern Baptist Convention minister (Hammer, 2008).

He continued his education at Wheaton College in Illinois, and while he was there, he met and married Ruth Bell, daughter of L. Nelson Bell, a missionary to China. Billy Graham thought he was interested in someone else, but when he saw Ruth, he said it was love at first sight, and a small little voice spoke to his heart, "This will be your wife." By the time Billy Graham had graduated from Wheaton in 1943, he had developed his trademark preaching style, a simple direct message of sin and salvation. He first believed what he was preaching and then wrapped it in his unique honesty and sincerity, which readily connected with the people. He and Ruth were married that same year in Montreat, North Carolina. He traveled the world and America for over fifty years, but she was the one who loved him, the one that he would return home to each and every time after being gone weeks and sometimes months (B. Graham, "Billy and Ruth Graham—A Love Story for the Ages," 2021).

After a brief period as pastor of Western Springs Baptist Church in the western suburbs of Chicago, Billy Graham felt the call to evangelism. He joined the staff of a new organization called Youth for Christ in 1945 and continued to develop ministerial and organizational skills. At the young age of twenty-nine, he became president of Northwestern Bible College in Minneapolis and held that post for about four years.

I would describe 1948 and the beginning of 1949 as the wilderness years for Billy Graham. Billy Graham's call to evangelism came at a very propitious time, as American Protestantism was deeply divided between different camps, including fundamentalism and modernism. During the 1925 Scopes Trial, the media successfully portrayed fundamentalist ministers as a bunch of uneducated country bumpkins. And on the other hand, Billy Graham had a stream of brilliant intellectuals who had his ear and were questioning the authority of the Bible. Oh, and yes, they were quite convincing. It is possible to attend religious seminaries and theological institutes that become so modernist, intellectual, and faith-

Faith, Healing, and Salvation

less that you would graduate from those places with less faith or no faith. However, Billy Graham had to get through this because he had an incredible call on his life to bring the simple message of salvation to America and the world and shake his generation (Balmer, 2023).

The Bible states in 2 Timothy 3:14–17 (NIV):

> But as for you, continue in what you have learned and have become convinced of, because you know those from whom you learned it, and how from infancy you have known the Holy Scriptures, which are able to make you wise for salvation through faith in Christ Jesus. All Scripture is God-breathed and is useful for teaching, rebuking, correcting, and training in righteousness, so that the servant of God may be thoroughly equipped for every good work.

And Billy Graham got it. After a period of wrestling with these issues, he went on a spiritual retreat and went off into the forest to get alone with God and pray. And so one evening in the dark shadows of the San Bernardino Mountains, he laid down his Bible on a stump in the forest and declared to God, in essence, "Lord, I accepted You by faith, and now I accept the authority of the inspired word of the Bible by faith" (Reardon, n.d.).

The Rise and Fall of the American Empire

He emerged from this retreat in California with a new peace and confidence, and not long after, a tent revival in Los Angeles began, which was on September 25, 1949. Billy Graham possessed a very charismatic combination of good looks, wit, humor, sincerity, and the ability to connect and communicate with people in a way that they understood. The first three weeks of the tent crusade in Los Angeles went very well, with high attendance. Then, there was a convergence of events, and many things began to happen very quickly. First, the whole event had been bathed in prayer and intercession before it had even begun.

The Christ for Greater Los Angeles Committee organized a series of revival meetings and invited Billy Graham to be the preacher. More than 1,000 prayer groups had been praying for the crusade's success and revival in Los Angeles. A very large tent that held 6,000 was erected but was quickly enlarged to 9,000, but it was still too small. Graham's preaching was simple yet electrifying, and he had found his stride. He moved like a quarterback in the center of the field, under the power and anointing of God, proclaiming, "I don't believe that any man can solve the problems and challenges of life without Jesus Christ. Across Europe, people know that time is running out. Now that Russia has the atomic bomb, an armament race has begun, driving us to destruction."

Not only did many hundreds of people come forward to receive salvation, but many celebrities and high-profile individuals, including Stuart Hamblen, Harvey Fritz, Louis Zamperini, and Jim Vaus, also came forward to receive salvation. Stuart Hamblen

Faith, Healing, and Salvation

announced to the world, on-air, of his conversion to Christianity at the Billy Graham crusade. Then, newspaper and magazine titans William Randolph Hearst and Henry Luce became involved. The local newspapers had already begun to cover the Los Angeles crusade, and then Hearst sent dozens of reporters from all over the country to cover the crusade. After about the third week, Billy Graham arrived at the huge tent and saw a giant mob of reporters and cameras and asked, "Hey, fellas, what's going on?" Then one reporter told him, "You have been kissed by William Randolph Hearst," and showed him the telegraph that Hearst had sent all over the country to his editors, which simply stated in news lingo, "Puff Graham."

The Los Angeles crusade exploded and was extended a further five weeks, and within days, the name, the photos, and the stories of Billy Graham were in every living room in America. At the same time, Henry Luce began to cover Billy Graham in all his magazines and would eventually feature him on the cover of *Time* magazine. God gave Billy Graham a platform of favor and influence to point people to him throughout the entirety of his ministry and life, which continues into the present through the Billy Graham Evangelistic Association led by his son, Franklin.

Hearst and Luce both got behind Graham because of his patriotism and anti-communism, as well as for being a good influence on the youth of America. Without fully understanding Christianity, Hearst and Luce were inspired and moved by Hamblen's conversions and all the Hollywood celebrities as well. And after an avalanche of media attention and the most successful crusade in the history of Los Angeles, the ministry of evangelist Billy Graham was born and is now in full gear. The collective consciousness of America once again began to think about God. And if William Randolph Hearst ever thought he was going to use Graham for his agenda, what happened is that he was used by God for a higher agenda. Ironically, Hearst and Graham never met ("70th Anniversary Greater Los Angeles Billy Graham Crusade of 1949," 2019).

One of the things that also occurred in 1948 was a series of meetings in Modesto, California, that Billy Graham had with George Beverly Shea, Cliff Barrows, and Grady Wilson, where they formulated "the Billy Graham Rule" and others. There had been so many scandals in the ministry and a lack of accountability that they felt it was wise to discuss these things. The core of the rule was never to be alone with a woman, to avoid the appearance of evil, and to avoid accusations. Later, in 1979, the Billy Graham Evangelistic Association helped form the Evangelical Council for Financial Accountability to address that issue as well. I think that it is noteworthy that in all the years of Billy Graham's ministry, there have never been any awful scandals that put another blot on ministers and ministry ("The Modesto Manifesto: A Declaration of Biblical Integrity," 2016).

One of the things that Billy Graham was good at was having an irenic view of the church. What that means is recognizing the importance of unity in the different factions of the Christian Church and declaring the common bond of all Christians under Christ. It

Faith, Healing, and Salvation

was very important for him to continue to develop this mindset to reach thousands and millions of people from every sphere and spectrum of life and the world. He did this without compromising Scripture or biblical truths and always pointed to and through Jesus as the way to heaven and salvation. And not everybody was happy with Billy Graham.

The liberal intellectual theologians were annoyed with the simplicity of his messages. Perhaps they would rather complicate them so no one could understand the Bible. And the staunch, stiff fundamentalists wanted him to remain in their "only us" inclusivity when Billy knew that there was a big, broken, dying world out there that needed Jesus.

The Billy Graham Evangelistic Association held many great crusades throughout America and the world, but one of the more monumental was the Billy Graham Crusade of 1957, held in Madison Square Garden, Times Square, and various locations in New York City. By this time, his ministry had grown to giant proportions, and people throughout America were looking for answers and something to believe in. There were as many as one hundred different language groups represented in New York City, and Billy Graham realized that if you touch New York City, you touch the world. No other city presented it as great a challenge to evangelize, and yet it was a strategic center of world influence that held great potential. There were weeks and months of preparation leading up to this event. They had to coordinate with the local police department and government officials. They enlisted the as-

The Rise and Fall of the American Empire

sistance of hundreds of local churches, prayer groups, volunteers, and counselors.

There were massive crowds of people, both indoors and out, and the whole city was stirred. The crusade itself lasted an astonishing sixteen weeks, and in 110 days, there were one hundred services attended by 2 million plus people, with more than 56,000 making decisions for Christ. Billy Graham's ministry continued to turn the heart of America back to God. On one of the crusade days, they dedicated the entire service to the city's Spanish-speaking population, with an interpreter assisting Billy Graham ("1957 New York Crusade," 2012). Then, in October of 1960, Dr. Billy Graham returned to New York City for another all-Spanish crusade, with Reverend Rogelio Archilla assisting with the interpretation and coordination of over 350 local Spanish-speaking churches.

Dr. Billy Graham returned to New York City and Madison Square Garden in 1969, with 240,000 in attendance and 10,000 coming forward to decide for Christ. Dr. Graham also returned to New York and Shea Stadium the following year, in 1970, with massive crowds and a large response. Also, in 1991, Dr. Billy Graham returned to New York City and held an amazing outdoor event on the great lawn of Central Park, which had 250,000 attendees. It is interesting that after over fifty-five years of ministry, with 417 crusades and rallies all over the world, once again, Dr. Billy Graham returned to New York City in 2005 for his final public crusade. The three-day event had about 242,000 in attendance, representing over one hundred different language groups, includ-

Faith, Healing, and Salvation

ing Spanish. According to the Billy Graham Library, Doctor Billy Graham preached the Gospel message to more than 215 million people in over 185 countries around the world (B. Graham, "List of Billy Graham's Crusades," n.d.).

It is written in Matthew 24:10–14 (NIV):

> At that time many will turn away from the faith and will betray and hate each other, and many false prophets will appear and deceive many people. Because of the increase of wickedness, the love of most will grow cold, but the one who stands firm to the end will be saved. And this gospel of the kingdom will be preached in the whole world as a testimony to all nations, and then the end will come.

One of the signs and indicators that Jesus emphasized in verse 14 was that the gospel would go out over all the earth to all nations preceding His second coming. God is good and desires that none should perish but that all should come to the saving knowledge of Jesus.

Dr. Billy Graham was one of the most important voices of the twentieth century, who played a big role in getting the gospel message out through every conceivable means to prepare for the soon second coming of Jesus. The Billy Graham Evangelistic

Association worked through crusades, magnetron video screens, television, film, radio, books, and the Internet and continues to have a voice and impact through the Billy Graham Library and the leadership of his son, Franklin Graham, over the Evangelistic Association.

Dr. Billy Graham grew into a man of great influence and even had a friendship with twelve different American presidents, some of them very close. They drew great comfort from his friendship and counsel during countless times of national crises. Dr. Billy Graham was truly America's pastor, and perhaps there will never be another like him. At the age of ninety-nine, Dr. Reverend William Franklin Graham died in his home in Montreat, North Carolina, on February 21, 2018. His beloved wife of sixty-four years, Ruth, preceded him in death in 2007 ("Billy Graham's Biography," 2021).

CHAPTER 26

1950s America

Cash, Elvis, and Boone

Near the end of the 1940s, at midnight on May 14, 1948, the provisional government of Israel proclaimed a new State of Israel. On that same date, the United States recognized the provisional Jewish government as the de facto authority of the Jewish state. United States President Harry S. Truman signed the recognition and statement on May 14, 1948 ("US Recognition of the State of Israel," 2021). A little backstory was the lifelong friendship of Harry Truman and Edward Jacobson, who met and worked together at the base canteen at the beginning of World War I. Jacobson was able to communicate Jewish issues and concerns more clearly to Truman, explain the Holocaust, and the importance of Jews having a homeland to return to from Europe after the end of World War II. President Harry S. Truman, when briefed by his staff on the matter, signed it without hesitation that same day ("Jacobson, Edward Papers," n.d.). Every Christian should clearly understand the weighty significance and prophetic timing of Israel once again being recognized as a state and nation after 2,000 years.

1950s America

Perhaps it was during this period that America was at the pinnacle of power and influence. Winston Churchill's observation in

The Rise and Fall of the American Empire

the middle of the century was that America sat atop the summit of the world ("For America, It Truly Was a Great War," 1995). After all, we did the impossible and dug our way out of the Great Depression. And even more impressively, we had thrust our military might along with the Allies against the invincible and unstoppable German war machine and successfully defeated them. And therein lies the problem. We start thinking and believing that by our own might, strength, and effort, we did it all by ourselves and begin to forget about God individually and as a nation. And it was a time of unprecedented optimism and prosperity as Americans felt anything was possible and the future looked bright.

Technology and industry were advancing, and economic prosperity was exploding, with the nation's gross national product more than doubling, going from 212 billion in 1945 to 504 billion in 1960. There was a significant amount of new and affordable housing being constructed in the suburbs, and with the help of low-cost mortgages and the G.I. Bill, many young men returned from the war, married their sweethearts, and purchased the American Dream. They had experienced enough of the daring, scary adventures of the Pacific and Europe and just wanted to settle down and have a family. And, boy, did they have families? ("Baby Boomers," 2019)

Not only was there an economic boom, but there was also a baby boom of 4 million new births each year. The population increased from approximately 150 million in 1950 to almost 180 million by 1960, with most of the increase being in suburbia.

1950s America

There were many good jobs available, and it wasn't uncommon to see middle-class families begin to purchase cabins in addition to their primary residence, boats, and often a second car for the wife (Pruitt, "The Post World War II Boom: How America Got into Gear," 2023).

And speaking of cars, the 1950s was the golden age of the automobile. Americans were perfectly car crazy and fell in love with their Chevrolets, Fords, Buicks, and the newfound freedom of mobility and hitting the road. Oh, and especially the American teenagers. Their conversations revolved primarily around cars and girls and maybe the new song by Buddy Holly on the radio. And then there were the drive-in movie theaters and restaurants. One of the funny tricks that the teenagers liked to play at the drive-in theater was how many extra kids you could hide on the floor covered up in the back seat or maybe a few in the trunk. The local hamburger stand was a great place to show off your car to the guys or maybe even talk to a girl. Everyone wanted a nice car, and for the teenagers, the louder and faster, the better (Heitmann, 2015).

Also in the early 1950s was the birth of a new music called rock 'n' roll and the emergence of many new and exciting talents like Fats Domino, Jerry Lee Lewis, the Platters, Buddy Holly, Pat Boone, and Elvis Presley. These were raw and energetic sounds, and for the first time, the music industry began to target American youth with the music and marketing ("The Birth and Rise of Rock 'n' Roll in the 1950s and 1960s," n.d.). In the 1950s, there were many new films and movie stars, such as Elizabeth Taylor, James

The Rise and Fall of the American Empire

Dean, and Marilyn Monroe. It was also the golden age of television, with *Westerns*, *The Honeymooners*, and *Leave It to Beaver* coming into the American living rooms. America developed its own style, character, and identity. If, in the past, in Europe, for example, art was traditionally referred to as architectural design, classical music, paintings, and sculpture, America broadened the meaning to pop art, which included film, music, and television (Ranker Editors, 2021).

Frankly, America was just plain cool and the envy of the world. Many world youths wanted to be like Americans, and their parents wanted to come to it for a better life as immigration continued. And perhaps that was one of the strengths of America—its diversity. People from Europe and all over the world came to it, bringing their own unique God-given talents, abilities, strengths, and giftings contributing to the whole. And yet, in the fifties, there was an ugly Cold War tension with our one-time ally Russia and its ideology of communism.

Franklin Roosevelt had attempted to develop some kind of relationship with Stalin and Russia through the 1940s, with an eye on the future, but it did not work out. Churchill had observed this maneuver by Roosevelt and had always believed that it was naive, like a man who believed that he could charm a snake and hold it under his power and influence. Russia had cooperated with Allied forces during World War II to accomplish a common goal, but its Communist ideology proved to be a formidable barrier to the palette of the average American (Roos, "FDR, Churchill, and Stalin:

1950s America

Inside Their Uneasy WW II Alliance," 2020).

In fact, most Americans hated communism, especially Senator Joseph McCarthy. McCarthy rose to public prominence in February of 1950 when he asserted in a speech that he had a list of members of the Communist party and members of a Spy Ring who were employed in the State Department (Joseph McCarthy, 2009). And while we were trying to eradicate communism at home, The North Korean military crossed the thirty-eighth parallel into South Korea, igniting America's battle to stop the spread of communism in Asia with the Korean War. And how is the spread of communism and socialism in America doing nearly seventy-five years later? Well, if you slowly and incrementally feed a populace of people the diet of thought, ideology, and belief that you want them to have, most begin to embrace it as truth in time without fully realizing what they have eaten.

In his book *Family and Civilization*, written in the 1930s by Harvard professor Carle C. Zimmerman, he discusses the various causes of societal breakdown, including the breakdown of the nuclear or traditional family (Zimmerman, 2007). Well, things were still solid in America in the 1950s, but how do you boil a frog in a pot of water? You simply, slowly, incrementally increase the heat until it is too late for the poor little guy. And then, there were the racial tensions, segregation, and problems in the 1950s that still exist in various forms to this day. For example, when the loyal patriotic Harlem Hellfighters returned to New York City after the war, instead of appreciation, they were still met by prejudice

The Rise and Fall of the American Empire

among many of their fellow New Yorkers ("The Harlem Hellfighters," 2018). In the next section, we will cover the lives and some of the stories of three entertainers who were contemporaries in the 1950s generation: Johnny Cash, Elvis, and Pat Boone.

John R. Cash

J. R. Cash was born on February 26, 1932, in Kingsland, Arkansas, at the beginning of the Great Depression, to cotton farmers Ray Cash and Carrie Cloveree. His father wanted to name him after himself, and his mother wanted to name him John, so they settled on J. R. When J. R. entered military service in 1950, he changed it to John R. and then later to Johnny. In 1935, when J. R. was three years old, his family moved to Dyess, Arkansas, and he remained in this home until he finished high school and entered the Air Force. His boyhood home remains in Dyess and was renovated in 2011 and added to the National Register of Historic Places.

During the Depression, the Cash family was very fortunate to be selected for "New Deal" Housing, and that is what the home in Dyess was. They were absolutely thrilled to receive this humble home in Arkansas, as many families did not have homes or jobs. Like Glen Campbell, some of Johnny Cash's earliest memories were looking at a mule from behind, plowing the cotton field. J. R. had three older siblings, Roy, Margaret Louise, and Jack, and three younger siblings, Reba, Joanne, and Tommy, to round out the family to an even seven. The Cash family was primarily of English

1950s America

and Scottish descent. The farm in Dyess was part of a New Deal colony established to give poor families the opportunity to work on land that they may later own. His family's economic and personal struggles during the Great Depression gave him a lifelong empathy for the poor and struggling and became a foundation and inspiration to much of his later songwriting.

In 1944, J. R.'s older brother Jack, with whom he was very close, had a terrible accident with an unguarded table saw at his job and died a week later. Johnny Cash related how, that day, he and his mother both had a sense of foreboding. Cash tried to talk his older brother Jack into going fishing with him, and his mother encouraged him to go too. However, Jack felt a certain obligation to work to help support the family, and he went on to work that day.

Later, Johnny Cash related that the day Jack died, the family gathered around him, and Jack spoke as if he was in between two worlds. As Jack lay dying, he was talking to his mom and the family and was saying things like, "Mama, can you see the light, Mama? Can you see the angels, Mama? Can you hear the...?" And then young Jack Cash died. This single incident probably affected Johnny Cash more than anything else in the entirety of his life.

Most American families believed in God in those days, as did the Cash family. But this one traumatic incident was the single greatest witness to Johnny that God and heaven were very real. Jack's death broke the family's hearts, including Ray, the stoic father who never hugged his children or told them that he loved them. Later, Ray Cash began to preach at the local church and grew closer in his faith and walk with God (Riddle, 2020).

Johnny Cash's early memories were gospel music and the radio. Songs would come on, and he would listen intently and be swept away into another world. His father did not understand or encourage his interest. But Johnny's mother and a childhood friend taught him how to play guitar, and he began to play, sing, and write songs as early as age twelve. When Johnny was a young teenager, his voice changed from a high tenor range to more of a deeper bass-baritone range. He would often sing all day long while working with his family on the farm, and one day, his mother asked him, "Was that you, Son?" She was quite surprised as he had transitioned down to a lower, deep, smooth register and said, "Yes, ma'am, that was me." And she said, "Son, God is going to use you and the gift of your voice to touch the world." In high school, he sang on the local radio station, and that experience never left him (Rossi, 2023).

Of the countless albums that Johnny Cash recorded and released in his lifetime, one was a collection of gospel songs called "My Mother's Hymn Book." Influenced by these early childhood memories, young Johnny grew to a remarkably tall and lanky six foot two inches, most of which was in his legs. Years later, when he would make music for Billy Graham at his crusades, they stood eye to eye (Allmond, 2021).

1950s America

Johnny Cash enlisted in the Air Force on July 7, 1950. After basic training at Lackland Air Force Base and technical training at Brooks Air Force Base in Texas, Cash was assigned to the 12th Radio Squadron Mobile of the US Air Force Security Service at Landsberg, West Germany. He worked as a Morse code operator, intercepting Soviet Army transmissions, which required developing a keen sense of rhythm and timing. He was one of the first Americans to be aware of Joseph Stalin's death via Morse code. While in Landsberg, Germany, he created a band called the Landsberg Barbarians ("Johnny Cash, Joseph Stalin, and the Great Morse Code Crack, 2014).

On July 3, 1954, he was honorably discharged as a staff sergeant and returned to Texas. While in Germany, the solitary nature of the assignment and the confinement to the base gave him a unique empathy for the pain and loneliness experienced by prisoners, which helped him in his Folsom Prison concerts and recordings later in life. He also had a surgery on the right side of his jaw to remove a cyst while in Germany, causing a very distinctive scar. He met Vivian, his first wife, prior to leaving, and after hundreds of letters, they soon wed upon his return ("Johnny Cash's Biography," n.d.).

In 1954, Johnny and Vivian Cash moved to Memphis, Tennessee, and he sold vacuum cleaners and appliances during the day while studying to be a radio announcer at night. He also practiced and played with Luther Perkins and bassist Marshall Grant, who were known as the Tennessee Two. Hoping to get a record contract, he auditioned for Sam Phillips, the owner of Sun Records in Memphis. Initially, Johnny Cash sang gospel songs for Phillips, but Sam told him that the Gospel market was not big enough to sell records. Cash eventually won over the producer, as Phillips liked Cash's original Rockabilly songs and his smooth bass voice. At that time, Sun Records changed John R. Cash or J. R. to his name, Johnny Cash.

In 1955, Cash made his first recordings at Sun, including "Hey Porter," which was released in late June and met with success on the country hit parade. Other artists who were signed at Sun Records at this time included Jerry Lee Lewis, Carl Perkins, and Elvis Presley. On December 4, 1956, Elvis dropped into the studio while Carl Perkins was cutting new tracks with Jerry Lee Lewis backing him on piano. Johnny Cash was also in the studio at the time, and the four started an impromptu jam session. Sam Phillips left the tape running, and the recordings, most of which were gospel songs, survived. They were eventually released under the title "The Million Dollar Quartet."

Cash later said that he was the farthest from the microphone and sang in a higher pitch to blend with Elvis. In the early years of Sun Records, Johnny and Elvis toured together for a brief time. Elvis believed in Johnny Cash and would say he would become world famous. One of the tricks that they would play was very funny; they would occasionally imitate each other in private and on stage (Frank, 2021).

1950s America

Johnny Cash's next record, "Folsom Prison Blues," made the country's top five. The song "I Walk the Line" became number one on the country charts and top twenty in pop. "Home of the Blues" followed, recorded in July 1957. Although he was Sun Records' most consistent and prolific artist at the time, Cash began to feel constrained by the small label. Sam Phillips also did not want Johnny Cash to record gospel, but Johnny did want to record it. In fact, it was very important to him. Elvis had already left the label, and Johnny Cash began to feel the pull also. In 1958, Johnny Cash left Sun Records and signed a big contract with Columbia Records, which let him record anything that he wanted, including gospel. His single "Don't Take Your Guns to Town" became a very big hit, and he also recorded a collection of gospel songs for his second album with Colombia. Ironically, Cash left behind a catalog of songs with Sun Records and had two record labels concurrently releasing his music and material. Sun Records continued to release its catalog of Johnny Cash material as late as 1964 (Cash, "The Story behind Johnny Cash and Sam Phillips: Sun Records," 2022).

About the time of the new contract with Columbia, Johnny and Vivian moved to California to further his career. Toward the end of the 1950s, his career and creativity blossomed as he began to become one of the most famous entertainers in the world. But at the same time, his home and personal life began to suffer and take a very dark turn. In his discussions and communication with Vivian, there was no give and take. He made it clear that his career would come first, and he went touring a lot. It was hard for Vivian to be happy for him and his new national fame when he was spending so little time with her and his daughters.

And to make matters worse, at that time in his life and career, Johnny Cash became heavily addicted to alcohol and drugs. It started out when someone first gave him amphetamines to help him stay up all night and drive. Then, he began to mix barbiturates, alcohol, and amphetamines in increasingly heavy daily doses and amounts. By Johnny Cash's own admission, it got to the point that he would take a terrifying one hundred pills a day and drink a full case of beer. Vivian Cash was a good woman, but it got to the point where she could no longer watch Johnny do this to himself and be around the children, so she divorced him in 1966 (Foy, 2018) ("Johnny Cash and Drugs: The Music Icon's Lifelong Struggle with Addiction," 2022).

Country music basically began in about 1922, with the earliest groups and singers. One of the famous early pioneers of country music was "The Carter Family," which Maybelle, Ezra, and June Carter were part of. President Jimmy Carter was also a cousin of the family (Dooley, 2019). "The Carter Family" joined Johnny Cash on tour, and there was an immediate attraction between him and June. It was supposed to be a professional relationship, and they were still both married. After Johnny and June had both gone through a divorce, June, Ezra, and Maybelle moved into his mansion to help him get off drugs. Johnny wanted to marry June, but she would not marry him until he was clean and sober.

1950s America

One night in 1967, Johnny was arrested in Walker County, Georgia, for drugs and a car accident. The next morning, Sheriff Ralph Jones had a long heart-to-heart talk with him, like a pastor or father, telling Johnny that he was destroying himself and his life. Something got through, and Johnny truly listened to Sheriff Jones (Summers, 2020). Cash credited that experience and the love and patience of June Carter for helping him begin to turn around and save his life. June went ahead and married him on March 1, 1968, but he did not end all drug use until 1970. Johnny Cash's journey included returning to his Christian faith and an altar call at Evangel Temple in Nashville. The birth of John Carter Cash also helped him by focusing on trying to be a good dad (Bertram, 2021).

Johnny Cash and June Carter Cash appeared several times on the Billy Graham Crusade TV specials, and Cash continued to include gospel and religious songs on his albums. Johnny's friendship with Billy Graham led to his production of a film about the life of Jesus called *Gospel Road*. It was released in 1973 and was a statement of his personal faith (Cash, *Gospel Road: A Story of Jesus*, 1973). Johnny Cash also had friendships with different US presidents, including Jimmy Carter, who was June Carter's cousin (Montalti, 2022).

Johnny Cash's life was as real, raw, ugly, and beautiful as they come. His struggle was, and is, all of ours: the struggle to follow God and not something else. He was a person who made many mistakes and even relapsed two more times in his life, but he loved God and cared about people. He was one of the few and rare artists in the world who could go into Folsom and San Quentin prisons and sing and talk to the guys and make a difference. Johnny Cash touched many lives and people and made this world a better place.

The Johnny Cash discography is huge, one of the largest ever, with ninety-one albums and 170 singles released on several record labels. He collaborated with many artists, including his friend Bob Dylan and The Highwaymen. He sold more than 90 million albums and had his own TV show on ABC network from 1969 to 1971. He spanned numerous genres, including folk, country, rock 'n' roll, blues, rockabilly, and gospel. He was the only man in history to be inducted into all three: the country, rock 'n' roll, and Songwriters Hall of Fame. Ironically, the first one to die was June Carter Cash, May 15, 2003, the one who never did drugs. One of the last things that she told Johnny was to keep working. And that is what he did, to keep going after June died. While experiencing profound pain and grief, he recorded sixty more songs and lived about four more months. But on September 12, 2003, the man in black, Johnny Cash, passed from this world into the next (Johnny Cash, 2023).

Elvis Presley

The Life, the Myth, the Man

Elvis Aaron Presley was at the center of the American scene in the 1950s. He was someone everyone could relate with, a nice young man from the country with a drawl. It just seems like people want a king, someone they can place on a pedestal that they can admire, and that "someone" became Elvis. He was born January 8, 1935, in Tupelo, Mississippi, and rose to become the most famous entertainer in the world. He personified coolness, as young men wanted to be like him, and young women wanted to be with him.

The first time Elvis appeared on stage was in 1953 at Humes High School, when he sang "Till I Waltz with You Again," and the kids reacted to his movements as much as his fledgling voice. Elvis marveled at how popular he became at school after that (Ott, "Elvis Presley's Musical Talents Took Root during a Lonely Childhood," 2022). And therein lies the problem with Elvis, the lifelong battle of either seeking the applause and approval of the world or the approval of God. And I think that, in this case, the world won.

The Presleys, like most American families in the 1930s and 1940s, went to church, and they brought young Elvis with them to the old First Assembly of God Pentecostal Church in Tupelo. And that is where Vernon Presley and Gladys Love Smith first met. But the backstory on that is a little bit funny and complicated. Gladys Love Smith had five different sisters, including one whose name was Clettes. At first, Vernon Presley dated Clettes, and Vester, his brother, dated Gladys. But Vester and Gladys did not get along very well, so Gladys, a little later, began to date Vernon. And never mind that he was seventeen and she was twenty-one. They simply drove over to the next county to get married. And Gladys stated her age to be nineteen, and Vernon said he was twenty-two.

That was in 1933, and then Elvis was born two years later in

1935. It was very unusual because Elvis had a twin brother, but he died at birth, and Gladys also had another miscarriage later, so Elvis was an only son. So, this was a big part of Elvis Presley's young life, the old Assemblies of God Church, the music, the prayer, and the power that marked and influenced him early on.

Elvis: Jailhouse Rock

The gospel music and its message got way down into his heart and soul, and as he listened to it on the radio and at church, he was mesmerized and carried away to somewhere else ("Vernon and Gladys Presley: Elvis Presley's Mother and Father," 2015).

1950s America

Gladys recalled that one time at their small church, two-year-old Elvis slipped off her lap, went up onto the platform, stood in front of the choir, and tried to sing along, but he did not know the words. Gladys's Uncle, Gains Mansell, was the pastor of the church she and Vernon attended in Tupelo, where Elvis was baptized in water and made a public confession of faith when he was nine. Then, a few years later, Elvis was baptized again at another church (Asay, 2018). Vernon and Gladys worked hard to give their only son, Elvis, a stable home, but Vernon made a bad mistake and was sent to prison in 1938.

Orville Bean had purchased a pig from Vernon, and when Vernon got the check, it was significantly less than what he thought he was going to receive from Orville, so he altered the check. He was sentenced to three years of hard labor at the Mississippi State Penitentiary at Parchman Farm. His sentence was reduced to eight months, but the damage was done. It traumatized young Elvis to see his father in handcuffs and a striped prison outfit each time he and his mother, Gladys, visited him. He and Gladys's living arrangements also became unstable as they lived in several temporary situations.

Gladys was trying to cope with a very difficult situation the best that she could, and she became a little overly protective of Elvis, especially while Vernon was in prison ("Vernon and Gladys Presley: Elvis Presley's Mother and Father," 2015). Throughout Elvis's life, he always seemed to have a touch of sadness and loneliness that no one else could resolve, especially after his mother's early death. And perhaps also an early childhood memory of growing up in the shadow of a twin brother, Jesse Garon, who almost was but died at birth ("Elvis Presley: The Tragic Story of His Twin Brother, Jesse Garon Presley," 2021).

On January 18, 1953, Elvis Presley went to the Memphis recording service at the Sun Record Company to record two double-sided demos, "My Happiness" and "That's When Your Heartache Begins," as a birthday present for his mother, Gladys, at a cost of $3.98. After Elvis had recorded this acetate, Marion Keisker, who worked at Sun Records, was very impressed with the demos and encouraged the owner, Sam Phillips, to record Elvis. Sam Phillips saw a unique raw quality in Elvis as if he could take from different streams of sound, including black artists, and create something original and new. Sam Phillips was also struck by Elvis's genuine humility. But Sam saw that humility was mixed with intense determination.

They began to experiment with recording Elvis in the studio, with a mix of originals, covers, and different things, and then one day, something special happened. Elvis began to sing "That's All Right," a blues song by Arthur "Big Boy" Crudup, and yet he took the song and reinvented it into a style all his own. Immediately, Sam knew that that was what he had been looking for from Elvis when he brought him into the studio. It was raw, it was soulful, and it was exciting and energetic: it was Elvis ("Elvis Presley Records 'That's All Right [Mama],'" 2023).

1950s America

The Presleys had originally left Tupelo for Memphis on November 6, 1948, for a new start and in search of a better life economically. Elvis and his parents packed up their belongings in the trunk of their 1939 Plymouth, and what they couldn't fit in the trunk, they crammed into the back seat with Elvis and strapped the rest onto the roof. Before leaving, Elvis bid farewell to his junior high class at Milam in Tupelo with a melancholy rendition of "Leaf on a Tree" with his guitar and his still high tenor voice, which had not transitioned or changed yet ("Early Childhood," n.d.). As a teenager, he developed an admiration for bass singers, who had exceptionally low vocal registers. Most gospel quartets had a bass vocalist or at least a lower baritone to stretch for the lower notes.

Elvis attended Humes High School in Memphis, where he was very shy, quiet, and introverted. He was considered the new kid and an outsider by the other students. When Elvis Presley was born, both his parents experienced remarkable otherworldly visions. His father, Vernon, who was just eighteen at the time, said that the moment Elvis was conceived, he blacked out and saw a vision of the night sky thronged with brilliant blue stars. During the birth, Elvis's twin brother, Jesse Garon, was stillborn, and Gladys had a near-death experience. At that time and moment, Gladys believed that somehow Elvis and Garon had become one and that he held the responsibility to live for both.

Gladys and Elvis's personalities were almost identical, and they seemed to develop an unhealthy codependency as he grew

The Rise and Fall of the American Empire

up. Gladys had suffered so much loss in her family and her life that she held onto the ongoing fear of losing her only child, Elvis. When he was a child, Elvis wanted a bicycle, but instead, Gladys bought him a guitar so he would not get hurt. She was overly protective and fearful as a result of her own life experiences and emotional issues.

When Elvis's career took off like a rocket, she became fearful of his touring, having an accident or something, and losing him. Gladys increasingly became an alcoholic and drug addict to deal with her emotional problems and fears. In 1957, after Elvis had become an international star, they moved into the fourteen-acre estate called Graceland in Memphis, Tennessee. When Elvis was touring, as he always seemed to be, the fans mobbed and tore at him. And after his chartered airplane lost an engine and crash-landed over the Ozarks, she forbade him to fly, and so he drove everywhere for a period. She prayed for her son but also battled constant anxiety and fear.

One night, she woke up in a fright after seeing Elvis in a burning car in the dream. The next day, Elvis called her from Texarkana and said his rented Cadillac had burst into flames, and he had barely made it out of the car alive.

Gladys best friend, Lillian, said that after Elvis became famous, she never had peace or another happy day. Soon after moving to Graceland, Elvis received a draft notice from the army, and Gladys begged him not to go, but Elvis felt that it was his duty, so he left for basic training. Not long after, Gladys Love Presley died and was buried on August 16, 1958, the same date Elvis would die nineteen years later. Elvis was never the same after his mother died, and he left the military a changed man. With his mother's death, he felt like he had lost everything that mattered to him and the one person who loved him and the one that he loved. His relationship with his father also probably changed, as Vernon soon remarried, and they were not as close (Comford, 2010).

While Elvis was in Bad Nauheim, Germany, the twenty-four-year-old met fourteen-year-old Priscilla Beaulieu at a party that he had at his rented home. The usual King of Cool just about stumbled over himself when he met Priscilla but eventually gained his composure. They did not get married until May 1, 1967, when she was just about to turn twenty-two. Their daughter Lisa Marie was born nine months later, February 1, 1968. Their marriage lasted just over six years, but Priscilla was a big part of his life from the time they met in 1959 to his death on August 16, 1977.

Many believed Elvis became addicted to opiates in 1967 when Doctor Nick began to prescribe them to him for pain. But it seems that he had already acquired a level of addiction as far back as the 1950s to both amphetamines and barbiturates because Priscilla stated that he would give them to her to stay up and for sleep. In the early years of his career, many of the artists, including Jerry Lee Lewis and Johnny Cash, had begun to take pills, and Elvis was probably exposed to them at that time (T. A. Picotti, 2023).

The Rise and Fall of the American Empire

Elvis was not unlike all of us, as he sought the meaning of life, looked for love, and searched for significance in all his endeavors. When times were low or when he was searching for answers, he would always turn to God and the comfort of gospel music. One day, Elvis asked Pat Boone where he went to church and how in the world he could go without getting mobbed. Pat Boone told Elvis that the people would eventually figure out why he was there and leave him alone as they settled into the service. But Elvis was not entirely convinced by Pat and often would decide with churches to show up late at night and sing gospel songs until the sun had risen (Marshall, 2015).

Of the fourteen Grammys that Elvis was nominated for, the three times that he won was for his gospel music. At one point in time in his career, he approached his management team about an idea that he had. He wanted to incorporate more gospel music into the shows, share his faith, and give a salvation altar call. But Elvis's team disagreed and talked him out of it (Patch Wooding, 2013).

Fresh off a performance on *The Ed Sullivan Show*, Elvis went to Sun Records, where Carl Perkins was recording tracks that day with Jerry Lee Lewis backing him up on piano. Elvis and Johnny Cash, who were also there that day, joined Carl and Jerry Lee in an impromptu jam that lasted into the night. Sam Phillips kept the tapes running, and even though it was not released until 1981, it became known as The Million Dollar Quartet Sessions. Elvis's contribution that day and night was mostly gospel songs that he knew and treasured from his youth. He did that a lot on movie sets and in different circumstances, as he loved to sing gospel music ("Million Dollar Quartet," December 4, 1956 [2008]).

Johnny Cash once said that the nature of pills is that once you start taking them, they begin to take you (Glossyfied.com Editors, 2022). Apparently, in 1967, Doctor Nick began to administer pain pills to Elvis, and he increasingly became addicted to an array of opiates and drugs. The list of pills and drugs and the amounts he began to take were frightening (Markel, 2018). Some people who met him and talked to him, including Elton John, said they would talk to him, but it was like no one was home (Fitzgerald, 2021).

A true friend is someone who tells you the truth. Did Colonel Tom Parker try to get him help? How about his family and friends? Perhaps Priscilla tried, and he continued to be in denial. Johnny Cash never went to Graceland because he said he wanted to give Elvis his privacy. Maybe the truth was, after Cash was clean, he did not ever want to go backwards. Addiction is a liar, and countless individuals and entertainers have been destroyed by it, including Elvis. Elvis Aaron Presley died on August 16, 1977, the same date that he had buried his beloved mother, Gladys, nineteen years earlier.

Elvis had numerous accolades and accomplishments in his lifetime. He had recorded over 700 different songs during his relatively short life. Starting with Elvis's first movie, *Love Me Tender*, Elvis starred in thirty-one feature films as an actor and two theatrically released concert documentary films, and most recently, the Baz Luhrmann film, *Elvis*, was released in 2022. More than 400 books have been published about the life and subject of Elvis. There have been over 250,000 Elvis impersonators since his death. It has been estimated by Graceland that more than 1 billion Elvis records worldwide have been sold.

It is estimated that Elvis performed in more than 1,600 concerts in his lifetime, with the last show being the evening of June 26, 1977, at Market Square Arena in Indianapolis. He also had three Network Television Specials. Elvis Presley was inducted into the Rock and Roll Hall of Fame in 1986, and his moniker was "The King of Rock and Roll." He was also inducted into the Country Music Hall of Fame in 1998, and he was also inducted into the Gospel Hall of Fame in 2001. He was also inducted into twenty other Hall of Fames, including the Rockabilly Hall of Fame (Connolly, 2017) (T. Picotti, 2022).

And most importantly was if his name was written in the book of life. When the Reverend Billy Graham was once asked if he had ever met Elvis, he stated, "No, but I believe that I will meet him in heaven" (Hanson, 2011).

Pat Boone

Patrick Charles Eugene Boone was born at the height of the Great American Depression on June 1, 1934, in Jacksonville, Florida. He rose to fame in the 1950s and 1960s as a teen idol, singer, movie star, television personality, and author. He was well known

1950s America

for his wholesome all-American image and good looks. Within the slippery slopes of the entertainment industry, he was a role model for American youth, with a solid foundation in his Christian faith. He had a vision when he first was married, and still was in college, to be a teacher and a preacher. But perhaps God allowed him to enter the entertainment sphere, where he ultimately had even more influence, a bigger platform, and a broader impact.

When Pat Boone was just two years old, his family moved from Jacksonville to Nashville, Tennessee, where his father, Archie Altman Boone, joined his uncle's construction company and was very fortunate to have a good job during the Depression. His mother, Margaret Virginia, raised Pat and his three siblings, Nick, Judy, and Marjorie Ann, at 1209 Lone Oak Road in Nashville, and after eighty-five years, the home is still occupied by members of the family.

Pat Boone is also a descendant of the legendary pioneer Daniel Boone, who was born in 1734 ("Was Daniel Boone an Ancestor of Pat Boone?" 2007). When the radio was on in the Boone household, one singer grabbed young Pat's attention, and that was the crooner Bing Crosby with a smooth, deep voice. In Nashville, Pat attended nearby David Lipscomb High School, where he met the love of his life, Shirley Lee Foley. Shirley was the daughter of the legendary Red Foley. Red Foley was one of the biggest stars in country music in the 1930s and 1940s, selling more than 25 million records, and was later inducted into the Country Music Hall of Fame. Shirley Foley was also a very beautiful young lady and a talented singer herself (Red Foly, 1967).

Pat continued to grow into a very bright, inquisitive, creative young man, and then a lot of different things began to happen quickly. After listening to Bing Crosby and other artists on the radio, he and his younger brother Nick began to sing at family gatherings. Nick also went on to be a successful singer and later a worship leader. And though Pat still did not seriously think of having a career as a recording artist, he began to enter talent contests and sing at different opportunities. He often ended up getting second place, but then he won first place in a particular contest that he had entered after high school and won a trip to New York City. First prize was the trip to New York and the exciting opportunity to audition for Ted Mack's *Amateur Hour*, which was the American idol of its day.

Viewers selected the winners on the show by sending in cards and letters, choosing their favorites. Much to his and Shirley's amazement, he won the contest three times in a row. And while he was competing on that show, incredibly, he also won *The Arthur Godfrey Talent Scout Show*. He had also obtained a small recording deal with Republic Records in Nashville, which then led to a more significant contract with Dot Records, which released his first album, and it went in the top ten. During all the excitement, Pat and Shirley were married on November 7, 1953, and were expecting their first child soon after ("Pat Boone Interview: Part 1 of 3," 2011).

1950s America

Then things began to move quicker. His first hit song, "Two Hearts, Two Kisses," began to get airplay on all the radio stations and sold 1,000,000 copies. Next was the song "Ain't That a Shame," which rocketed Pat Boone to teen stardom and went to number one. He then had one or more singles on the charts for 220 consecutive weeks, which is an industry record that stands to this day. He went on in his career to record more than 2,300 songs, which is another industry record that probably still stands to this day. For Pat Boone, success did happen overnight, and it happened dramatically. He may not have become the teacher-preacher that he envisioned while in college, but God gave him a huge platform of even greater influence than he could have ever imagined. He ended up getting three different stars on the Hollywood Walk of Fame for music, television, and film.

Numerous books and biographies were written about Pat Boone, but he himself also authored many books, including his first one at age twenty, *Twixt Twelve and Twenty*, for teenagers, which sold millions of copies. He starred in over twenty-six major motion pictures, starting at an early age. He sold 45 million records, with thirty-eight albums in the top forty. While he was graduating magna cum laude from Columbia University, he was the youngest person in America with his own weekly musical variety show, *Pat Boones Chevy Showroom*, which ran for three years on ABC. At this time, his picture was on TV Guide, with his cap and gown on at graduation. All this, and married with four young children, Cherry, Lindy, Debby, and Laury (Cole, 2023).

The Rise and Fall of the American Empire

There were many new and exciting stars in the 1950s, including Marilyn Monroe, James Dean, and even young Ricky Nelson, but the two biggest stars were Elvis and Pat Boone. Pat Boone recalled the first time that he had met Elvis Presley. Pat was only six months older than Elvis, with just eleven months head start on his recording career, but Pat had gained a lot of ground in that time, as Elvis was just getting started. Pat Boone was headlining a sock hop in Cleveland, Ohio, attended by three thousand teenagers and hosted by renowned DJ Bill Randle.

Pat Boone had already made three albums, had several hits, was a rising teen idol, and the kids were there to see him. But when DJ Bill Randle met Pat at the airport, he told him that a new kid was going on before him. So, Pat asked, "Is it anyone I know?" Randle said, "No, you wouldn't have heard of him. His name is Elvis Presley." So, Pat said, "Really? I've seen his name on a jukebox in Dallas, but he's a hillbilly. He's country." Randle said, "Yeah, he is known as a rockabilly down south, and he's on a show called *Louisiana Hayride* once a week." Pat Boone said that at the time, he was singing hillbilly songs with a kind of rock beat, which was intriguing to him.

But when Pat Boone went backstage to meet the opening act, he was taken aback. Even though Pat was only six months older than Elvis, he had maturity and a calmness about him. His first impression of Elvis was that "he looked like a scared young kid." Almost an unusual nervousness about going on stage, much less meeting and talking to Pat. Some entertainers call it stage fright.

His shirt collar was turned up, his pants were a little too long, and he was wearing white scuffed-up buck shoes that looked like Pat's.

The other impression Pat got was that Elvis had a bit of a "bad boy" image, the kind of young man that a mother would not want her daughter to go out with. That pre-show nervousness was something Elvis dealt with for the entirety of his career, and he was somewhat introverted and shy. Pat Boone shook his hand and said, "Bill Randle thinks big things may be ahead for you," and Elvis quietly said, with his head slightly lowered, "I don't know about that, but I hope so." He just leaned back against the wall, trying to relax, as his band closed in around him, talking to him. Pat thought to himself, *Wow! He is nervous; he may mess up out here in front of all these 3,000 kids.* Elvis told Pat years later that he was a little intimidated to meet him because he was already a big star, and all he had so far was a single with a B-side on Sun Records. Nevertheless, Pat was struck by Elvis's unique look, which, unlike his clean-cut image, was more like a James Dean rebel persona, even before he was famous.

The first song Elvis performed was an up-tempo "Blue Moon of Kentucky," for which the audience gave him a nice hand. But the second song that he sang was "That's All Right (Mama)," which is now recognized as his official breakout debut single, and it really rocked the house. That nervousness he had went down through his whole body and legs. The crowd loved it and wanted more, but that was all he had was those two songs, Boone recalled. So, Elvis left with his band, and then Pat Boone went on and sang the three hit songs that he had at the time. And so that night, Pat got most of all the screams, and that was the last and only time that Pat and Elvis appeared together on stage.

Pat Boone said that he and Elvis became and remained good friends, even as Elvis skyrocketed to fame. They had a friendly competition in the 1950s and would go back and forth on the charts. Pat Boone charted forty-one times during that period, and Elvis charted forty times. There was a period when Pat and Elvis were both renting homes in Belair, California, filming movies at 20th Century Fox, having dinner together, and hanging out. They would even have informal tag football games with Ricky Nelson and others.

Pat Boone said that the last time he saw Elvis and talked with him was at the Memphis Airport in July 1977, just one month before he died. Pat and his family waited for him at the gate, and he was able to talk to him for a few minutes before he boarded. When Elvis learned that Pat was heading to Orlando instead of Vegas, he said to him, "You're going to Orlando! That's the wrong way, man." Then Elvis turned to his entourage and said, "This man is always going the wrong way." And Pat responded, "It depends on where you're coming from."

One month later, Pat was in a barbershop getting a haircut when two men rushed in, shouting Elvis had died. And Pat yelled back, "Get out of here; that is not a funny joke." But sadly, it was not. As the years went on, Pat Boone remembered the last time he saw his friend and their brief conversation. He knew that Elvis was just kidding with him, but those words stuck with him. If following God was the wrong way, then he would continue to swim upstream against the currents of life, Las Vegas, and the world. Pat Boone was a great role model and influenced many people and entertainers, including Elvis (Nolasco, "Pat Boone Recalls Meeting Pal Elvis Presley: He Was Just a Scared Young Kid," 2020).

Around 1960, Shirley suggested to Pat that they move to California, as they had thought about it before, during the time that they had rented out a second home in Bel Air in the late 1950s. Nashville was growing as a center for the country and other styles of music, but if they moved to California, Pat could continue to develop his career in film, television, and music.

When Pat Boone moved to Beverly Hills-Hollywood, he didn't have to tell everyone that he was a Christian. They all knew it already, and his influence would only continue to grow. One of the decisions that the Boone family made was to bring Tennessee ways to California. They attended church regularly, kept prayer time, and even held a growing Bible study in their home. In the Bible study the Boones hosted at their Beverly Hills home, they had a close-knit group of celebrities who prayed and read the Bible together, including Jonathan Winters, Zsa Zsa Gabor, Glenn Ford, Doris Day, and Priscilla Presley. The Boones didn't even have a fence around the Beverly Hills property, not until Debby Boone became famous and it became necessary. There were times when Elvis, when he was in town, would drive right up to the front of the house, walk around to the back, and play at the swimming pool with the Boone children (Paulson, 2023).

There was a time, soon after he had come to California, that Pat was introduced to some very powerful anointed ministers and churches, including Kathryn Kuhlman and George Otis. It was about this time that Pat Boone, Shirley, and his four children all got the baptism in the Holy Spirit with evidence of speaking in glossolalia. With Pat, he said that if first came out singing, singing in the Holy Spirit. He said that it was a wonderful experience that helped and strengthened his family. When he discussed it with Elvis, Elvis reminded him that he had always believed in the gifts of the Spirit, the power of God, and miracles, having grown up attending a small Assemblies of God Pentecostal Church ("Ortega Law," 2022).

One of the ministers that Pat Boone befriended was a man named George Otis. Pat called him the Electric Man because sometimes you could feel the power of God in or come out of his hand. On a particular day, Ronald Reagan was with Pat Boone, George Otis, and another minister. When Ronald Reagan was about to take his leave from them that day, George Otis asked Reagan if they could first have a word of prayer. After Ronald Reagan agreed, George Otis and the other minister grasped his hands and began to pray. After a little time of a nice prayer with the governor, George Otis stopped and looked into Reagan's eyes. His face and his voice changed, and he said, "My son, if you continue to walk upright with me, you will live at 1600 Pennsylvania

1950s America

Avenue in time."

Ronald Reagan initially tried to run for president in 1976 but was not successful, and said, "I tried, but it didn't work out." Reagan told Boone years later that the words of George Otis kept rolling around in his head many times, so he attempted to run for president one more time in 1980. Ronald Reagan was elected the fortieth president of the United States of America and served from January 20, 1981, to January 20, 1989 (Slosser, 2022).

When Pat Boone was very young, he was signed to 20th Century Fox and began to make movies. Many of the films Boone participated in helped 20th Century Fox turn their financial fortunes around because there was a time when they were on the ropes and on the verge of bankruptcy. Then 20th Century Fox approached Boone with their idea for his next film role. They had an idea for a film that they would call *The Stripper* based on a play called *A Loss of Roses*. They had a bright new film director named Franklin J. Schaffner who would helm the project, and they would cast Pat Boone with Marilyn Monroe.

The script was about an aging, struggling actress who accepts a job as a stripper to survive, and the role Boone would play would be the wide-eyed teenager who is initially infatuated with her. Pat Boone told 20th Century Fox, "Sure, I would love to do a movie with Marilyn Monroe, but not this one. It is an ungodly immoral story." Not happy, 20th Century Fox put the heat on Boone, threatening to cancel his contract and ruin his musical career. He thought about it for a while, then basically told them, "You do what you need to do, but I am not going to do this movie." Shortly after that, Marilyn Monroe died of a barbiturate overdose, and they let Pat off the hook. Then, later, casting Joanne Woodward and Richard Beemer in the film, it turned out to be a colossal flop (Nolasco, "Pat Boone Says 'Moral Values' Are Missing from Today's Hollywood Films: America's Image Is Being Destroyed," 2022).

Pat Boone has stated that many young people come to Hollywood with stars in their eyes and even sometimes sell their souls to make it. He has said that is not a good idea. He has even advised most young people to stay out of the entertainment business, that they would usually be better off leading a normal life. Another notable film that Pat Boone starred in with James Mason and Arlene Dahl in 1958 was Jules Verne's *Journey to the Center of the Earth*, adapted from the storyline of the 1864 novel of the same name. In one scene, Boone's character, Alec McKuen, and costars were latched to a raft that was swirling around in water and being deluged with water while it was being pulled to the center of the earth. And if that wasn't dangerous enough, in another scene, Boone (Alec McKuen) leaps into a tunnel and begins to be covered by hundreds of pounds of sand-like material.

The director forgot about Pat down in the tunnel as he was checking the cameras and the film they had just shown. The sand-like material had reached all the way up to his mouth, and he could not move and began to run out of air. After a short time, a man yelled from the catwalk, "You'd better get Pat Boone out of there!" So, they dug and pulled him out as quickly as possible, but he nearly died in the filming of that particular scene ("Pat Boone's Incredible Story," 2019).

Another powerful film was *The Cross and the Switchblade*, adapted from the book written by David Wilkerson with the same name. It is the true story of a small-town Pennsylvania preacher who was called by God to go into the streets and alleys of New York City to reach the drug addicts and gang members, played by Pat Boone. And Nicky, the gang member, played by Eric Estrada, was another prominent role in the movie. David Ray Wilkerson, whose early days in New York City as a young man, went on to found Times Square Church, Teen Challenge, World Challenge, and many other great works (Vision Video, 2020). Pat Boone stated, "Moral values are missing from today's Hollywood film and music scene, and the image of the once great America is being destroyed by the content of today's films and music" (Nolasco, "Pat Boone Says 'Moral Values' Are Missing from Today's Hollywood Films: America's Image Is Being Destroyed," 2022).

Pat and Shirley Boone successfully reared and guided their four daughters, Cherry, Lindy, Debby, and Laury, in the glare of Hollywood's spotlight, and now also have sixteen grandchildren and seventeen great-grandchildren. His beloved wife, Shirley, died on January 11, 2019, and as the saying goes, behind every great man is a great woman. I personally believe that Pat Boone has made a big difference and made an incredible contribution to this world and to several generations. And after seventy years in the entertainment industry, Pat realizes that he may be running his final lap right now. And he is still doing the same things, like his new album, "Country Jubilee," his new book, *If*, his latest movie, *The Mulligan*, and numerous other projects. The same consistent thing Patrick Charles Eugene Boone has done for the entirety of his life is to try to point people to God and take as many people to heaven with him as he can.

Some other interesting facts about Pat Boone are that he loves the nation of Israel, has led over twenty tours to the Holy Land, and wrote the song "This Land Is My Land," an Israel theme song. He has raised some 600 million for charities and the disabled. He has recorded numerous gospel songs and albums, opening the market to others. Later in life, he hosted many different evangelical radio and television programs and was inducted as a member of the Gospel Music Hall of Fame in 2003. He was also an avid golfer and basketball player, playing in the Senior Basketball Olympics until age eighty-five. He also helped start the American Basketball Association, owning a couple of the teams. His team, the Oakland Oaks, won the championship, led by All-star Rick Barry. And we fully expect to see Pat Boone continue to make more three-point shots as he is blazing the trail on his final lap (Cole, 2023).

1950s America

Major W. David Doiron had different duties during the Vietnam War, including flying the wounded back to the States

CHAPTER 27

The End of Innocence, JFK, MLK, Chavez, and the 1960s

One of the songs that captured the essence of 1960s America was "American Pie." There was a saying that emerged earlier in the century that said, "As American as baseball, hot dogs, motherhood, and apple pie." It was a phrase that described the things that best represent American culture, that were of an element of order, a constant, a predictability (Rummel, 2016). And so, the song "American Pie," written by Don McLean when he was twenty-four years old, 1969 to 1970, reflected the rapid and deep cultural changes, profound disappointment, disillusion, and loss of innocence of that generation.

For decades, people have discussed the meaning and symbolism of the lyrics and pressed the artist for insight. And for all its catchy sing-along jauntiness, there's little to cheer about in "American Pie" because it is largely devoid of hope. The song did a superb job of connecting with the collective consciousness of 1960s America, which was cynical and disillusioned by the Vietnam War and traumatized by the assassination of John F. Kennedy. And some would argue that the decline of American culture began well before the 1960s, and they have a very good point. And yet, this change and decline rapidly accelerated in the 1960s.

There is general agreement that "American Pie" is indeed about the cultural and political decline of the US in the 1960s, the end of innocence, and a farewell to the American Dream. But that has always been both one of the beauties and mysteries of this song, and McLean has given the listener great latitude for their own interpretation. He especially enjoys it when an interviewer tells him at the beginning of an interview that after considerable examination of the lyrics, they have indeed unlocked the meaning and the mysteries.

At that point, he will wryly say, "Oh, please do explain it to me then." So, what exactly was revealed the day the music died? Was it exclusively referring to the 1959 plane crash of Buddy Holly, the Big Bopper, and Ritchie Valens? Or was there a broader meaning that also applied to the day McLean's father died and when his whole world came crashing down? Not to mention the pain of watching his older sister, Betty Ann, destroy herself and her life through addiction. Who was the jester who sang for the king and queen in a coat that he borrowed from James Dean?

The Vietnam War, Social Revolution, Bob Dylan, Elvis Presley, JFK, Mick Jagger, Martin Luther King, Charles Manson, the Hells Angels, The Beatles, hallucinogenic drugs, evil, and the Trinity of God are all in the song. But does Don McLean even understand the totality of what he penned? If we are indeed witnessing the decline and fall of American civilization, what is causing it? Is it Mick Jagger's fault, John Lennon's, or maybe Charles Manson's? Every great world empire has a time and life, and then

The End of Innocence, JFK, MLK, Chavez, and the 1960s

it will fall; there is no stopping it. The only kingdom that is eternal, that will stand forever and never fail, is the Kingdom of God.

The Bible states that the most cataclysmic event in human history is nearing the second coming of Christ. The powers of darkness are aware of the times and have only been accelerating their activities and efforts over the last decades, including during the tumultuous 1960s. So, if the song "American Pie" ultimately lacked hope, and it is not wise to place one's hope exclusively in this present temporal world that is passing away, remember that there is always hope in God, His eternal purposes, and Kingdom (Windsor, 2022).

JFK

John Fitzgerald Kennedy was born May 29, 1917, in Brookline, Massachusetts, and rose to be the thirty-fifth president of the United States from January 20, 1961, to his death and assassination on November 22, 1963. JFK's family included his parents, Joseph P. Kennedy, Rose Kennedy, his eight brothers, sisters, and their spouses. His father, Joseph Patrick Kennedy, the patriarch of the family, had been involved in everything from Wall Street Investments, early Hollywood Film company investment and re-organization, real estate, and various business investments.

From 1934 to 1935, he was the first chairman of the Securities and Exchange Commission. And from 1938 to late 1940, he was the United States ambassador to the United Kingdom. During his time and involvement in politics, he began to aspire to see one of his sons rise to the presidency. He had hoped that his son, Joseph Jr., would be the one, but he died on August 12, 1944, in World War II. He did live to see his son JFK rise to the presidency, his son RFK become attorney general and senator, and his son Ted rise to the Senate. But he also lived through the heartbreak of outliving three sons and a daughter (W. R. Manchester, 2023).

From the time that John Kennedy, or Jack, as the family called him, was very small, he was sickly. At two years of age, he nearly died of scarlet fever. He did enjoy sports like his other siblings, but he would prefer to read books in his room when he was young. Even at a young age, he had a perceptive intelligence, a unique creative wit, and boyish charisma. With his family's privilege and wealth, he was educated at private schools where, in the beginning, he consistently earned mediocre grades. One thing that he did well at the time was aggravating the faculty along with the other troublemakers in the school.

His father, Joseph, who was very competitive and ambitious, worried that Jack might never reach his potential. After leaving Choate Preparatory Academy, he enrolled in Princeton University but was soon hit with serious illness and left. For years, he had dealt with weakness, weight loss, and gastrointestinal issues, but this time, they were able to successfully diagnose and treat Addison's disease, which had nearly killed him several times.

After he got his health and strength back, he began to attend Harvard, where his older brother Joe had already been attending.

The End of Innocence, JFK, MLK, Chavez, and the 1960s

Jack Kennedy began his first semester at Harvard in the fall of 1936. And though he possessed intelligence and academic ability, he was yet to apply himself seriously and instead focused on the social scene and the freshman football team. He may very well have been the skinniest young man on the football team, but he was tenacious and competitive. During the summer after his freshman year at Harvard, he toured Europe and began to demonstrate a mature interest in politics and international matters (Matthews, 2011).

Two years later, he traveled even more extensively in Europe, all the while writing long, detailed letters to his father, who was at the time ambassador to the United Kingdom. By early 1940, when Jack began his last semester at Harvard, he began to write his thesis titled "Why England Slept," which was published and became a national bestseller. JFK asserted, in the volume, that it was Britain's isolationist character that had led to the early attitude of appeasement toward Germany and its fuhrer, Adolf Hitler. The published work was successful, yet had a mixed reception but, at minimum, demonstrated that Kennedy was developing as a critical thinker with international perspective and political insight (J. Kennedy, 2016).

With the war raging in Europe, John F. Kennedy joined the Navy and the American war effort. At this time, his father, Joseph, began to have a vision that he could help his eldest son, Joe Jr., who was a pilot during World War II, rise to be president. But it was never to be for young Joe Junior. When he took off in formation on August 12, 1944, with copilot Lieutenant Wilford J. Willy, their 22,000 lb. load of torpex high explosives detonated in flight, killing them instantly. Joseph Kennedy Sr. was shattered, and so was his dream of pushing Joe Jr. to the White House and the presidency (Joseph Kennedy Jr., 2018).

John F. Kennedy, not unlike many young men of World War II, had close calls and barely made it back alive, while others did not, like Joe Jr. It was 1941 when John F. Kennedy joined the US Navy and their efforts against Japan in the South Pacific.

JFK

Commanding the patrol torpedo craft, US PT 109 Lieutenant Junior Grade John Kennedy and his crew participated in the early campaigns in the Allies' protracted struggle to push back the

Japanese from their conquests throughout the island chains of the Pacific Ocean. The assignment of the small and fast PT boats was to attack Japanese supply shipping and to support the US Army and Marine Corps assaults onshore.

On August 2, 1943, PT 109 was running Ghost Mode at night to avoid detection, and it was struck by the Japanese destroyer *Amagiri*, traveling at forty knots, and was cut in half. Kennedy's entire crew was tossed into the dark ocean waters, thinking perhaps that this was it. Eleven crew members spent a total of fifteen hours bobbing in the ocean waters. First, Kennedy was able to tow injured crew member McMahon four miles to a small island to the southwest, then the rest of the ditched crew. After four days on the small island, they were astonishingly able to send a message written on a coconut carried by local indigenous islanders to an Australian spy, and then they were finally rescued on August 8.

This was one of those against-all-odds experiences in JFK's early life that helped shape his character and that of many other young, brave soldiers who placed themselves in harm's way defending America during World War II. JFK received a Purple Heart and the Navy and Marine Corps Medal for his heroism and rescue of most of his crew. Later, Kennedy's political supporters made a great deal of JFK's military honors and heroism, but he basically shrugged it off, stating that he and most of his crew just survived when others did not (Roos, "The Navy Disaster that Earned JFK Two Medals for Heroism," 2018).

The Rise and Fall of the American Empire

After a very long and drawn-out battle in Europe and further protracted in the Pacific, JFK was finally able to go home. JFK had returned to the States a bonafide war hero, and then the light came on in Joseph Kennedy Sr.'s mind. He encouraged JFK to enter politics as he was an easy sell to the media and the public. From 1947 to 1953, JFK represented the Massachusetts 11th Congressional District in the US House of Representatives for three full terms. He further rose to US Senator from Massachusetts and served two full terms from 1953 to 1960. Rose Kennedy had named JFK after her father, John Francis Fitzgerald, mayor of Boston.

Soon after being elected senator, JFK, at thirty-six years of age, married the young, charming, and lovely Jacqueline Bouvier, a writer with The Washington Times Herald. Soon after marriage, JFK's back pain became so acute that he had to have two back surgeries. While he was still recovering, he wrote the Pulitzer Prize biography *Profiles in Courage* in 1957. JFK's popularity and public profile continued to rise so much that he was nearly chosen to run as the vice president in 1956. Instead, JFK decided to wait and run for president in the next election.

JFK began to travel and campaign all around the United States on the weekends. On July 13, 1960, the Democratic Party nominated JFK as its candidate for president, and he also selected Lyndon B. Johnson as his running mate. On November 8, 1960, after a very close race with Republican Richard Nixon, John F. Kennedy was elected the thirty-fifth president of the United States. JFK was also the youngest president ever elected to the office. JFK's rise

The End of Innocence, JFK, MLK, Chavez, and the 1960s

was meteoric, but his star was one that was soon shot down.

Joseph Kennedy Sr. was a master of image as he carefully cultivated the Kennedy Camelot. America didn't just have a president and first lady; they were almost regarded as royalty nationally and internationally. Everybody wanted to get close to JFK, including big stars like Frank Sinatra. But his brother Robert F. Kennedy, as attorney general, put the nix on that and told him that he needed to distance himself from Sinatra.

Kennedy's Camelot and White House was the pride of America and the buzz of political leadership and royalty internationally. They were invited to Buckingham Palace in June of 1961 by Queen Elizabeth and Prince Philip, and things went reasonably well. And they were invited back, but JFK would never make it back.

John F. Kennedy was assassinated on November 22, 1963, in an open motorcade in Dallas, with the first lady sitting right next to him. Not only was Jacqueline Kennedy totally traumatized by the horrific events of that moment, but so was all of America. It was truly the end of innocence for America, as the hideous hand of evil reached out to kill the president before all the eyes of America and the world. Just two hours after the death of the president, the first lady stood in her blood-stained clothing with Vice President Lyndon B. Johnson as he took the oath of office and assumed the presidency. There was a somber mood that descended upon America following the assassination of JFK, and there was nonstop media coverage broadcast for days after the event. It was a pivotal moment in American history, and everything changed ("Life of John F. Kennedy," n.d.).

Three days later, on November 25, 1963, the state funeral was held the same day as the president's son John Junior's birthday. The news of his father's death was explained to little John John, but the three-year-old boy did not understand and continued to request to be taken to see his dad. While at Saint Matthew's Cathedral for the president's funeral Mass, John Junior began to cry and had to be taken to another room to calm down. To distract him, one Secret Service agent tried to show him how to salute, but he was having trouble getting it. But then a marine colonel took over the lesson to teach John Junior how to salute, and he started to get it right.

After the Mass, the funeral procession of cars was to begin to make their way to Arlington National Cemetery. The children were considered too young for this part of the ceremony, especially after John Junior's crying in the Mass. But before John Junior and Carolyn left their mother for the day, photographers captured them outside the cathedral, watching their father's coffin go by. At that very moment, three-year-old John Junior spontaneously stepped forward and used the salute that he had just perfected, in absolute soldier form, as his father's coffin went by (Burak, 2023).

As the decades wore on, countless books were written about JFK and his assassination, hypothesizing on what really occurred

The End of Innocence, JFK, MLK, Chavez, and the 1960s

("Assassination of John F. Kennedy," 2023). Just this last week, RFK Jr., who is running for president, casually stated his opinion on his uncle's death. He is most certainly entitled to his views and insight and would know more than most, as both his father and uncle were assassinated. President Abraham Lincoln began to see it more and more clearly as he neared the end of his life: evil was real, and there was a battle over the White House and for the soul of America (Wilentz, 2018).

Cesar Chavez

Cesario Estrada Chavez was born on March 31, 1927, in the small agricultural town of Yuma, Arizona. Cesario was named after his paternal grandfather, Cesario Chavez, who had crossed from Mexico into Texas in 1898. Cesario had a wood hauling business near Yuma, Arizona, and in 1906, he purchased a farm in the North Gila Valley in the Sonoran Desert. Cesario had brought his wife, Dorotea, and eight children from Mexico with him, and the youngest child was Librado, Cesario Estrada Chavez's father. Cesario's name was anglicized to Cesar in Yuma in the 1930s at his school. Librado married Juana Estrada Chavez in the early 1920s, who was from Ascension, Chihuahua.

Juana had crossed into Picacho, California, with her mother as a baby before moving to Yuma, Arizona. In Yuma, Juana worked as a farm laborer and then had her first child, Rita, in August 1925. In November 1925, Librado and Juana purchased a series of buildings near the family home, which included a pool hall, store, and

The Rise and Fall of the American Empire

living quarters. Cesar Chavez was the second child of Juana and Librado, born two years later. Librado and Juana began to have financial problems and were forced to sell most of their assets and then move in with the widowed Dorotea. Librado and Juana went on to have a total of six children, and although they had very humble lives, they were comfortable and never went hungry. The family spoke Spanish, and Cesar was raised Catholic. In those early years, young Cesar began to attend Laguna Dam School in Yuma in 1933. And as often was the case of that generation, Young Cesario was forbidden to speak Spanish, was made to learn English, and his name was also changed to Cesar (Shelton, 2018).

At the height of the Great Depression, Cesar's grandmother Dorotea died, and his parents lost the family home and farmstead. This was something that young Cesar never forgot: how his father tried to fight the banks, the lawyers, and the Anglo-American power structure and felt that it was an injustice to him and his family. And this was probably one of those seminal moments and experiences that helped shape him into the future leader and activist that he became. Also influenced by his Catholicism, he increasingly viewed the poor as a source of moral goodness and fabric of society and the rich and powerful as something else.

Perhaps it was survival, as the Chavez family joined the growing number of American migrants who were moving to California during the Great Depression. They first moved to Oxnard, where the family worked as avocado pickers. Young Cesar continued to attend school and work with the family in the fields ("Cesar

The End of Innocence, JFK, MLK, Chavez, and the 1960s

Chavez's Biography," 2019). As an agricultural worker in California, Cesar moved and changed schools many times, attending Miguel Hidalgo Junior High the longest. He routinely experienced prejudice in school, and the children also made fun of him because of his poverty. He finished junior high school in 1942 and then became a full-time farm worker until he enlisted in the military.

When Cesar Chavez enlisted in the US Navy in 1944, America was still trying to finish the job in the Pacific against Japan. Cesar's first stop in the Navy was the training center in San Diego. Then, he crossed the enormous span of the Pacific and was stationed in Sipan at the US base there for six months. Later, Cesar moved to Guam, where he was soon promoted to the rank of seamen first class and continued to mature and develop as a leader. He then went back to the States and was stationed in San Francisco when he decided to leave the Navy and was honorably discharged in 1946. The young, uniformed Cesar sought out his family in Delano, California, where they had relocated and joined them in farm labor. It was also about this time that he met Helen Fabela, and they would soon get married and start a family.

In 1947, Cesar Chavez joined the National Farm Labor Union, and in his first taste of resistance, he began to picket the cotton fields around Corcoran near Delano, California. About that time, the Union called a strike against the DiGiorgio Grape Fields, forming caravans that marched along the perimeter, and Cesar Chavez took the lead in one group. They encouraged the workers in the fields to join them in their strike caravan (Pawell, 2015).

The Rise and Fall of the American Empire

The injustices of man against man seem to be endless throughout the course of human history in war and in everyday life. God has made man and all the different peoples of the earth, and He will judge the nations, and He will judge us individually according to our response to Him and how we treat our fellow man.

Throughout time and each generation, God will raise up individuals who are part of the solution and who are change agents. In the sphere of human rights and civil rights, God raised up different individuals, like Martin Luther King Jr. and Cesar Chavez, who made a big difference in their time and generations.

The plight of approximately 3 million farm workers in America may have improved to a big degree from the very harsh environments of the early years, but there is still a long way to go. The average life expectancy of a farmworker is still only forty-nine years old, and though Cesar Chavez lived to a comparatively old sixty-six years of age, he lived a very hard and stressful life, representing the interests of the agricultural laborer ("Cesar Chavez: American Labor Leader," 2023).

So, this is how Cesar Chavez grew up. He and his family lived and experienced the life of farm workers, and what made it even harder was the distant, fading memory of how his parents and grandparents had once owned their own home, farm, land, buildings, and assets. And it was not just the Chavez family; there were many mom-and-pop farms lost in the Great Depression and ensuing decades for various reasons that were increasingly being

The End of Innocence, JFK, MLK, Chavez, and the 1960s

bought up by big businesses and corporations. And the farm workers were treated like dispensable mules—modern slaves, and so began the lifelong vision and work of Cesar Chavez to do something about it (Cesar Chavez, 2023).

Cesar had lived and experienced the deplorable conditions in the farm labor camps. The workers bore the brunt of the elements day in and day out, laboring long hours for meager wages, often being exposed to dangerous, deadly chemicals in fields without access to adequate food, water, or shelter. And if you dare complain about the dire conditions, the back-breaking labor, the sexual harassment, the lack of educational opportunities for your children, much less no benefits, you could lose your job and easily be replaced by a bracero. The braceros worked for even less money and were treated even more harshly. The bracero program concluded on December 31, 1964, as mechanization became more widespread and as the Unions gained more strength and control ("US and Mexico Sign the Mexican Farm Labor Agreement," 2019). Yet, as recently as 2019, almost half of the agricultural workers were foreign-born, and more than 27 percent were undocumented.

Cesar Chavez dedicated his life to improving the treatment, pay, and working conditions for farm workers, but it was a long, arduous road and process, like a David and Goliath battle. During the 1950s, Cesar Chavez worked as a community and labor organizer. Along with Dolores Huerta, Chavez founded the National Farm Workers Association in 1962. This Union joined with the Agricultural Workers Organizing Committee in its first strike against grape growers in California in 1965. A year later, the two unions merged and were renamed the United Farm Workers ("United Farm Workers," 2023). In early 1968, Chavez called for a national boycott of California table grape growers and the battle for improved compensation and labor conditions, which would last for years. At the end of that battle, Chavez and his Union won several important victories for the workers when many growers signed contracts and made concessions with the Union. He continued to face many challenges through the years from other growers and, ironically, the Teamsters Union. All the while, he continued to oversee the Union and look for ways to help farm workers and advance the cause.

As a labor leader, Chavez employed nonviolent means like marches, boycotts, and even hunger strikes to bring attention to the plight of farm workers. He also brought about a national awareness of the dangers of pesticides to workers' health, looking for improvements and alternatives. His lifelong dedication to his work and cause earned him numerous friends and supporters, including Robert F. Kennedy and the Reverend Jesse Jackson. He was looked upon as a modern-day folk hero among the workers and their families, and the legend only grew in time. Some believe that Chavez's long hunger strikes weakened him and contributed to his early death on April 23, 1993, in San Luis, Arizona. In 2014, US President Barack Obama declared Cesar Chavez's birthday, March 31, to be recognized as a federal commemorative holiday.

There have been numerous books and films about Cesar

The End of Innocence, JFK, MLK, Chavez, and the 1960s

Chavez, including the documentary films *Cesar Chavez* and *Cesar's Last Fast*. He once fasted for thirty-six days straight to bring attention to workers' rights. The American Friends Service Committee nominated Cesar Chavez three times for the Nobel Peace Prize. At the start of the Biden administration, a bust of Chavez was placed on a table directly behind the Resolute Desk in the Oval Office.

Many schools, libraries, and parks bear his name, including Cesar Chavez High School in Arizona. There is a portrait of Chavez at the National Portrait Gallery in Washington, DC. In 2003, the US Postal Service honored Chavez with a postal stamp. In 2004, the National Chavez Center was opened on the UFW National Headquarters campus in Keene by the Cesar E. Chavez Foundation. It currently consists of a visitor center, museum, Memorial Gardens, and his gravesite on 187 acres ("Cesar Chavez's Biography and Career Timeline," 2023).

Martin Luther King Jr.

Martin's original name was Michael King Jr, and he was born on January 15, 1929, in Atlanta, Georgia. Martin Luther King Jr. was a Baptist minister and social activist who led the Civil Rights movement in the United States from the mid-1950s until his assassination in 1968. His tireless and determined leadership was fundamental to that movement's success in ending the legal segregation of African Americans in the South and other parts of the United States.

The Rise and Fall of the American Empire

MLK rose to national prominence as head of the Southern Christian Leadership Conference, which promoted nonviolent tactics such as protests and marches, including the massive march on the Washington, DC, National Mall in 1963 to achieve another level of civil rights. Sixty years later, America still has a long way to go, as there are many issues and much division remaining. Martin Luther King Jr. was awarded the Nobel Peace Prize in 1964 and numerous other awards and honors. In this short biography, we will look at the brief but remarkable life of one man who shook 1960s America (Carson, 2023).

It seems to me that, ultimately, you cannot pass a law to legislate hatred and prejudice. These are things of the heart that are often taught and indoctrinated into people at an early age. I believe that the only accurate understanding of life, mankind, the different races, and the purpose of God in all of this is found in the Bible and the word of God. Three characteristics of God are that He is life, light, and love. He doesn't just have love; He is love. The first of the Ten Commandments teaches us to love God and put Him first and then to love your neighbor as yourself. The Bible doesn't say to love your neighbor only if they agree with you on everything and they're the same color. So is the problem the Chinese people, or maybe it is the Africans and all the dark people? Perhaps it is the Russians, or maybe it is the Mexicans? After all, they look so strange and speak a different language. There is an ideology that is being taught today, first to their youth and children, that Israel and the United States must be destroyed to hasten the return of the twelfth Imam, Mahdi. Is that the spirit of God to hate, kill, and destroy?

The Civil Rights Act of 1964 in the United States explicitly banned all discrimination based on race, including racial segregation in schools, businesses, and public accommodations. That certainly was a big step forward, but America is full of more hatred, misunderstanding, and division than ever before. And there is even great contention and division in the church. Will there be hatred, prejudice, and division in heaven? If not, then perhaps it would be good if we began to understand these things more clearly while we are alive and here on earth. In every generation, God raises up people to be solutions to the different problems in the world. And in the sphere of human and civil rights, he raised up individuals like Cesar Chavez and Martin Luther King Jr.

King was born Michael King Jr. on January 15, 1929, in Atlanta, Georgia, the second of three children to Michael King Sr. and Alberta Williams. King's older sister was named Christine, and his younger brother was Alfred Daniel, or A. D. King. Alberta's father, Adam Daniel Williams, was a minister in the rural towns of Georgia, then moved to Atlanta in 1893. The following year, Adam Williams became the pastor of the Ebenezer Baptist Church in Atlanta. King Sr. was born to sharecroppers James Albert and Delia King of Stockbridge, Georgia, and was of African Irish descent. When Michael King Sr. was hardly twelve years old, he left his parents' farm and walked on foot to Atlanta, where he worked and put himself through high school.

The Rise and Fall of the American Empire

After finishing high school, Michael King Sr. enrolled at Morehouse College to study and prepare for the ministry. Soon after, Michael King Sr. met Alberta Williams, and they began courting in 1920 and then were married on November 25, 1926. Until Jennie's death, Alberta's mother, they both lived on the second floor of Alberta's parents' two-story Victorian house, where Michael King Jr. was born.

Shortly after marrying Alberta Williams, Michael King Sr. became assistant pastor of the Ebenezer Baptist Church. After Senior Pastor Williams died in the spring of 1931, Michael King Sr. assumed the role of senior pastor in the fall of that same year. After Pastor King took over Ebenezer Baptist, with great support from his wife, Alberta, the church grew from 600 to 3,000 members in attendance.

In 1934, the church sent Michael King Sr. on a multinational trip, including to Berlin, Germany, for the meeting of the Congress of the Baptist World Alliance (BWA). At that time, he visited sites in Germany that honored the Reformation leader Martin Luther, and he was very moved and inspired by Luther's legacy. Also, during this time, King Sr. and other BWA delegates witnessed the rise of Nazism and found it to be very disturbing. In reaction, the BWA issued a resolution stating, "This Congress deplores and condemns as a violation of the law of God the Heavenly Father, all racial animosity and every form of oppression or unfair discrimination toward the Jews, toward colored people or towards subject races in any part of the world." When Jesse Owens ac-

The End of Innocence, JFK, MLK, Chavez, and the 1960s

complished the incredible feat of winning four gold medals in the 1936 Olympics in Berlin, Adolf Hitler refused to shake his hand. Interestingly, upon returning home in August of 1934, King Senior changed his name legally to Martin Luther King Sr. and his five-year-old son's name to Martin Luther King Jr. (King, Martin Luther Sr., n.d.).

As a child, Martin Luther King Jr. and his two siblings would take turns reading the Scriptures aloud in family Bible studies. And after dinner, Jennie, the children's grandmother, would read Bible stories to them, trying to make it both interesting and instructional. Sometimes in life, the very thing that bothers us could be the thing that we are called to change. Prior to starting school, MLK had become friends with a white boy whose father owned a business across the street from his family's home. In September of 1935, both children began their schooling. MLK had to go to Yonge Elementary, an all-Black school, while his friend went to a different school exclusively for White children.

Soon afterwards, the parents of MLK's friend put an end to their friendship. They told him that he was colored, and their son was White, and they could no longer play together. When MLK told his parents what had happened, they had a long discussion with him about the history of slavery and racism in America. MLK's six-year-old mind tried to understand the hatred, violence, and oppression that Black people had faced in the US. His first response at the time was to be determined to hate every White person, but his parents told him that it was his Christian duty to love everyone (Eig, 2023).

So, MLK grew up in the segregated environment of Atlanta in the 1930s, watching his father's life like that of an illustrated sermon. MLK Sr. tried to walk in love and respect towards his fellow man, but he would not tolerate any guff or disrespect and would stand up to it. Once, when MLK accompanied his father to a downtown shoe store, the clerk told them that they had to sit in the back of the store. MLK Sr. refused to move and said, "We'll either buy shoes sitting here or won't buy any shoes at all." As he and MLK Jr. left the store, he said, "I don't care how long I have to live with this system; I will never accept it." In 1936, MLK Sr. led hundreds of local African Americans in a civil rights march to the City Hall in Atlanta to protest voting rights discrimination. MLK Sr. was a real father as well as a role model to MLK Jr. (Bishop, 2019).

By the time MLK was five years old, he had already begun to memorize verses from the Bible and quote them. He also loved gospel music and hymns and would begin to attend events with his mother, where she played piano, and he would sing along with others. One of his favorite hymns was "I Want to Be More and More Like Jesus." He began to develop his strong voice singing and later joined the junior choir in the church. He also liked opera and began to play the piano as well. Besides his regular education, he also would read dictionaries to further understand and learn new words. In time, he became a very gifted speaker and communicator. Sometimes, he got into fistfights with other boys in the

The End of Innocence, JFK, MLK, Chavez, and the 1960s

neighborhood but began to realize that often, he could reason with them and avoid knocking each other on the head. In September of 1940, eleven-year-old MLK was enrolled in the Atlanta University Laboratory School for his seventh grade. While there, he took violin and piano lessons and showed a particularly keen interest in History and English classes.

On May 18, 1941, MLK's maternal grandmother died, and it greatly traumatized him. Yet MLK Sr. did his best to talk to him and let him know it was not his or anybody else's fault that she had died. Shortly thereafter, MLK Sr. decided to move the family to a two-story brick home on a hill that overlooked downtown Atlanta with beautiful views, especially at night. As MLK grew into his adolescent years, he continued to observe the racial humiliation that he and other families endured in the segregated South.

In 1942, he became the youngest assistant manager of a delivery station for the *Atlanta Journal*. That year, MLK skipped the ninth grade and was enrolled in Booker T. Washington High School, where he got very good grades. In high school, MLK joined the debate team and continued to develop his strong voice and public speaking skills. On April 13, 1944, in his junior year at Booker T. Washington High School, MLK gave his first public speech, which essentially stated Black America still wore chains. He won the contest, but ironically, on the way home, MLK and his teacher were forced by the bus driver to stand in the back of the bus so white passengers could sit down.

The Rise and Fall of the American Empire

At age fifteen, the very bright MLK was admitted into Morehouse College, where his father and maternal grandfather had attended. That summer, prior to attending Morehouse, he took a job in Connecticut with friends and students and was amazed at how different it was. He felt like after they had passed Washington, DC, there was no more discrimination at all. Up to that time, he had only experienced segregation, and in Connecticut, MLK could eat where he wanted, sit where he wanted, and even attend a mostly White church there without any problems or issues (The Martin Luther King Jr. Research and Education Institute, Stanford University, n.d.).

The summer prior to his last year at Morehouse, under the mentorship of Baptist Minister and President Benjamin Hayes, MLK chose to go into the ministry to serve humanity. MLK graduated from Morehouse with a BA in sociology. In 1948, at nineteen, MLK furthered his education by enrolling in Crozer Theological Seminary in Upland, Pennsylvania, where he was elected student body president. MLK graduated from Crozier in 1951 with a bachelor of divinity. His next stop was Boston University, where he began his doctoral studies in systematic theology. While pursuing doctoral studies, MLK worked as an assistant minister at Boston's Historic Twelfth Baptist Church. At the age of twenty-five, Martin Luther King Jr. became the pastor of the Dexter Avenue Baptist Church in Montgomery, Alabama. The following year, he received his PhD degree on June 5, 1955.

While MLK was attending Boston University, he had been in-

The End of Innocence, JFK, MLK, Chavez, and the 1960s

troduced to Coretta Scott, an undergraduate student and activist at Antioch University. Martin and Coretta were married on June 18, 1953, and had four children: Yolanda, Martin Luther III, Dexter Scott, and Bernice. In December of 1959, MLK moved back to Atlanta at the request of the SCLC, where he co-pastored Ebenezer Baptist with his father and helped expand the civil rights movement across the South.

On December 1, 1955, Rosa Parks was arrested for refusing to give up her seat on a city bus. This and other similar incidents led to the Montgomery Bus Boycott, which lasted 385 days. It was urged and planned by E. D. Nixon and led by MLK Jr., who was barely twenty-six years old and rather reluctantly took the leadership role in this boycott. Not long after, his home was bombed, and he was also put in jail for driving five mph over the speed limit. MLK Jr.'s role in the bus boycott thrust him into national attention, and he soon became the best-known spokesman for the civil rights movement. They called off the boycott after the United States District Court issued a ruling in Browder v. Gayle that prohibited racial segregation on all Montgomery buses. Blacks resumed riding the buses again and were legally allowed to sit wherever they wanted, front, back, or center.

In 1957, MLK Jr. and other civil rights activists founded the Southern Christian Leadership Conference, SCLC. The group had been inspired by the evangelistic crusades of the Reverend Billy Graham, who befriended MLK. And the SCLC was also created to harness the moral authority and organizing power of black church-

The Rise and Fall of the American Empire

es to conduct nonviolent protests in the service of civil rights reform. The first time that MLK addressed a national audience was at the SCLC's 1957 Prayer Pilgrimage for Freedom.

MLK believed that organized, nonviolent protest against the system of Southern segregation, known as Jim Crow laws, would lead to extensive media coverage of the struggle for Black equality and voting rights. Media coverage of the daily indignities and deprivation suffered by Southern Blacks and of segregationist violence and harassment of civil rights workers and marchers produced a wave of sympathetic public opinion and support that convinced the majority of Americans that the civil rights movement was the most important issue in American politics in the early 1960s. MLK and his team of civil rights leaders organized and led marches for Blacks' right to vote, desegregation, labor rights, and other basic civil rights. Most of these rights were successfully enacted into law with the passage of the Civil Rights Act of 1964 and the 1965 Voting Rights Act (Ott, "Martin Luther King Jr.," 2024).

On September 20, 1958, MLK was stabbed by a mentally deranged woman while signing copies of his new book, "Stride Toward Freedom," at Blumstein's department store in Harlem. He underwent emergency surgery and was hospitalized for weeks but survived (Klein, 2019). Towards the end of MLK Jr.'s life, he was in flight reminiscing with one of his SCLC associates and friends about some of the things they had gone through together. His friend believed that he had gone to jail forty-two times, while MLK smiled and said that he had only gone to jail nineteen times.

His friend recalled the worst possible food in the jails, while MLK laughed and said that he had gotten some really good food, especially at one jail ("Martin Luther King Jr. Was Arrested Twenty-Nine Times for These So-Called Crimes," n.d.). Then MLK's face changed as he began to recall every time that he felt endangered, as he was speaking publicly, or the countless times that he had led a march through the most harrowing of circumstances. In one city, they were marching down a narrow tree-lined street as local police went ahead of the marchers, trying to get all the hundreds of armed men out of the trees. They were marching in nonviolence, yet frequently were met by violent responses wherever they went (Eig, 2023).

MLK and the SCLC crisscrossed the country for years, holding meetings in churches and other locations, organizing marches, protests, strategies, and different events. Often, Black Power members or militant Blacks attended these meetings, insisting that nonviolence did not work. However, MLK and the SCLC organizers argued and insisted that it did work, that maybe they were not batting 100 percent or even 50 percent, but they continued to make progress slowly but surely. Even within the anomaly of MLK's assassination, the SCLC continued to maintain the position that their nonviolent marches and strategies had indeed worked and made good progress ("Martin Luther King and the Founding of SCLC," n.d.).

After Martin Luther King Jr.'s assassination on April 4, 1968, many American cities and towns erupted in violent protests and riots lasting for days on into the weekend, with the National Guard and local police forces trying to quell the chaos ("Martin Luther King Jr.'s Assassination," 2010). MLK and the SCLC led countless marches, including the Albany Movement in 1961, the Birmingham Campaign in 1963, and the huge march on Washington in 1963, with over 250,000 in attendance. It was at this Jobs and Freedom event that the legendary gospel singer Mahalia Jackson called out to MLK while he was speaking, "Martin, tell them about the dream!" And he spontaneously incorporated "I Have a Dream" into the message. It spoke to the heart and aspirations of the broken Black community of 1960s America, perhaps in a unique way and convergent time in history (Chang, 2021).

Martin Luther King Jr. was awarded the Nobel Peace Prize in 1964, the same year that President Lyndon B. Johnson signed the Civil Rights Act into law. A week after MLK's assassination, one of the final pieces of Civil Rights Era legislation was enacted, the Fair Housing Act. Posthumously, MLK received the Presidential Medal of Freedom in 1977 and the Congressional Gold Medal in 2004. There are numerous memorials, buildings, sculptures, and various monuments dedicated to Martin Luther King Jr. in the United States and internationally. In 1980, the US Department of the Interior designated MLK's boyhood home in Atlanta, as well as several nearby buildings, such as the Martin Luther King Jr. National Historic Site. Doctor Martin Luther King Jr. Memorial Gardens in Raleigh, North Carolina, is the first of many parks devoted to MLK and the Civil Rights Movement. Martin Luther

The End of Innocence, JFK, MLK, Chavez, and the 1960s

King Jr. College Preparatory High School in Memphis, Tennessee, is one of many schools named in honor of MLK. The Martin Luther King Jr. Memorial Library and The Doctor Martin Luther King Jr. Library in San Jose, California, are named in his honor.

MLK was the first African American honored with his own memorial at the National Mall in Washington, DC. A bust of Doctor King was added to the Gallery of Notables in the United States Capitol in 1986. The beginning of Doctor King's "I Have a Dream" speech is etched into the steps of the Lincoln Memorial, at the very place where he stood before 250,000 people and a televised audience of millions. There are countless other memorials and sculptures throughout the United States and the world. And although we will never entirely be "free at last" until we are released from the constraints of this present world, Doctor Reverend Martin Luther King Jr. moved the hopes and dreams of many Americans forward amidst the turbulent 1960s (Eig, 2023) ("Martin Luther King Jr.'s Achievements," 2020).

350

CHAPTER 28

CBN, TBN, Daystar, and the Close of the Twentieth Century

Here in America, we enjoy many privileges and freedoms that we can potentially take for granted. Just take a little tour of the world, and you can see that many other peoples and nations are not nearly as well off as Americans. We also have freedom of speech and religion, whereas, in many other countries, you must fall in line with the ideology of the government or perhaps the main religious entity or group. Here in America, you can believe what you want to believe, go to the church of your choice, and worship as you like, at least for now. And if you are already a Christian, you can pray, read your Bible and Christian books, and have access to a plethora of great teachers, ministers, and ministries, including CBN, TBN, and Daystar Television, to get strong in the Lord and in your faith.

Most Bible teachers today teach that there is no prophetic fulfillment remaining to prevent the return of Jesus. While I agree with that in principle, I believe that the final harvest of souls in the last days is of paramount importance to God. Since the advent of the newspaper, mass printings of the Bible, radio, television, film, the World Wide Web, and other forms of media communication, the speed of spreading the gospel message worldwide to all people has greatly accelerated. Not to mention the explosion of gospel, Christian, and worship music in the last fifty years. Three media platforms that have performed an indispensable role in spreading the gospel message over the last fifty-plus years are CBN, TBN, and Daystar Television. We will start with CBN and its founder since they go back to the farthest in history and time.

Christian Broadcasting Network

The founder of CBN was Marion Gordon Robertson, who was born on March 22, 1930, in Lexington, Virginia. Pat Robertson's career and ministry spanned well into six decades, and he was a very influential figure in many spheres, including politics. He stated that he had become a born-again Christian at the end of the 1950s while having dinner at a restaurant in Philadelphia with author and World War II veteran Cornelius Vanderbreggen (Cornelius "Cornie" Vanderbreggen Jr., 2015). Some of the great works that Pat Robertson founded were the Christian Broadcasting Network, Regent University, Operation Blessing, The International Family Entertainment Incorporated, The American Center for Law and Justice, The Founders Inn and Conference Center, and the Christian Coalition.

Pat Robertson had also written more than twenty-six bestselling books, including *The End of the Age*, written in 1995. He was also the host of the popular show *The 700 Club* up until 2021. Pat Robertson ran for president in 1988, perhaps seeing a void in Reagan Republicanism and, although unsuccessful in his attempt, continued to grow in political knowledge, savvy, and insight. Pat Robertson was one of the most high-profile voices of his generation, holding and pointing to conservative Christianity and a biblical standard in a culture that seemed ever more determined to depart from it in America.

Pat Robertson was born right at the beginning of the Great American Depression to conservative Virginia Senator Absalon Willis Robertson and Gladys Churchill, who was a musician (Pat Robertson, 2023). When he was still a baby, his older brother, Willis Robertson Jr., would pat him on the cheeks and say, "Pat, Pat, Pat." As he grew into an adolescent, his childhood nickname stayed with him, and he was not particularly fond of his real first name, Marion ("Nickname Pat," n.d.).

When Pat was eleven years old, he enrolled in the McDonogh Preparatory School outside Baltimore, Maryland. From 1940 to 1946, he attended the McCallie School in Chattanooga, Tennessee, where he graduated at the top of his class with honors. Pat then attended Washington and Lee University, where he continued to excel academically, graduating magna cum laude. In 1948, the draft was reinstated, and Robertson was given the choice of the Marines or Army, so he joined the US Marine Corps prior to being drafted. Not long after, Pat Robertson was shipped out to Korea, where he was stationed at Headquarters Command just above the thirty-eighth parallel at Heartbreak Ridge. Pat Robertson was awarded three battle stars for his service in the Korean War and was promoted to first lieutenant in 1952.

Upon his return to the United States, Pat Robertson continued his education and graduated from Yale Law School at the top of his class in 1955. After becoming a born-again Christian in the late fifties, Pat Robertson attended the New York Theological Seminary, where he received a master of divinity degree in 1959 and soon after entered the ministry. God called Pat Robertson to an incredible lifelong work, and after he became a spirit-filled Christian, it changed everything. His vision up until that time was just to go into business, start a corporation, and make a lot of money. He had so much talent, ability, energy, vision, and motivation, but he put it all in God's hands. He had stated that prior to becoming a Christian, there truly was an emptiness, a void, and a lack of satisfaction in his life and endeavors. But like a convergence, this remarkable man with so much potential submitted it to God—to a much higher and bigger purpose. Pat said that in the beginning, one of the most important things that he learned was how to be led by God and to obey Him (Pat Robertson, 2023).

About four years prior to M. G. Pat Robertson's death on June 8, 2023, at his home in Virginia Beach, Virginia, White House correspondent and his granddaughter, Abigail Robertson, interviewed him. Even at almost ninety years of age, Pat seemed to radiate the essence of what was important in life. Even after falling off a horse and a light stroke, Pat had an amazing attitude and flowed in the wisdom of a life serving God and humanity. Abigail Robertson asked him questions and walked him through the highlights of the previous sixty years of his life. One of the things that he had made clear was that he had a radical transformation and encounter with

CBN, TBN, Daystar, and the Close of the Twentieth Century

God that changed his life and priorities from the beginning. He was spirit-filled and learned how to hear from God and follow the leading of the Lord. Perhaps in an early test of obedience, he sold everything out of his apartment in Queens, New York, and then gave the money to a minister in Bedford-Stuyvesant to distribute to the poor and needy. Then he had the leading of the Lord return to Virginia and tell them what great things the Lord had done for him.

Returning to Virginia, he had the opportunity to preach at a small church, and after he was done, a leader in the church told him that he would support him in a radio ministry that he had yet to do. Also, he ran into an old friend from high school, who told Pat the vision God had given him, which confirmed what God had been showing to Pat Robertson. His friend told him to go get to a television station, that it would be easy. He laughed about that years later, knowing nothing about television nor even owning one himself. So, when Pat Robertson learned that the tiny UHF station in nearby Portsmouth, Virginia, was available, he sent the owner a letter asking him how much he would want for it. In the meantime, Pat began to pray about the purchase and asked God how much he should spend to purchase tiny WYAH-TV and the small amount of space and equipment. Tim Bright said that he wanted $37,000 for everything, and Pat proceeded with the purchase, feeling confident that it was an answer to prayer.

On October 1, 1961, CBN made their first televised broadcast from tiny WYAH-TV in Portsmouth. Because they were yet to have a monitor in the studio, Pat would run down the street to the barbershop and check the television there to make sure that the signal was working and coming through. Not long after the first TV station, CBN picked up its first radio station and its small signal. Pat knew that the Word of God said, "Do not despise these small beginnings" (Zechariah 4:10a, NLT).

Ronald Reagan

From the very start, he had a vision to develop a network, and they continued to grow and progress little by little, one step at a time. In one of Pat Robertson's first efforts to raise funds for the

CBN, TBN, Daystar, and the Close of the Twentieth Century

projects and vision, he requested $10 a month from 700 viewers to help support the ministry financially.

This was the genesis of what was to become known as *The 700 Club*. Not only was this successful but there began to be reports from viewers throughout the area of God moving in unique and supernatural ways to confirm God's purpose and blessing on CBN. People reported miracle healings, the power of God in their homes, and God speaking to them during this time. The police department even called Pat Robertson and asked him what was going on. The officer sounded a little frightened and asked him if it was the Second Coming, but Pat assured him that it was just a revival.

Since CBN's founding in 1960, they have grown to cover the earth with the good news of salvation in Jesus. They have broadcast programs in over seventy languages to nearly every nation on earth. And since M. G. Pat Robertson's death, his son Gordon has taken over the helm of CBN as CEO, and Robert Allman is the news director. One of the mainstays of CBN has been *The 700 Club*, which has been the longest-running program in the country in the variety format.

Pat Robertson ran for president in 1988 after growing up in a family where his father was a Virginia senator and after befriending Ronald Reagan. And even though Pat failed to become president, he succeeded in translating his experience, network, and knowledge into creating the politically powerful Christian coali-

The Rise and Fall of the American Empire

tion to effectuate positive change and influence in America politically. Up until that time, Christians had held the erroneous belief that politics is wrong, dirty, and corrupt and that we need to stay out of it.

Pat Robertson was a pioneer in understanding that Christians need to effectively climb every mountain and sphere of influence, including politics. And the very reason Pat Robertson rubbed some people wrong and was attacked by the media was because he was a very strong and powerful Christian who was making a difference. CBN has reached and touched countless millions of people, and continues to, with the Gospel message of Christ. Another great work founded by CBN was Operation Blessing in 1978. Operation Blessing is a nonprofit humanitarian organization that has provided disaster relief, medical aid, clean water, hunger relief, community development, and orphan care to millions of people all over the world.

Another notable work established by Pat Robertson in 1977 is the highly-ranked private Christian university, Regent University, in Virginia Beach, Virginia. From its inception in 1977, Regent has educated and trained thousands of Christians to represent Christ in their respective fields of endeavor. Throughout its dramatic growth as a global Center for Christian thought and action, the university has remained steadfast to its mission of Christian leadership to change the world. The Reverend Billy Graham once stated that "the most important legacy that a man can leave behind is one that is rich in character and faith." M. G. Pat Robertson's beautiful and brilliant wife of sixty-eight years, Adelia "DeDe" Elmer, preceded him in death by one year, and besides leaving behind the amazing CBN family to carry on the work, they also had four children, fourteen grandchildren, and twenty-four great-grandchildren. One of the last things that Pat Robertson said to Abigail Robertson in the 2019 interview was that he believed the work of getting the gospel out to everyone all over the world was just about done (Robertson, "Abigail Robertson's Long-Ranging Interview with Pat Robertson," 2023) (Levenson and Watson, 2023).

TBN

Trinity Broadcasting Network is the world's largest international Christian television network based in California and the United States. TBN has become synonymous with Christian television since its modest beginning on May 28, 1973, with one small part-time station airing a few hours of Christian television throughout Los Angeles each day.

Paul Franklin Crouch, born March 30, 1934, in Saint Joseph, Missouri, along with his wife, Janice, were the founders and visionaries of TBN. Yet the call to evangelism and mission work began generations back in the Crouch family in the early 1900s. An Iowa farmer's wife loaded up a revival tent in the rumble seat of her Model T and preached the gospel from Texas to the Canadian border ("The Story of TBN: Fifty Years in the Making," 2023). That was Paul Crouch Sr.'s grandmother. Paul Crouch Sr.'s parents, Andrew and Sarah Crouch, were born in the late 1800s and were Assemblies of God missionaries to Egypt. Paul spent some of his early childhood there.

Another fact about the early years of the Crouch family that few are aware of is that they have deep roots in the Assemblies of God church. Paul's father, Andrew F. Crouch, two uncles, and an aunt were all present in 1914 at Hot Springs, Arkansas, at the General Council founding of the Assemblies of God ("History," 2023). And though the times and the technology have changed, the mission remains the same: to lead people to Christ and strengthen them in their faith.

Paul Crouch Sr. was the third son of Andrew and Sarah Crouch, and his mother and grandparents raised him after his father, Andrew, died when he was only seven years old. Paul's two older brothers were John Mark and the Reverend Philip Crouch, who went on to be the president of Central Bible College for many years. When Paul Crouch Sr. was young, he became very interested in amateur radio and announced to the family that he would use such technology to send the gospel around the world. Paul not only graduated in 1955 from Central Bible College in Springfield with a degree in theology but also received three honorary doctorates. A doctor of literature (DLitt) on May 29, 1981, from the California Graduate School of Theology, Glendale, California, a doctor of divinity on May 29, 1983, from the American Christian Theological Seminary, Anaheim, California, and a doctor of laws degree on May 5, 1985, from Oral Roberts University, Tulsa, Oklahoma.

CBN, TBN, Daystar, and the Close of the Twentieth Century

Soon after meeting in 1957, Paul Crouch and Janice Bethany were married in Missouri and had two sons, Paul Crouch Jr. and Matthew Crouch. Paul began his early career in broadcasting by helping to build an educational AM station KCBI on campus while a student at Central Bible Institute and Seminary. In 1957, Paul became a radio announcer at KRSD in Rapid City, South Dakota, and was soon promoted to program director. He was then promoted to manager of sister station KRSD-TV, the NBC affiliate in Rapid City.

In 1961, Paul Crouch Sr. was appointed by the General Council of the Assemblies of God to organize and operate their newly formed Department of Film and Television Production in Burbank, California, which he did for four years from 1965 to 1970. Paul Crouch was also the general manager of KREL Radio in Corona, California. After departing KREL, Paul Crouch became the general manager of KHOF-FM and KHOF-TV in San Bernardino, California ("Crouch Family's Deep Roots in Assemblies of God," 2013).

Behind every great man, there is usually a supportive and remarkable woman, like Janice Wendell Bethany Crouch. Jan was born May 14, 1938, in New Brockton, Alabama, the same day that Israel was recognized as a nation ten years later. Jan Crouch was the daughter of Reverend and Mrs. Edgar W. Bethany and grew up in Columbus, Georgia. Her father served as an Assemblies of God pastor and was the founding president of Southeastern University in Florida. Her parents prayed for her and her future, and she was

The Rise and Fall of the American Empire

a daughter of destiny. While Jan was attending Evangel College in Springfield, Missouri, she met Paul Crouch, and soon after, they were married. Later, during the TBN years, Jan always brought a warmth and genuine kindness to the viewers that they could always connect with ("Founders' Biographies," 2018).

Both Paul and Jan grew up in families where God was the number one priority: to serve Him and to reach people for Christ. But the belief of many of the old timers in the first part of the twentieth century was that television and movies were evil, a tool of the devil. But then Pat Robertson, Paul Crouch, and many other ministers began to think, *What if you use these new mediums of technology as a vehicle to spread the gospel?* For the first nineteen centuries, since the time of Christ, the spreading of the good news had mostly been word of mouth and small gatherings. Then, around the turn of the century, electric amplification was invented to speak to larger groups of people. And with the advent of radio, ministers found that they could reach audiences of hundreds and thousands of people.

With the invention and introduction of television, ministers began to envision speaking to and reaching thousands and millions of people. And I believe that was the essence of the early vision of Paul and Jan Crouch, with TBN Christian Television being an alternative to secular programming. This seems to be one way that we have seen the acceleration of the gospel message going around the world, with film, the worldwide web, music, TV, and major media platforms like CBN, TBN, and Daystar Television. Each

CBN, TBN, Daystar, and the Close of the Twentieth Century

time TBN got a new satellite or station, Paul Crouch Sr. would announce it on air with great excitement and genuine enthusiasm.

From the early years of just one UHF station and the monumental struggles that nearly knocked them out before they could even get off the ground, TBN began to grow and expand with phenomenal success. They had and have so many great shows and ministry personalities, with a wide variety of content from children, young adult, teaching, and evangelism, strengthening the body of Christ in addition to the local church. Legendary shows like *Praise the Lord* and *Behind the Scenes* would give the viewers an idea of what was going on worldwide with the church and the ministry of TBN. Matt Crouch has diligently continued the work and ministry and is currently TBN's president and head of operations after his father, Paul Crouch Sr., died in November 2013. Currently, TBN and its twenty-six global networks and affiliates reach every inhabited continent, utilizing eighty-plus satellites and more than 20,000 television and cable affiliates, as well as via the Internet. From the early vision of young Paul Crouch of spreading the good news around the world with radio, TBN has truly given "The Winds a Mighty Voice." Only eternity will reveal the number of persons saved, healed, edified, and ministered to these last fifty-plus years through the wonderful work of TBN ("The Legacy of TBN," 2023) (Crouch Family's Deep Roots in Assemblies of God," 2013).

Daystar Television Network

When Jesus had risen from the dead, He instructed His eleven disciples to go to a certain mountain in Galilee and meet Him there. One of the last directives He gave them is recorded in Matthew 28:18–20 (NIV):

> Then Jesus came to them and said, "All authority in heaven and on earth has been given to me. Therefore go and make disciples of all nations, baptizing them in the name of the Father and of the Son and of the Holy Spirit, and teaching them to obey everything I have commanded you. And surely I am with you always, to the very end of the age."

This is commonly referred to as the Great Commission, where Jesus called on His followers to preach the gospel to all nations and people, work miracles in Jesus's name to testify to the gospel, baptize new believers, and disciple those who receive Christ. Well, whose job is that anyway? I imagine that it is every believer's responsibility and every member of the body of Christ to fulfill a part and purpose, from the individual believer to the role of the local church to the fivefold ministry and media platforms like CBN, TBN, and Daystar Television.

Marcus Daron Lamb was born October 7, 1957, in Cordell, Georgia, and subsequently was raised in Macon, Georgia, and along with his wife, Joni Trammell, co-founded the Daystar Television Network. Marcus was raised in the church and made a commitment to Jesus at a very early age. According to the Daystar biography, in the summer of 1973, at the age of fifteen, he began preaching as an evangelist. He had sufficient credits to graduate from high school in 1974. After his junior year, and on full scholarship, he began to attend Lee University in Cleveland, Tennessee, at age sixteen. Then, at the age of nineteen, Marcus began his final senior semester at Lee and graduated magna cum laude. Later in life, Marcus Lamb received two honorary doctorates, as well as an Alumnus of the Year Award from Lee University.

In December of 1981, Marcus Lamb founded Word of God Fellowship in Macon, Georgia. After Marcus met Joni Trammell of Greenville, South Carolina, they were married in 1982. Marcus and Joni began to travel, and they ministered in more than twenty states. Many began to refer to Marcus Lamb as "the walking Bible" because of his extensive knowledge, memory, and use of the Scriptures in his sermons.

While in Israel in 1983, God spoke to Marcus Lamb and instructed him to start a Christian television station in Montgomery, Alabama. So, in 1985, WMCF-TV, "45 Alive" was launched in Montgomery. Not only was it the first Christian TV station in the state, but Marcus was also the youngest person in the country to build a full-power television station. That success and experience enabled the Lambs to move to the larger market of Dallas in 1990 and build KMPX-TV 29. Through divine favor and a series of miracles, TV 29 went on the air full power in September of 1993.

The Rise and Fall of the American Empire

The Daystar Television Network officially launched in 1997 with a live broadcast of T. D. Jakes's New Year's Eve service at the Potter's House Church in Dallas, Texas.

Currently reaching over 108 million households in the United States and over 2 billion people worldwide, Daystar is the fastest-growing faith-based television network in the world. They are the rising star, that is, day star, in faith-based television. Daystar is available on all major satellite and cable systems in the US and can be seen in every country around the world. In 2006, Daystar had the notable privilege of becoming the first and only Christian television network to be broadcast in the nation of Israel.

And although Marcus Daron Lamb died on November 30, 2021, the work and ministry of Daystar Television continues with Joni, family, and the Daystar staff and family ("Marcus Lamb's Biography," 2023). Pat Robertson, the founder of CBN, stated at the time, "We mourn the passing of Marcus Lamb, a great man of God, whose life will be remembered by millions." Jentezen Franklin, the senior pastor of Free Chapel, also stated,

> Generations of Christians have had the dream of reaching the world with the gospel in their generation. Marcus Lamb did it. He also welcomed the rest of us along on the journey with him through the extraordinary network he created. The truth is that very few Christians have had more

> of an impact in a single lifetime, and the
> impact of his life will carry on forever.

Prior to his passing, Marcus had laid out a plan for Joni, in case anything were to happen to him, for the future and continuation of Daystar (Warren, 2021).

Joni Trammell was born on July 19, 1960, in Colleyville, Texas, and subsequently lived in Greenville, South Carolina, through her formative years. She is the president and cofounder of Daystar Television Network. Her family were members of the Tremont Avenue Church of God, where she met Marcus Lamb when he came to Tremont to minister during a revival. Marcus and Joni were married in 1982 and had three gifted, amazing children together, Jonathan, Rachel, and Rebecca, who have all been involved with Daystar in different capacities since the passing of Marcus Lamb (Joni Lamb, 2024).

Joni Trammell Weiss was recently remarried to the well-known minister Dr. Doug Weiss, who will most certainly strengthen the family and the ministry (*Healing Time with Dr. Doug Weiss*, 2023). Daystar has a lineup of daily shows to edify the viewers with seasoned generals like John Hagee, Perry Stone, and Rick Renner. Rick Renner brings an international dynamic and perspective into his teaching, as he has established churches in Russia and Ukraine as well. There are so many excellent programs on Daystar, such as *Jewish Voice*, *Ministry Now*, and *Joni Table Talk*. *Joni Table Talk* consistently has a variety of gifted and insightful teachers who can discuss matters that concern everyone in the church. Individuals like Jimmy Evans, Joseph Z, and Lance Wallnau strengthen the listeners and bring them up to speed to understand the times and current events. In the early days, Joni sang in the church and was a worship leader and talented recording artist. She now has an awesome group of musicians and the Daystar singers, along with anointed guests like David and Nicole Binion and Martha Munizzi.

If we had just one prophetic sign and indicator that we were at the end of the age and the return of Christ was near, that would be one thing. But when we have a convergence of every sign, all at once, the Bible tells us to be ready, to be prepared, for our Lord is at the door. It is God's will for you to finish strong, fulfill your destiny, and run and complete your race. For such a time as this, you have come into the kingdom to do His will, whatever it is. And in addition to our personal devotion and the strength of the local church, Daystar and Christian television have been very important tools to edify, connect, strengthen, and prepare the body of Christ ("Marcus Lamb's Biography," 2023).

CBN, TBN, Daystar, and the Close of the Twentieth Century

Major Lynn Gordon Ray

CHAPTER 29

Let the Heroes Arise

There are some things that are simply beyond our scope and control. Nobody knows for sure how things are going to go on the international scene and in the world. We don't know exactly when the return of Christ will occur, and we don't want to make the mistake of trying to put a date on that. But we also do not want to make the mistake, in this critical time in history, of being apathetic and indifferent, complacent, and cold, disregarding Scripture and the warnings of the Lord. So, what can we do to serve the Lord and make a difference in this generation? Well, I say, "Let the heroes arise." Let's do what we know to do and be about the Father's business until He returns or until we finish our individual race. Yes, the current trajectory of America and its decline is alarming, but we can't throw up our hands or throw in the towel.

You might be limited in your influence or resources and think, *What can I do to make a difference?* Well, we can all pray, as one person standing in the courts of intercession with God can make a big difference. And we can pray over ourselves and our families, our community and children, our churches, and our nation. Let's try to encourage people and speak life over them, as it's so easy to hate and beat up people, but we don't want to be like that. Let's speak to the young people about hope and vision and let them know they can be part of God's solution for the world. Support your local church and help them fulfill their vision. Get strong

The Rise and Fall of the American Empire

in the Lord now, while you can, because there are more storms ahead. Not everyone is called specifically into the ministry, but you can be a light and a witness in your sphere of endeavor.

When Pat Boone moved from Tennessee to Hollywood in the late 1950s, he didn't have to announce to everyone that he was a Christian, as they already knew and were watching him. The current speaker of the House, Mike Johnson, has been aware of the hand of God on his life and that God has raised him up for this time (Piccotti, 2023). Demos Shakarian started the Full Gospel Businessmen Fellowship in 1952 with a small meeting each week at Clifton's Cafeteria in Los Angeles, which spread over the following decades to touch and impact multiplied thousands of businessmen in America to live for Christ ("Our History," 2020).

One man born in 1929, Hal Lindsey, wrote a book, *The Late Great Planet Earth*, and this single work alone went on to sell an estimated 35 million copies by 1999 and was translated into more than fifty different languages. In 1977, a movie version narrated by Orson Welles ran in theaters nationwide, and all of America was thinking about the apocalypse ("Hal Lindsey: Media Ministries," 2023). As of September 2023, there are 900 Christian colleges in America training our future leaders. Wheaton College alone has a rich history that goes back to its founding by the Wesleyans in 1853, and Michaele Whelan is its current president. Wheaton College's mission statement is "For Christ and His Kingdom" (President & College Leadership, 2023).

The Christian film industry has been exploding, with movies like *The Sound of Freedom*, *The Passion of Christ*, *The Chosen*, and *Jesus Revolution* entering the consciousness of America

(Brown, 2024). And while *Jesus Revolution* hit the movie theaters, which is a movie about revival among the youth fifty years ago, a new revival swept through many American universities, including Asbury, saving thousands (Brown, 2024). There has also been an exponential increase in gospel, Christian, and worship music, with artists like Lauren Daigle, Mercy Me, Michael W. Smith, Amy Grant, and Israel Houghton entering the ears in churches, cars, and living rooms of America. Israel Houghton was one of the worship leaders at Lakewood Church in Houston, along with Martha Munizzi and others ("101 Best Christian Artists of All Time," 2013).

Lakewood Church was originally founded by the firebrand John Osteen and his wife, Dodie. After John's passing, the family successfully carried on Lakewood into a new time and generation, with the children and grandchildren operating in many positions and duties in the church, looking to impact and serve the community in Houston, Texas, and throughout the world. Lisa Osteen is a great Bible teacher, and Sr. Pastor Joel Osteen is very inspiring, encouraging, and evangelistic. His brother Paul and sister April are also excellent bible teachers ("Our History," 2023). There are many great churches throughout the United States that are making a difference and impact, such as the Church for the Nations in Phoenix, Arizona. Pastor Dr. Michael Maiden is a very gifted and prophetic minister with a vision to establish 10,000 churches throughout America and the world. And as the name conveys, the church is composed of a very diverse composite of people from every race, color, and many countries of the world. And isn't that what heaven will be like, every race, nation, tongue, and country represented? There will not be any segregation or prejudice in heaven (*My Church, My Family*, 2023).

And there are many heroes all over America, like pastors and their staff who faithfully serve the Lord in their congregations year after year, or little grandmothers in Texas, Oklahoma, and Tennessee who pray and intercede daily for their children and grandchildren and the future of this great nation. Moms and dads in the cities and in the country who work and keep their wheels spinning while they love and raise their children in the Lord. And the police and firemen throughout America who protect and serve their communities in increasingly uncertain times. Firemen are like evangelists, trying to pull and save everyone that they can from the fire. And like the pilgrims and pioneers who went before us, carving the trails of hope and vision, led by God. Also, the great military veterans and soldiers of past and present bravely guarding our shores. "Let the heroes arise…"

Major Lynn Gordon Ray flying over Mt. Saint Helen

CHAPTER 30

Destiny to Win

God never promised mankind a pain-free, problem-free journey through life and route to heaven. But He did promise us that He would never leave or forsake us on this journey (Hebrews 13:5, NIV). We can have a great confidence and trust in God as we focus on Him and His promises, knowing that it's our destiny to win. The world has been shaking, and it could very well intensify (Hebrews 12:25–29, NIV). But God and a great cloud of witnesses are cheering us on because they want us to overcome and finish strong. Run your race with perseverance, fixing your eyes on Jesus (Hebrews 12:1–3, NIV).

The apostle Paul stated, "For our light and momentary troubles are achieving for us an eternal glory that far outweighs them all" (2 Corinthians 4:17, NIV). The spirit of God had already taken the apostle Paul to heaven once to allow him to see it, and he realized that no matter what temporal adversities and afflictions he faced, there awaited him an eternal place of rest and reward. That enabled him to press through anything and everything (2 Corinthians 12:1–10, NIV). The battle that is raging around us is first spiritual and manifests in the natural. This battle is only intensifying as we approach the end of the age.

I had once thought to myself privately and determined in my heart that I would go out swinging, fighting to the end. And then I heard Paul Crouch Jr. say the same thing publicly (Crouch, 2023). Mature Christianity puts on the armor of God, keeps it on, and keeps moving forward regardless of the circumstances and what you see, hear, or feel. Jesus won the victory, and all who follow Him will share in that victory (Revelation 21:1–8, NIV).

Every believer and member of the body of Christ is important, and we get more done and are more effective when we are in unity. And I'm not talking about pleasing and appeasing people, watering down the truth so we can all get along, or embracing a culture where you compromise biblical truth. But I am talking about knowing your identity and being aware that the body of Christ and believers is composed of many different members serving in various capacities for a greater kingdom purpose (1 Corinthians chapter 12, NIV). And there are many of us who have had great losses, hurt, trauma, and woundedness, but God is faithful and a healer of the brokenhearted. Yes, there is an ultimate healing that we will experience in heaven, but God starts the process in the here and now.

For some of you, the enemy has hit you so hard that he's tried to derail the calling, the purpose, and destiny for your life. But get back up and keep praising and worshiping God in the journey you're on; you're going to make it; it's your destiny to win. And remember to travel light, letting go of the cares of this world, including bitterness, offense, hate, and unforgiveness, keeping your eyes on the high calling and the prize (Philippians 3:12–16, NIV). Winston Churchill, from his underground bunker in London during World War II, cried out to the English people on the BBC to never give in, never give in, as it was their destiny to be victorious (Churchill, 1941).

We must have a soldier's mindset as we enter this time in history (2 Timothy 2:1–7, NIV). Do not be overly concerned with or entangled in the affairs of this present world, but rather be focused on eternity, conducting our lives within that mindset. Dr. Bill Hammond recently said, "This current generation has to toughen up, or you won't make it." And he also had an admonition to the pastors and said that he hoped that they were getting the people ready for what was coming ("Bishop Bill Hamon's 2023 Word of the Lord," 2023).

Now is the time to strengthen yourself spiritually by staying in prayer and the Word of God, keeping your lamp full of oil, and being ready for His return. Develop spiritual survival skills. One of the most important things to develop is the ability to hear from God and be led by Him. One of the keys to that is walking in a right relationship with God and fellowship with the Holy Spirit. The safest place in the world might not be a physical location, but rather, to be as close to God as possible in your walk with Him. I believe that we are going to see an increase in various forms of persecution in the United States. It has gone one step beyond a culture war to spiritual doors that have been opened in this nation, where we have seen the return of idols, or rather ancient evil spirits and gross darkness covering almost every sphere in America.

So, how much time does America have left? Well, I believe that we are currently in a window and season of grace, where if the church keeps advancing, occupying, and holding the line, we can continue to see the doors and windows for the harvest to remain open. Otherwise, we could see a rapid deterioration of many factors take place. The enemy would love to push the United States into World War III and international conflict. If there is an agenda by very powerful people to topple America, darkness is always going to be behind that. The Antichrist spirit is continuing to look for ways to accelerate and advance its agenda. In America, the digitization of money would be one more step towards control, along with controlling the distribution of food and water.

It states in Revelation 20:10 (NKJV): "The devil, who deceived them, was cast into the lake of fire and brimstone where the beast and the false prophet are. And they will be tormented day and night forever and ever." And then Revelation 20:11–15 (NKJV) talks about the Great White Throne Judgment:

> Then I saw a great white throne, and he who sat on it, from whose face the earth and the heaven fled away. And there was no place for them. And I saw the dead, small and great, standing before God, and books were opened. And another book was opened, which is the Book of Life. And the dead were judged according to

> their works, by the things which were written in the books. The sea gave up the dead who were in it, and Death and Hades delivered up the dead who were in them. And they were judged, each one according to his works. Then Death and Hades were cast into the lake of fire. This is the second death, and anyone not found written in the Book of Life was cast into the lake of fire.

It is written in 2 Peter 3:9–10a (NKJV): "The Lord is not slack concerning His promise, as some count slackness, but is longsuffering toward us, not wishing that any should perish, but that all should come to repentance. But the day of the Lord will come as a thief in the night...." What Peter is saying here is that the Lord will return as He promised, but since He would that none should perish, He is delaying His return until the final harvest is drawn in, including you, if you have not asked Jesus to be your Lord and Savior. So, please, if you have not done that yet, pray now so you do not go to that dreadful place called the lake of fire forever.

Jesus, come into my life and heart, be my Lord and my Savior. Change and transform me into who You want me to be by the power of the Holy Spirit. I repent of my sins and choose to follow You all the days of my life. Amen.

Chapter 21 of the book of Revelation talks about God making

all things new, a new heaven and new earth, and the holy city, the New Jerusalem, coming down out of heaven. Revelation 21:3–5 (NKJV) states,

> And I heard a loud voice from heaven saying, "Behold, the tabernacle of God is with men, and he will dwell with them, and they shall be his people. God himself will be with them and be their God. And God will wipe away every tear from their eyes; there shall be no more death, no sorrow, no crying. There shall be no more pain, for the former things have passed away."
>
> Then He who sat on the throne said, "Behold, I make all things new." And He said to me, "Write, for these words are true and faithful."

God does not send anyone to hell; you must choose to reject Jesus to end up there. So, choose life, choose Jesus, and keep praying for America because it is your destiny to win.

Destiny to Win

"DESTINY TO WIN"

There's a call of God upon us

to leave our present blessing,

a move into the destiny of God,

to lose our present comforts

for a greater blessing future;

your birthing into destiny will require.

It's our destiny to win,

to wear the victor's crown;

yet our lives, we must lay down

at His feet;

it's our destiny to win,

to wear the victor's crown;

yet our lives, we must lay down

at His feet.

The Master's plan requires of us

to lose our lives to gain them;

submit our desires to greater plan of God.

Oh, could you not tarry

an hour for the power

He longs to fill His warriors with

the victory He's equipped us to win.

It's our destiny to conquer,

to wear the victor's crown;

yet our lives, we must lay down

at His feet.

It's our destiny to conquer,

The Rise and Fall of the American Empire

to wear the victor's crown.

A living sacrifice we are to Him.

Whoooh!

There's a call of God upon us

to leave our present blessing,

a move into the destiny of God,

to lose our present comforts

for a greater blessing future;

your birthing into destiny will require.

It's our destiny to win,

to wear the victor's crown;

yet our lives, we must lay down

at His feet.

It's our destiny to win,

to wear the victor's crown;

yet our lives, we must lay down

at His feet, at His feet…

It's our destiny to win,

to wear the victor's crown;

yet our lives, we must lay down

at His feet.

it's our destiny to win,

to wear the victor's crown;

yet our lives, we must lay down

at His feet, at His feet…

It's our destiny to win,

to wear the victor's crown;

Destiny to Win

yet our lives, we must lay down
at His feet.
It's our destiny to triumph,
to wear the victor's crown;
yet our lives, we must lay down
at His feet.
It's our destiny to triumph;
it's our destiny to conquer;
it's our destiny to win, to win…

D. S. Prescott

July 7, 1983

To hear the audio version of "Destiny to Win," go to Douglas Prescott's YouTube channel.

EPILOGUE

One of my hopes and objectives with *The Rise and Fall of the American Empire* was to combine history and stories of people from all walks of life to show how God has moved in America in multitudes of ways from the very beginning. I believe that the early Pilgrims and pioneers foundationally dedicated America to God and His purposes. But is America still a Christian nation? That would certainly be a good discussion as an increasing number and percentage of Americans no longer identify with Christianity. Besides trying to create an interesting book with many stories, one of my main purposes was evangelism. If you are already a believer, I hope that this book edified and encouraged you in some way. And if you, like the prodigal, have fallen away, jump back on the Gospel train because hell's train is quickly accelerating towards doom. And if you have never considered the claims of Christ before, get into the New Testament and read the words of Jesus as He can change and transform your life. And if you love America, let's do what we can to hold the line while we still have time.

Love in Christ,

D. S. Prescott

ABOUT THE AUTHOR

D. S. Prescott was born on October 28, the same day that the Statue of Liberty was dedicated at Ellis Island, that great symbol of freedom and America itself. There were still many horses and cattle in Arizona in the late 1950s, where he was born. You could still hear the call of the wild in the desert mountains and see a wisp of connection to the memories of the old West.

D. S. Prescott lived for a time, in his youth, on a small ranch outside of Kingman, Arizona, at the foot of the Hualapai Mountains. It was a time when there was still prayer in school and the pledge of allegiance when you looked people in the eye and said, "Yes, sir," and "No, ma'am."

Yes, it was a different America sixty years ago when the children would gather and sing "You're a Grand Old Flag"!

At age thirteen, at a campus crusade for Christ Rally, D. S. Prescott made his first commitment of faith. Then, in his early twenties, he began to earnestly study the scriptures and consistently attend church.

After a few years, and after receiving the baptism of the Holy Spirit, D. S. Prescott went to Israel to live and share his faith with the people. Prior to living in Israel, he also joined a group of 300k individuals who would pray for America and intercede for the world harvest. It was during this time in Israel that he had a vision to sing for the Lord. Upon returning to Arizona and the States, he also began to develop his writing skills, penning some 600 songs and recording "The Winds of Change" EP.

D. S. Prescott was also in the choir and praise teams and was a worship leader through the years. Even as early as 1981, he had the idea for *The Rise and Fall of the American Empire* and wrote out the preliminary outline. He also has numerous insightful books waiting to go into production behind his first book. He is also in the early stages of raising up ZPF, Zackary Prayer Force, a group of intercessors committed to praying for the youth and children of America.

D. S. Prescott still resides in Arizona with his wife, Arnelly, and family.

BIBLIOGRAPHY

n.d.

2012. "1957 New York Crusade." The Billy Graham Library, June 1. Accessed September 16, 2023. https://www.billygrahamlibrary.org/1957-new-york-crusade.

2019. "70th Anniversary Greater Los Angeles Billy Graham Crusade of 1949." The Billy Graham Library, September 25. Accessed September 16, 2023. https://www.billygrahamlibrary.org/70th-anniversary-greater-los-angeles-billy-graham-crusade-of-1949.

2022. "A Short History of Jamestown." Washington, DC: National Park Service, September 16. Accessed Jun 3, 2023. https://www.nps.gov/james/learn/historyculture/a-short-history-of-jamestown.htm.

n.d., "A True Declaration of the Estate of the Colonie in Virginia, with a Confutation of Such Scandalous Reports as Have Tended to the Disgrace of So Worthy an Enterprise." Virtual Jamestown. Accessed June 3, 2023. www.virtualjamestown.org/exist/cocoon/jamestown/fha/J1059.

n.d., "About Pastor Benny Hinn." Grapevine, Texas: Benny Hinn Ministries. Accessed July 10, 2023. https://www.bennyhinn.org/about/.

n.d., "About Pastor Benny Hinn." Grapevine, Texas: Benny Hinn Ministries. Accessed August 1, 2023. https://www.benny-hinn.org/about.

n.d., "About Richard Roberts Ministries." Richard Roberts Ministries. Accessed September 13, 2023. https://www.richardroberts.org/about.

2009. "Abraham Lincoln." New York, New York: History.com, October 29. Accessed June 14, 2023. https://www.history.com/topics/us-presidents/abraham-lincoln.

2022. "Abraham Lincoln's Assassination." New York, New York: History.com, January 28. Accessed June 15, 2023. https://history.com/topics/american-civil-war/abraham-lincoln-assassination.

2021. "Adolf Hitler's Biography." New York, New York: Biography.com, March 26. Accessed September 9, 2023. https://www.biography.com/political-figures/adolf-hitler.

2022. "Aimee Semple McPherson." Chicago, Illinois: Encyclopedia Britannica, March 10. Accessed July 12, 2023. https://www.britannica.com/biography/Aimee-Semple-McPherson.

n.d., "Aimee Semple McPherson's Biography." Encyclopedia of World Biography. Accessed July 11, 2023. https://wwwnotablebiographies.com/Ma-Mo/McPherson-Aimee-Semple.html.

n.d., "Aimee Simple McPherson: Foursquare Phenomenon." Christianity Today. Accessed July 11, 2023. https://www.christianitytoday.com/history/people/denominational-founders/aimee-semple-mcpherson.html.

2023. "Allied Invasion of Sicily." Chicago, Illinois: Encyclopedia Britannica, August 25. Accessed September 1, 2023. https://www.britannica.com/topic/Allied-Invasion-of-Sicily.

2023. "Allies Prepare for D-Day." New York, New York: History.com, June 13. Accessed September 2, 2023. https://www.history.com/this-day-in-history/allies-prepare-for-d-day.

Allmond, Joy. 2021. "Johnny Cash's Faith and Friendship with Billy Graham." Billy Graham Evangelistic Association, February 22. Accessed October 2, 2023. https://www.billygraham.org/story/johnny-cash-faith-and-friendship-with-billy-graham.

Almagia, Roberto, 2023. "Amerigo Vespucci: Italian Navigator." Chicago, Illinois: Encyclopedia Britannica, May 2. Accessed June 1, 2023. https://www.britannica.com/biography/Amerigo-Vespucci.

Andrews, Evan, 2016. "The Siege of Leningrad." New York, New York: History.com, September 8. Accessed August 4, 2023. https://www.history.com/news/the-siege-of-leningrad.

Asay, Paul, 2018. "The Complex Christian Legacy of Elvis Presley." Aleteia, August 18. Accessed October 4, 2023. https://aleteia.org/2018/08/18/the-complex-christian-legacy-of-elvis/.

2023. "Assassination of John F. Kennedy." History.com, April 25. Accessed October 10, 2023. https://www.history.com/topics/us-president/jfk-assassination.

2020. "Assassination Plot against Hitler Fails." New York, New York: History.com, July 17. Accessed September 9, 2023. https://www.history.com/this-day-in-history/assassination-plot-against-hitler-fails.

2019. "Baby Boomers." History.com, June 7. Accessed October 1, 2023. https://www.history.com/topics/1960s/baby-boomers-1.

Bakalian, Anny. 2023. "How Armenians Came to America and What They'll Never Forget." New England Historical Society.com. Boston, Massachusetts: New England Historical Society.com. Accessed July 4, 2023. https://newenglandhistoricalsociety.com/how-armenias-came-to-america-and-what-theyll-never-forget/.

Balmer, Randall, 2023. "Billy Graham: American Evangelist." Illinois, Chicago: Encyclopedia Britannica, August 18. Accessed September 15, 2023. https://www.britannica.com/biography/Billy-Graham.

Bibliography

2022. "Bataan Death March." New York, New York: History. com, December 12. Accessed August 12, 2023. https://www.history.com/topics/world-war-ii/baatan-death-march.

2022. "Battle of Britain." New York, New York: History.com, November 15. Accessed August 3, 2023. https://www.history.com/topics/war-world-ii/battle-of-britain-1.

2020. "Battle of the Bulge." New York, New York: History.com, July 22. Accessed September 9, 2023. https://www.history.com/topics/worl-war-ii/battle-of-the-bulge.

Bertram, Colin. 2021. "Johnny Cash Described His Love for June Carter as 'Unconditional': Inside Their Love Story." Biography.com, March 3. Accessed October 3, 2023. https://www.biography.com/musicians/johnny-cash-june-carter-love-story-relationship.

2021. "Billy Graham's Biography." Biography.com, May 6. Accessed September 16, 2023. https://www.biography.com/religious-figures/billy-graham.

2022. "Billy Sunday." Chicago, Illinois: Encyclopedia Britannica, September 2. Accessed July 3, 2023. https://www.britannica.com/biography/Billy-Sunday.

2016. "Biography of Kathryn Kuhlman." Believers Portal. September 15. Accessed August 2, 2023.

2016. "Biography of Kenneth E. Hagin." Believers Portal, September 16. Accessed September 12, 2023. https://www.believersportal.com/biography-kenneth-e-hagin/.

2016. "Biography of Oral Roberts." Believers Portal, September 6. Accessed September 12, 2023. https://www.beliviersportal.com/biography-oral-roberts/.

Bishop, David. 2019. "The Shoes of Martin Luther King Jr.'s Childhood." Woeful Living, January 21. Accessed October 16, 2023. https://www.wowfulliving.com/the-shoes-of-martin-luther-king-jrs-childhood.

Bland, Sean. 2020. "Admiral John S. McCain and the Triumph of Naval Airpower." Washington, DC: Naval Historical Foundation, April 21. Accessed August 14, 2023. https://www.navyhistory.org/2020/04/admiral-john-s-mccain.

2019. "Block Island." Chicago, Illinois: Encyclopedia Britannica, July 23. Accessed June 7, 2023. https://www.britannica.com/place/Block-Island.

Blumhofer, Edith, 2006. "Azusa Street Revival: Historiography of Pentecostalism." The Christian Century, March 7. Accessed July 6, 2023. https://christiancentury.org/article/2006-03/azusa-street-revival.

Boissoneault, Lorraine. 2015. "L'Anse Aux Meadows and the Viking Discovery of North America." *Jstor Daily.* New York, New York: Ithaka Harbors, Inc., July 23. Accessed

Bibliography

June 1, 2023. https://daily.jstor.org/anse-aux-meadows-and-the-viking-discovery-of-north-america.

Bolton, David A., n.d. "History of Mission San Diego de Alcala." California Mission Foundation. Accessed Jun 8, 2023. https://californiamissionsfoundation.org/mission-san-diego-de-alcala/.

2023. "Bombing of Hiroshima and Nagasaki." New York, New York: History.com, April 18. Accessed September 11, 2023. https://www.history.com/topics/worl-war-ii/bombing-of-hiroshima-and-nagasaki.

Brill, Marlene Targ, 2010. *America in the 1900s.* Minneapolis, Minnesota.
—. 2010. *America in the 1900s.* Minneapolis, USA: Twenty-First Century Books.

Brown, Kevin, 2024. "What the Asbury Revival Taught Me about Gen Z." Christianity Today, February 12. Accessed February 15, 2024. https://www.christianitytoday.com/ct/2024/march/asbury-revival-taught-me-about-gen-z-casual-christianity.html.

Burak, Emily, 2023. "The Story behind John F. Kennedy Jr.'s Salute at JFK's Funeral." Town and Country, November 22. Accessed November 23, 2023. https://www.townandcountrymag.com/society/tradition/a45836421/john-jr-salute-father-jfk-funeral-true-story.

2022. "California Gold Rush." New York, New York: History. com, August 10. Accessed June 13, 2013. https://www. history.com/topics/19th-century/gold-rush-of-1849.

Carson, Clayborne and Lewis, David L., 2023. "Martin Luther King Jr." Chicago, Illinois: Encyclopedia Britannica, October 5. Accessed October 14, 2023. https://www.britannica.com/biography/Martin-Luther-King-Jr.

Cash, Johnny, 1973. "Gospel Road: A Story of Jesus." March 31. Accessed October 3, 2023. https://www.johnnycash.com/film/gospel-road-a-story-of-jesus/.

Cash, Johnny, 2022. "The Story behind Johnny Cash and Sam Phillips: Sun Records." The Trail, July 28. Accessed October 3, 2023. https://www.folsomcasharttrail.com/the-trail/blog/the-story-behind-johnny-cash-and-sam-phillips-sun-records.

Cauchi, Tony., n.d. "William Seymour and the History of the Azusa Street Outpouring." Revival Library. Accessed July 6, 2023. https://revival-library.org/%20revival-heroes/20th-21st-century-heroes/american-pentecostal-heroes-main/william-seymour/.

2023. "Cesar Chavez." History.com, September 26. Accessed October 13, 2023. https://www.history.com/topics/hispanic-history/cesar-chavez.

2023. "Cesar Chavez's Biography and Career Timeline." PBS,

Bibliography

August 24. Accessed October 14, 2023. https://www.pbs.org/wnet/americanmasters/cesar-chavez-biography-and-career-timeline/28703.

2019. "Cesar Chavez's Biography." Biography.com, September 9. Accessed October 13, 2023. https://www.biography.com/activists/cesar-chavez.

2023. "Cesar Chavez: American Labor Leader." Chicago, Illinois: Encyclopedia Britannica, August 8. Accessed October 13, 2023. https://www.britannica.com/biography/Cesar-Chavez.

Chang, Rachel, 2021. "How Mahalia Jackson Sparked Martin Luther King Jr's 'I Have a Dream' Speech." A&E Networks, March 29. Accessed October 18, 2023. https://www.biography.com/musicians/mahalia-jackson-i-have-a-dream-influence.

2020. "Charles Grandison Finney: American Evangelist." Chicago, Illinois: Encyclopedia Britannica, May 22. Accessed June 12, 2023. https://www.britannica.com/biography/Charles-Grandison-Finney.

2020. "Charles Lindbergh." New York, New York: History.com, May 6. Accessed July 8, 2023. https://www.history.com/topics/exploration/charles-a-lindbergh.

2017. "Chester W. Nimitz." Chicago, Illinois: Encyclopedia Britannica, January 17. Accessed August 13, 2023. https://www.britannica.com/biography/Chester-W-Nimitz.

2023. "Chiang Kai-shek." Chicago, Illinois: Encyclopedia Britannica, August 14. Accessed August 15, 2023. https://www.britannica.com/biography/Chiang-Kai-Shek.

2023. "Civil War." New York, New York: History.com, April 20. Accessed June 16, 2023. https://www.history.com/topics/american-civil-war/american-civil-war-history.

Cole, Rachel, 2023. "Pat Boone." Encyclopedia Britannica, May 28. Accessed October 8, 2023. https://www.britannica.com/biography/Pat-Boone.

Comford, David, 2010. "Elvis, Gladys, and Their Double Doomdate." The Wrap, August 15. Accessed October 5, 2023. https://www.thewrap.com/there-goes-my-everything-elvis-gladys-rip-20137/.

Connolly, Ray, 2017. *Being Elvis: A Lonely Life.* New York: Liveright Publishing Corporation.

2015. "Cornelius 'Cornie' Vanderbreggen Jr." Find a Grave, March 1. Accessed October 18, 2023. https://www.findagrave.com/memorial/143202847/cornelius-vanderbreggen.

Bibliography

2013. "Crouch Family's Deep Roots in Assemblies of God." Charisma News, December 6. Accessed October 19, 2023. https://www.charismanews.com/news/us/crouch-family-s-deep-roots-in-assemblies-of-god/.

Cunningham, John M., 2023. "Roaring Twenties." Chicago, Illinois: Encyclopedia Britannica, June 23. Accessed July 6, 2023. https://www.britannica/topic/Roaring-Twenties.

Current, R. N., 2023. "Abraham Lincoln." Chicago, Illinois: Encyclopaedia Britannica, April 11. Accessed June 15, 2023. https://www.britannica.com/biography/Abraham-Lincoln.

D-Day Veterans. 2004. "Bob Littlar's D-Day: 2nd Battalion King's Shropshire Light Infantry." London: BBC, April 16. Accessed September 7, 2023. https://www.bbc.co.uk/history/ww2peopleswar/stories/39/a2524439.shtml.

n.d., "D. L. Moody." Chicago, Illinois: Moody Bible Institute. Accessed July 1, 2023. https://www.moody.edu/about/our-bold-legacy/d-l-moody.

Dawson, Shay, 2015. "Harriet Tubman: 1822–1913." National Women's History Museum. Washington, DC. Accessed June 12, 2023. https://www.womenshistory.org/education-resources/biographies/harriet-tubman.

De Arteaga, William, 2019. "Demos Shakarian and His Ecumenical Businessmen." 50 Pentecostal Theology, October 27. Accessed July 4, 2023. https://www.pentecostaltheology.

com/demos-sakarian-and-the-his-ecumenical-business-men.

Deak, Megan, 2023. "The Portuguese Colonization of the Americas." Montreal, Quebec: World Atlas, January 25. Accessed June 7, 2023. https://www.worldatlas.com/history/the-portuguese-colonization-of-the-americas.html.

Dean, Mack, 2021. "Battle of Bastogne Facts." World War II Facts, April 17. Accessed September 9, 2023. https://www.worldwar2facts.org/battle-of-bastogne.html.

Dooley, Sean, 2019. "The History of Country Music." Liveaboutdotcom, May 23. Accessed October 3, 2023. https://www.liveabout.com/the-history-of-country-music-934030.

2021. "Doolittle Leads Air Raid on Tokyo." New York, New York: History.com, April 15. Accessed August 12, 2023. https://www.history.com/this-day-in-history/doolittle-leads-air-raid-on-tokyo.

2023. "Dunkirk Evacuation." Chicago, Illinois: Encyclopedia Britannica, Jun 30. Accessed August 3, 2023. https://www.britannica.com/event/Dunkirk-evacuation.

Dunn, R. S., 2023. "John Winthrop: American Colonial Governor." Chicago, Illinois: Encyclopedia Britannica, April 1. Accessed June 9, 2023. https://www.britannica.com/biography/John-Winthrop-American-colonial-governor.

Bibliography

2009. "Dust Bowl." New York, New York: History.com, October 27. Accessed July 8, 2023. https://www.history.com/topics/great-depression/dust-bowl.

2021. Dwight D. "Eisenhower's Biography." New York, New York: A&E Networks, April 13. Accessed September 5, 2023. https://www.biography.com/political-figures/dwight-d-eisenhower.

2021. "Dwight L. Moody." Chicago, Illinois: Encyclopedia Britannica, May 8. Accessed July 1, 2023. https://www.britannica.com/biography/Dwight-L-Moody.

n.d., "Early Twentieth Century US." New York, New York: History.com. Accessed July 2, 2023. https://www.history.com/topics/early-20th-century-us.

n.d., "Early Childhood." Graceland.com. Accessed October 4, 2023. https://www.graceland.com/early-childhood.

Eccles, W., 2022. "Jacques Cartier." Chicago, Illinois: Encyclopedia Britannica, May 3. Accessed June 7, 2023. https://www.britannica.com/biography/Jacques-Cartier.

Eig, Jonathan, 2023. *King: A Life.* New York: Farrar, Strauss and Giroux.

Eisenger, Sara, 2023. "Local Renewal of Historic 1607 Covenant with God." Prod. Soo Leader. Sault Ste. Marie, Michigan: Sooleader.com, April 25. Accessed June 3, 2023. https://

www.sooleader.com/local-news/local-renewal-of-historic-1607-covenant-with-god-6903153.

Eliot Morison, Samuel, 2011. *Of Plymouth Plantation: 1620–1647.* New York, New York: Alfred A. Knopf. Accessed Jun 5, 2023.

2023. "Elvis Presley Records 'That's All Right (Mama).'" History.com, July 6. Accessed October 4, 2023. https://www.history.com/this-day-in-history/elvis-presley-records-thats-all-right-mama.

2021. "Elvis Presley: The Tragic Story of His Twin Brother, Jesse Garon Presley." Outsider.com, February 24. Accessed October 4, 2023. https://www.outsider.com/entertainment/elvis-presley-the-tragic-story-of-his-twin-brother-jesse-garon-presley/.

Fairchild, Mary, 2019. "George Whitefield—Spellbinding Evangelist of the Great Awakening." New York, New York: Learn Religious, June 25. Accessed June 9, 2023. https://www.learnreligions.com/george-whitefield-4689110.

Finney G., Charles, 1988. "Lectures on Revival." Minneapolis, Minnesota: Bethany House Publishers. Accessed May 29, 2023.

Fitzgerald, Claire, 2021. "Elvis Presley Played a Role in Elton John Becoming Sober." The Vintage News, November 3. Accessed October 5, 2023. https://www.thevintagenews.com/2021/11/03/elvis-presley-elton-john-meeting.

Bibliography

1995. "For America, It Truly Was a Great War." The New York Times Magazine, May 7. Accessed October 1, 2023. https://www.nytimes.com/1995/05/07/magazine/for-america-it-truly-was-a-great-war.html.

n.d., "Fort Nassau: A Tour of New Netherland." New York, New York: New Netherland Institute. Accessed June 7, 2023. https://www.newnetherlandinstitute.org/history-and-heritage/digital-exhibitions/a-tour-of-new-netherland/delaware/fort-nassau.

2018. "Founders' Biographies." Trinity Broadcasting Network. Accessed October 20, 2023. https://tbnfounders.org/founders-biographies/.

Foust, Michael, 2009. "Pistol Pete's Faith Gets New Spotlight." Baptist Press, April 2. Accessed August 2, 2023. https://www.baptistpress.com/resource-library/news/pistol-petes-faith-gets-new-spotlight/.

Foy, Chris, 2018. "Johnny Cash's Long Struggle with Drugs and Sobriety." FHE Health, August 27. Accessed October 3, 2023. https://fherehab.com/news/johnny-cashs-struggle-with-addiction/.

Frank, F., 2021. "The Truth about Elvis Presley's Friendship with Johnny Cash." Grunge, December 20. Accessed October 3, 2023. https://www.grunge.com/595910/the-truth-about-elvis-presleys-friendship-with-johnny-cash.

2020. "Franklin D. Roosevelt." New York, New York: Biography.com, March 12. Accessed July 8, 2023. https://www.biography.com/political-figures/franklin-d-roosevelt.

Fraser, Rebecca, 2017. *The Mayflower: The Families, the Voyage, and the Founding of America.* New York, New York: St. Martin's Press. Accessed May 30, 2023.

2021. "George Whitefield: British Clergyman." Chicago, Illinois: Encyclopedia Britannica, June 18. Accessed June 8, 2023. https://www.britannica.com/biography/George-Whitefield.

2021. "Germany Surrenders Unconditionally to the Allies at Reims." New York, New York: History.com, May 4. Accessed September 9, 2023. https://www.history.com/this-day-in-history/germany-surrenders-unconditionally-to-the-allies-at-reims.

Gilbert, A. 2023. "Battle of Crete." Chicago, Illinois, May 13. Accessed August 4, 2023. https://www.britannica.com/topic/battle-of-crete.

Glass, Andrew, 2018. "Truman Sworn in as 33rd President, April 12, 1945." Politico.com, April 12. Accessed September 10, 2023. https://www.politico.com/story/2018/04/12/harry-truman-sworn-in-as-33rd-president-april-12-1945-511037.

Bibliography

Glossyfied.com Editors, 2022. "Johnny Cash and Drugs: The Music Icon's Lifelong Struggle with Addiction." Glossyfied.com, December 17. Accessed October 5, 2023. https://www.glossyfied.com/johnny-cash-and-drugs-the-music-icons-lifelong-struggle-with-addiction/.

Gopnik, Adam and Wilfred and Beeman, Richard Owen, 2023. "Imperial Organization." Chicago, Illinois, May 15. Accessed June 8, 2023. https://www.britannica.com/place/United-States/Imperial-organization.

Görlitz, Walter Otto Julius, 2023. "Erwin Rommel." Chicago, Illinois: Encyclopedia Britannica, August 7. Accessed September 1, 2023. https://www.britannica.com/biography/Erwin-Rommel.

Graham, Billy, 2020. "America at the Crossroads." Decision: The Evangelical Voice, September 21. Accessed September 14, 2023. https://www.decisionmagazine.com/billy-graham-america-at-the-crossroads.

Graham, Billy. 2021. "Billy & Ruth Graham—A Love Story for the Ages." The Billy Graham Library, August 13. Accessed September 15, 2023. https://www.billygrahamlibrary.org/blog-love-story-for-the-ages/.

Graham, Billy, n.d. "List of Billy Graham's Crusades." Wikiwand.com. Accessed September 16, 2023. https://www.wikiwand.com/en/List_of_Billy_Graham%27s_crusades.

—. 1981. *Till Armageddon: A Perspective on Suffering.* Waco, Texas: Word Books.

Graham, Franklin Toney, Donna Lee, 2018. *Through My Father's Eyes.* Nashville: W Publishing Group.

2009. "Great Depression." New York, New York: History.com, October 29. Accessed July 9, 2023. https://www.history.com/topics/great-depression/great-depression-history.

Greenspan, Jesse, 2014. "Landing at Normandy: The 5 Beaches of D-Day." New York, New York: A&E Networks, June 6. Accessed September 5, 2023. https://www.history.com/news/landing-at-normandy-the-5-beaches-of-d-day.

Greenspan, Jesse, 2018. "Remembering the Great San Francisco Earthquake of 1906." New York, New York: A&E Networks, October 19. Accessed July 4, 2023. https://www.history.com/news/remembering-the-great-san-francisco-earthquake-of-1906.

Groeneveld, Emma, 2018. "Leif Erikson." Prod. World History Encyclopedia. Horsham: World History Publishing Ltd, September 20. Accessed June 1, 2023. https://www.worldhistory.org/Leif_Erikson.

Groom, Winston, 2015. "The Generals: Patton, MacArthur, Marshall, and Winning of World War II." Washington: National Geographic.

Bibliography

Hagin, Kenneth E., 2021. "Full Testimony of How Kenneth E. Hagin Received His Miraculous Healing on His Deathbed." Therismos Foundation, September 25. Accessed September 12, 2023. https://www.youtube.com/watch?v=BCKNeDPscDk.

—. 1997. *The Healing Anointing.* Tulsa: Kenneth Hagin Ministries.

Hagin, Kenneth E., n.d. *The Healing Anointing.* Tulsa, Oklahoma: Kenneth Hagin Ministries.

Hagin, Kenneth, 1997. *The Healing Anointing.* Tulsa: Kenneth Hagin Ministries.

2023. "Hal Lindsey: Media Ministries." Daystar Television Network. Accessed November 5, 2023. https://daystar.com/hal-lindsey.

2008. *The Early Years of Billy Graham.* Directed by Robby Benson. Produced by Cinedigm. Performed by Armie Hammer. Accessed September 14, 2023. https://www.amazon.com/Billy-Early-Years-Graham/dp/B07DD11CVF.

Hanson, Alan, 2011. "Elvis Presley Endured Criticism from Religious Leaders in 1950s." Elvis History Blog, February. Accessed October 5, 2023. http://www.elvis-history-blog.com/elvis-religious-criticism.html.

2021. "Harry S. Truman's Biography." New York, New York: Biography.com, April 15. Accessed September 11, 2023. https://www.biography.com/political-figures/harry-s-truman.

2021. "Harry S. Truman's Biography." New York, New York: Biography.com, April 15. Accessed September 10, 2023. https://www.biography.com/political-figures/harry-s-truman.

Hassler, W. W. and Weber, Jennifer L., 2023. "American Civil War: United States History." Chicago, Illinois: Encyclopaedia Britannica, May 11. Accessed June 16, 2023. https://www.britannica.com/event/American-Civil-War.

2023. *Healing Time with Dr. Doug Weiss.* Daystar Television Network. Accessed November 2, 2023. https://daystar.com/doug-weiss.

Heitmann, John, 2015. "The Golden Age of the Automobile in America: The 1950s: The Automobile and American Life." March 27. Accessed October 1, 2023. https://www.automobileandamericanlife.blogspot.com/2015/03/the-golden-age-of-automobile-in-america.html.

2023. "Henry Hudson." History.com. New York, New York: A&E Networks, June 6. Accessed June 7, 2023. https://www.history.com/topics/exploration/henry-hudson.

Bibliography

"I Am God's Witness," 2022. "The True Life Miracle Story of Kathryn Kuhlman's Death." August 19. Accessed August 2, 2023. https://www.youtube.com/watch?v=8-NxGd-JRbb4.

2021. "I Went to Hell: Kenneth E. Haggin's Testimony." Pentecostal Theology, July 13. Accessed September 12, 2023. https://www.pentecostaltheology.com/i-went-to-hell-kenneth-e-hagins-testimony.

2022. "In 1603, Martin Pring Escapes New England with His Tail between His Legs." Boston, Massachusetts: New England Historical Society. Accessed June 1, 2023. https://newenglandhistoricalsociety.com/in-1603-martin-pring-escapes-new-england-with-his-tail-between-his-legs/.

n.d., "Invasion of Manchuria." Independence, Missouri: Harry S. Truman Library. Accessed August 10, 2023. https://www.trumanlibrary.gov/education/presidential-inquiries/invasion-manchuria.

2021. "Isoroku Yamamoto, Japan's Mastermind of the Pearl Harbor Attack, Is Born." New York, New York: History.com, April 1. Accessed August 12, 2023. https://www.history.comthis-day-in-history/yamamoto-isoroku-japans-mastermind-of-the-pearl-harbor-attack-is-born.

n.d., "Jacobson, Edward Papers." Harry S. Truman Library and Museums. Accessed October 1, 2023. https://www.

trumanlibrary.org/library/personal-papers/edward-jacob-son-papers.

2019. "Java Sea." Chicago, Illinois: Encyclopedia Britannica, March 5. Accessed August 12, 2023. https://www.britannica.com/place/Java-Sea#ref250491.

2023. "John Curtin." Chicago, Illinois: Encyclopedia Britannica, July 1. Accessed August 12, 2023. https://www.britannica.com/biography/John-Curtin.

2009. "John Paul Jones." New York, New York: History.com, October 29. Accessed June 11, 2023. https://www.history.com/topics/american-revolution/john-paul-jones.

2023. "Johnny Cash." New York, New York: Biography.com, September 12. Accessed October 3, 2023. https://www.biography.com/musicians/johnny-cash.

2022. "Johnny Cash and Drugs: The Music Icon's Lifelong Struggle with Addiction." Glossyfield, December 17. Accessed October 2023. https://www.glossyfied.com/johnny-cash-and-drugs-the-music-icons-lifelong-struggle-with-addiction/.

n.d., "Johnny Cash's Biography." The Famous People. Accessed October 2, 2023. https://www.thefamouspeople.com/profiles/john-r-cash-1978.php.

2014. "Johnny Cash, Joseph Stalin, & the Great Morse Code

Crack." Saving Country Music, June 29. Accessed October 2, 2023. https://www.savingcountrymusic.com/johnny-cash-joseph-stalin-the-great-morse-code-crack/.

2024. "Joni Lamb." Alchetron, January 30. Accessed February 2, 2024. https://www.alchetron.com/Joni-Lamb.

2018. "Joseph Kennedy Jr." History.com, August 21. Accessed October 10, 2023. https://www.history.com/topics/us-presidents/joseph-kennedy-jr.

2009. "Joseph McCarthy." New York, New York: History.com, October 29. Accessed October 1, 2023. https://www.history.com/topics/cold-war/joseph-mccarthy.

n.d., "Kathryn Kuhlman's Biography." The Famous People. Accessed August 2, 2023. https://www.thefamouspeople.com/profiles/kathryn-kuhlman-18990.php.

Keegan, John, 2023. "Normandy Invasion World War II." Chicago, Illinois: Encyclopedia Britannica, May 30. Accessed September 7, 2023. https://www.britannica.com/event/Normandy-Invasion/Breakout-August-1944.

Kennedy, John, 2016. *Why England Slept.* Mountain View: Ishi Press.

Kennedy, Lesley, 2020. "Caesar Who? The Founding Father You've Probably Never Heard Of." New York, New York: A&E Networks, September 18. Accessed June 11,

2023. https://www.history.com/news/founding-father-you-never-heard-of-caesar-rodney.

Kiger, Patrick, 2021. "How Thomas Paine's 'Common Sense' Helped Inspire the American Revolution." New York, New York: A&E Networks, June 28. Accessed June 11, 2023. https://www.history.com/news/thomas-paine-common-sense-revolution.

Kiger, Patrick J., 2019. "Who Were the Sons of Liberty?" Prod. History.com. New York, New York: A&E Networks, August 19. Accessed June 9, 2023. https://www.history.com/news/sons-of-liberty-members-causes.

King, Daniel, 2021. "Charles F. Parham: The Topeka Outpouring of 1901, Pentecostal Origin Story." Morinville, Alberta: YouTube, January 25. Accessed July 4, 2023. https://king-ministries.com/podcast-episodes/charles-f-parham-the-topeka-outpouring-of-1901-pentecostal-origin-story/.

n.d., "King, Martin Luther Sr." The Martin Luther King Jr. Research and Education Institute, Stanford University. Accessed October 16, 2023. https://kinginstitute.stanford.edu/king-martin-luther-sr.

Klein, Christopher, 2019. "How an Assassination Attempt Affirmed MLK's Faith in Nonviolence." A&E Networks, January 15. Accessed October 17, 2023. https://www.history.com/news/martin-luther-king-1958-assassination-attempt.

Bibliography

Klett, Leah Marie Ann, 2020. "Tommy Barnett on Most Important Thing He's Learned about Holy Spirit over Decades-Long Ministry." The Christian Post, April 19. Accessed July 12, 2023. https://www.christianpost.com/news/tommy-barnett-on-most-important-thing-hes-learned-about-holy-spirit-over-decades-long-ministry.html.

Kuhlman, Kathryn, 2020. "Kathryn Kuhlman/What Matter Most/Heroes of the Faith/Oral Roberts University/1974." YouTube, December 3. Accessed August 1, 2023. https://www.youtube.com/watch?v=HKNqELlE17o.

Laird Simons, M., n.d. "Dwight Lyman Moody." *Christian Biographies.* Wholesome Words Home. Accessed July 1, 2023. https://www.wholesomewords.org/biography/bio-moody.html.

Leidner, Gordon, 2012. "The Religious Beliefs of America's Founding Fathers: Christians or Deists." December 31. Accessed June 11, 2023. https://greatamericanhistory.net/blog/the-religious-beliefs-of-americas-founding-fathers-christians-or-deists/.

Leidner, Gordon, n.d. "The Religious Beliefs of America's Founding Fathers: Christians or Deists."

Levenson, Eric and Michelle and Williams, David Watson, 2023. "Pat Robertson, Christian Televangelist and One-

Time Presidential Candidate, Dies at Age 93." CNN, June 8. Accessed October 19, 2023. https://www.cnn.com/2023/06/08/us/pat-robertson-death/index.html.

2009. "Lewis and Clark Expedition." New York, New York: History.com, November 9. Accessed June 12, 2023. https://www.history.com/topics/19th-century/lewis-and-clark.

2019. *Life Application Study Bible.* Grand Rapids, Michigan: Zondervan.

n.d., "Life of John F. Kennedy." John F. Kennedy Presidential Library and Museum. Accessed October 11, 2023. https://www.jfklibrary.org/learn/about-jfk/life-of-john-f-kennedy.

n.d., "Lincoln Quotes." Springfield, Illinois: Abraham Lincoln Presidential Library and Museum. Accessed July 7, 2023. https://presidentlincoln.illinois.gov/lincoln-quotes.

Lincoln, Abraham, 2013. "The Railsplitter—Lincoln's Writings: The Multi-Media Edition." Prod. Dickinson College. Carlisle, Pennsylvania. Accessed June 13, 2023. https://housedivided.dickinson.edu/sites/lincoln/.

Lindop, Edmund and Goldstein, Margaret J., 2010. *America in the 1920s.* Minneapolis: Twenty-First Century Books.

Little, Becky, 2022. "Pearl Harbor Wasn't Japan's Only Target." New York, New York: A&E Networks, December 5.

Bibliography

https://www.history.com/news/pearl-harbor-japan-at-tacks-territories.

2019. "Louisiana Purchase." New York, New York: History.com, June 6. Accessed June 12, 2023. https://history.com/top-ics/19th-century/louisiana-purchase.

Lovelace, Alex, 2023. "George Patton, United States General." Chicago, Illinois: Encyclopedia Britannica, February 23. Accessed September 8, 2023. https://www.britannica.com/biography/George-Smith-Patton/aditional-info#his-tory.

Manchester, William and Reid, Paul, 2012. *The Last Lion: Winston Spencer Churchill, Defender of the Realm.* New York: Little, Brown and Company.

Manchester, William, 2023. "Joseph P. Kennedy." Encyclopedia Britannica, September 2. Accessed October 10, 2023. https://www.britannica.com/biography/Joseph-P-Kenne-dy.

2023. "Manhattan Project." New York, New York: History.com, July 21. Accessed September 10, 2023. https://www.his-tory.com/topics/worl-war-ii/the-manhattan-project.

2023. "Marcus Lamb's Biography." Daystar Television Network. Accessed November 1, 2023. https://daystar.com/about-marcus-lamb.

Markel, Howard, 2018. "Elvis's Addiction Was the Perfect Prescription for an Early Death." Pbs, August 16. Accessed October 5, 2023. https://www.pbs.org/newshour/health/elvis-addiction-was-the-perfect-prescription-for-an-early-death.

Marshall, Stacie, 2015. "This 'King' Knew Who the Real King Was. So, These Struggles He Shared Really Hit Me Hard." God updates.com, January 19. Accessed October 5, 2023. https://www.godupdates.com/elvis-shares-his-struggles-with-faith/.

n.d., "Martin Luther King and the founding of SCLC." History on the Net. Accessed October 17, 2023. https://www.historyonthenet.com/martin-luther-king-jr-and-the-founding-of-sclc.

2010. "Martin Luther King Jr.'s Assassination." New York, New York: History.com, January 28. Accessed October 17, 2023. https://www.history.com/topics/black-history/martin-luther-king-jr-assassination.

2020. "Martin Luther King Jr.'s Achievements." Chicago, Illinois: Encyclopedia Britannica, October 20. Accessed October 18, 2023. https://www.britannica.com/summary/Martin-Luther-King-Jr-s-Achievements.

n.d., "Martin Luther King Jr. Was Arrested 29 Times for These So-Called Crimes." Black History. Accessed October 17, 2023. https://www.blackhistory.com/2019/11/martin-luther-king-jr-was-arrested-29-times-crimes.html.

Bibliography

Martin, Larry and Linda, n.d. "The Azuza Street Revival." Azusa Street. Accessed July 4, 2023. https://azuzastreet.org/The_Revival_Begins.htm.

Matthews, Chris, 2011. *Jack Kennedy: Elusive Hero.* New York: Simon & Schuster.

McGee, Suzanne, 2022. "When Russia Colonized North America." New York, New York: A&E Networks, September 12. Accessed June 8, 2023. https://www.history.com/news/russia-settlements-north-america-alaska-fur-trade.

McKenzie, Margo, 2014. "Thomas Dorsey's Biography." Inspirational Christians, November 29. Accessed July 07, 2023. https://www.inspirationalchristians.org/influencers/thomas-dorsey-biography.

Mead, Wendy, 2020. "Seven Facts about Franklin D. Roosevelt." Edited by Biography.com. New York, New York: A&E Networks, June 18. Accessed September 9, 2023. https://www.biography.com/political-figures/franklin-roosevelt-biography-facts.

Medianews Group, 2021. "Michigan Native Kym Douglas Adds Humor, Joy to Lifestyle Reporting." The Oakland Press, June 17. Accessed September 13, 2023. https://www.theoaklandpress.com/2020/03/09/michigan-native-kym-douglas-adds-humor-joy-to-lifestyle-reporting/.

The Rise and Fall of the American Empire

2023. *Mein Kampf.* Chicago, Illinois: Encyclopedia Britannica, July 3. Accessed August 3, 2023. https://www.britannica. com/topic/Mein-Kampf.

Melton, Gordon, 2023. "Pentecostalism." Chicago, Illinois: Encyclopedia Britannica, June 21. Accessed July 5, 2023. https://www.britannica.com/topic/Pentecostalism.

Michals, Debra, 2015. "Margaret Cochran Corbin: 1751–1800." Washington, DC: National Women's History Museum. Accessed June 10, 2023. https://www.womenshistory. org/education-resources/biographies/margaret-co-chran-corbin.

Miguel, Ken, 2016. "Survivors Recall Horror of 1906 Great Earthquake in San Francisco." *abc7news.com.* Glen-dale, California, April 18. Accessed July 4, 2023. https:// abc7news.com/110th-anniversary=of-1906-earth-quake-in-san-francisco/1297723.

2008. "Million Dollar Quartet, December 4, 1956." Sun Records, December 5. Accessed October 5, 2023. https://www. sunrecords.com/million-dollar-quartet-dec-4-1956/.

Montalti, Victoria, 2022. "Eleven Celebrities Who Are Related to US Presidents." Business Insider, May 10. Accessed October 3, 2023. https://www.businessinsider.com/celeb-rities-related-to-us-presidents.

Bibliography

Murillo, Mario, 2021. "The Price of God's Miracle-Working Power." December 26. Accessed August 2, 2023. https://mariomurillo.org/2021/12/26/the-price-of-gods-miracle-working-power-2/.

Nasuti, Guy J., 2019. "Operation Neptune; The US Navy on D-Day: 6 June 1944." Washington, DC: Naval History and Heritage Command, May 28. Accessed September 1, 2023. https://www.history.navy.mil/browse-by-topic/wars-conflicts-and-operations/world-war-ii/1944/overlord/operation-neptune.html.

2010. "Netherlands Reformed Church: Dutch Protestant Denomination." Chicago, Illinois: Encyclopedia Britannica, April 16. Accessed June 7, 2023. https://www.britannica.com/topic/Netherlands-Reformed-Church.

n.d., "Nickname Pat." The Official Site of Pat Robertson. Accessed October 18, 2023. https://www.patrobertson.com/FastFacts/nickname.asp.

2019. "Noah's Ark." Answers in Genesis, Agosto 8. Accessed July 10, 2023. https://answeringingenesis.org/noahs-ark.

Nolasco, Stephanie, 2020. "Pat Boone Recalls Meeting Pal Elvis Presley: He Was Just a Scared Young Kid." Fox News, July 24. Accessed October 8, 2023. https://www.foxnews.com/entertainment/pat-boone-elvis-presley.

Nolasco, Stephanie, 2022. "Pat Boone Says 'Moral Values' Are Missing from Today's Hollywood Films: America's Image Is Being Destroyed." Fox News, April 26. Accessed October 8, 2023. https://www.foxnews.com/entertainment/pat-boone-moral-values-hollywood-movies-the-mulligan.

Nowell, Charles E., 2023. "Spain's American Empire: The Conquests." Chicago, Illinois: Encyclopedia Britannica, April 28. Accessed June 7, 2023. https://www.britannica.com/topic/Western-colonialism/Spanish-American-empire.

Offner, Arnold A., 2000. "Truman Responds." Annapolis, Maryland: US Naval Institute, June. Accessed September 11, 2023. https://www.usni.org/magazines/naval-history-magazine/2000/june/truman-responds.

Olsen, Ted, 2003. "Weblog: Kenneth Hagin, 'Word of Faith' Preacher Dies at 86." September 1. Accessed September 12, 2023. https://www.christianitytoday.com/ct/2003/septemberweb-only/9-22-11.0.html.

2022. "Omar N. Bradley." New York, New York: History.com, January 27. Accessed September 6, 2023. https://history.com/topics/world-war-ii/omar-bradley.

Ortega Law, Jeannie, 2022. "Pat Boone Says Being Baptized with the Holy Spirit Gave His Marriage a Second Chance." The Christian Post, April 15. Accessed October 8, 2023. https://www.christianpost.com/news/pat-boone-talks-being-baptized-in-the-holy-spirit.html.

Bibliography

Ott, Tim, 2022. "Elvis Presley's Musical Talents Took Root during a Lonely Childhood." A&E Networks, June 6. Accessed October 4, 2023. https://www.biography.com/musicians/elvis-presley-childhood-high-school.

Ott, Tim. 2024. "Martin Luther King Jr." Biography.com, January 15. Accessed January 18, 2024. https://www.biography.com/activists/martin-luther-king-jr.

n.d., "Our History." St. Augustine, Florida: City of St. Augustine. Accessed June 7, 2023. https://www.citystaug.com/693/Our-History#:~:text=Founded%20in%201565%2C%20St.,The%20Spanish%20established%20at%20St.

2020. "Our History." Irvine, California: Full Gospel Business Men's Fellowship International. Accessed November 5, 2023. https://wwwfgbmfi.org/our-history.

n.d., "Overview." Washington, DC: Library of Congress. Accessed July 2, 2023. https://www.loc.gov/classroom-materials/united-states-history-primart-source-timeline/progressive-era-to-new-era-1900-1929/overview.

2023. "Pacific War." Chicago, Illinois: Encyclopedia Britannica, June 30. Accessed August 15, 2023. https://www.britannica.com/topic/Pacific-War.

2022. "Panama Canal." New York, New York: History.com, September 6. https://www.history.com/topics/landmarks/panama-canal.

2011. "Pat Boone Interview: Part 1 of 3." Foundation Interviews, May 19. Accessed October 7, 2023. https://www.youtube.com/watch?v=R5_Fp4RxtZ0&t=49s.

2019. "Pat Boone's Incredible Story." Studio 10, September 15. Accessed October 8, 2023. https://www.youtube.com/watch?v=dnn9acQm5cM7t=2s.

2023. "Pat Robertson." Encyclopedia Britannica, September 1. Accessed October 18, 2023. https://www.britannica.com/biography/Pat-Robertson.

2023. "Pat Robertson." The Christian Broadcasting Network. Accessed October 18, 2023. https://www2.cbn.com/person/pat-robertson.

Patch Wooding, Dan, 2013. "Pat Boone, the Great Rock and Roll Survivor, and His Friendship with Elvis Presley." June 28. Accessed October 5, 2023. https://patch.com/california/ranchosantamargarita/pat-boone--the-great-rock-and-roll-survivor--and-his-friendship-with-elvis-presley_12e2dca5.

Paulson, Bob, 2023. "Focused on What Matters Most: Pat Boone Is on a Mission to See People Saved." Decision, March 1. Accessed October 8, 2023. https://decisionmagazine.com/focused-on-what-matters-most/.

Pawell, Miriam, 2015. *The Crusades of Cesar Chavez: A Biography.* New York: Bloomsbury Press.

Bibliography

Pearce Rotondi, Jessica, 2023. "What Caused the Korean War, and Why Did the US Get Involved?" New York, New York: A&E Networks, June 26. Accessed September 11, 2023. https://www.history.com/news/korean-war-causes-us-involvement.

2022. "Pearl Harbor." New York, New York: History.com, December 6. Accessed August 10, 2023. https://www.history.com/topics/world-war-ii/pearl-harbor.

n.d., "Philippe Kieffer's Biography." D-Day Overlord. Accessed September 7, 2023. https://www.dday-overlord.com/en/battle-of-normandy/biographies/france/philippe-kieffer.

Piccotti, Tyler, 2023. "What You Need to Know about Mike Johnson, the New Speaker of the House." New York, New York, October 26. Accessed October 30, 2023. https://www.biography.com/political-figures/a45654212/mike-johnson.

Pickles, Dorothy, 2023. "Charles de Gaulle." Chicago, Illinois: Encyclopedia Britannica, June 20. Accessed September 2, 2023. https://www.britannica.com/biography/Charles-de-Gaulle-president-of-France.

Picotti, Tyler and Kettler, Sara, 2023. "How Priscilla Presley Went from Elvis's 'Young Love Interest' to His 'Living Doll.'" A&E Networks, February 23. Accessed October 5, 2023. https://www.biography.com/musicians/elvis-priscilla-presley-relationship-marriage-divorce.

Picotti, Tyler, 2022. "Elvis Presley." A&E Networks, October 31. Accessed October 5, 2023. https://www.biography.com/musicians/elvis-presley.

2023. "President & College Leadership." Massachusetts: Wheaton College Massachusetts. Accessed November 5, 2023. https://www.wheatoncollege.edu/about-wheaton-college/college-leadership/.

2006. "Pre-War Japanese Military Preparation 1941." US Army Center of Military History, November 1. Accessed August 10, 2023. https://history.army.mil/books/wwii/MacArthur%20Reports/MacArthur%20V2%20P1/Ch1.htm.

Price, David A., 2023. "Jamestown Colony: English Colony, North America." Chicago, Illinois: Encyclopedia Britannica, May 11. Accessed June 1, 2023. https://www.britannica.com/place/Jamestown-Colony.

Pruitt, Sarah, 2023. "How Codebreakers Helped Secure US Victory in the Battle of Midway." New York, New York: A&E Networks, June 7. Accessed August 13, 2023. https://www.history.com/news/battle-midway-codebreakers-allies-pacific-theater.

Pruitt, Sarah, 2023. "The Post-World War II Boom: How America Got into Gear." A&E Networks, August 10. Accessed October 1, 2023. https://www.history.com/news/post-world-war-ii-boom-economy.

Bibliography

Pruitt, Sarah, 2020. "Why Did Japan Attack Pearl Harbor?" New York, New York: A&E Networks, May 13. Accessed August 5, 2023. https://www.history.com/news/why-did-japan-attack-pearl-harbor.

Randall, Keith, 2019. "James Earl Rudder's Legacy Was Born 75 Years Ago at D-Day." Texas A&M University Division of Marketing & Communications, June 5. Accessed September 7, 2023. https://today.tamu.edu/2019/06/05/james-earl-rudders-legacy-was-born-75-years-ago-at-d-day/.

Ranker Editors, 2021. "Forty Famous Movie Stars of the 1950s." Ranker.com, April 26. Accessed October 1, 2023. https://www.ranker.com/list/1950s-movie-stars/ranker-film.

Reardon, Patrick Henry, n.d. "The Day God Settled the 'Bible Question' for Billy Graham." Christianity Today. Accessed September 15, 2023. https://www.christianitytoday.com/history/issues/issue-83/turning-point.html.

1967. "Red Foley." Country Music Hall of Fame and Museum Nashville, November 4. Accessed October 7, 2023. https://www.countrymusichalloffame.org/about/collections/oral-history/red-foley.

Renner, Rick, 2020. *Last Days Survival Guide: A Scriptural Handbook to Prepare You for These Perilous Times.* Shippensburg: Harrison House.

The Rise and Fall of the American Empire

2009. "Revolutionary War." New York, New York: History.com, October 29. Accessed June 11, 2023. https://www.history.com/topics/american-revolution/american-revolution-history.

Riddle, Jonathan, 2020. "The Death of Jack Cash (Johnny Cash's Brother)." October 24. Accessed October 2, 2023. https://www.youtube.com/watch?v=Ocei8jnI2-s.

Robert, Cecil, 2017. *The Azusa Street Mission and Revival.* Nashville, Tennessee: Thomas Nelson.

Roberts, Oral, 1952. *Oral Roberts' Life Story.* Tulsa: Oral Roberts Evangelistic Association.

Roberts, Richard, 2020. "The Story of Oral Roberts's Ministry—How It Began." Richard Roberts, October 29. Accessed September 12, 2023. https://www.youtube.com/watch?v=JwZbzO8pfOI.

Roberts, Richard, 2023. "Wake Up—A Prophetic Message by Oral Roberts." May 2. Accessed September 14, 2023. https://www.youtube.com/watch?v=un0wykY4r-mg&t=2s.

Robertson, Pat, interview by Abby Robertson, 2023. "Abby Robertson's Conversation with Her Grandfather and CBN Founder Pat Robertson: Full Interview." Virginia Beach, Virginia: Christian Broadcasting Network, June 19. Accessed June 20, 2023. https://www.youtube.com/watch?v=E3ZVRYsNB4c.

Bibliography

Robertson, Pat, interview by Abigail Robertson, 2023. "Abigail Robertson's Long-Ranging Interview with Pat Robertson." YouTube, September 19. Accessed October 19, 2023. https://www.youtube.com/watch?v=8xz5G3Ri94E.

Ronner, C. D. and Pells, Richard H., 2023. "Great Depression." Chicago, Illinois, July 3. Accessed July 10, 2023. https://www.britannica.com/money/topic/Great-Depression.

Roos, Dave, 2020. "FDR, Churchill, and Stalin: Inside Their Uneasy WW II Alliance." A&E Networks, June 12. Accessed October 1, 2023. https://www.history.com/news/big-three-allies-wwii-roosevelt-churchill-stalin.

Roos, Dave, 2019. "How Many Were Killed on D-Day?" New York, New York: A&E Networks, June 3. Accessed September 7, 2023. https://www.history.com/news/d-day-casualties-deaths-allies.

Roos, Dave, 2018. "The Navy Disaster that Earned JFK Two Medals for Heroism." December 3. Accessed October 10, 2023. https://www.history.com/news/jfk-wwii-purple-heart-torpedo-boat.

Rosenberg, Jennifer, 2019. "The History of Prohibition in the United States." New York, New York: Thought Co, October 14. Accessed July 7, 2023. https://www.thoughtco.com/history -of-prohibition-1779250.

Rossi, Jason, 2023. "Johnny Cash's Mother Was Floored When She Heard Him Sing at 17 Years Old." Showbiz Cheat Sheets, January 20. Accessed October 2, 2023. https://www.cheatsheets.com/entertainment/johnny-cash-mother-floored-sign.html.

Ruffle, John, 2023. "Oral Roberts' Final Speech to ORU Staff & Students from His Newport Beach, California Home." Youtube.com, August 9. Accessed September 13, 2023. https://www.youtube.com/watch?v=kC_OX1GN4h4.

Rummel, Sally, 2016. "As American as 'Baseball, Hot Dogs, Apple Pie, and Chevrolet.'" *Times*, Fenton, Michigan, July 27. Accessed October 10, 2023. https://www.tctimes.com/as-american-as-baseball-hot-dogs-apple-pie-and-chevrolet/article_dd7083ea-3efe-11e6-8531-43492d385b75.html.

Schneider, Keith, 2009. "Oral Roberts, Fiery Preacher, Dies at 91." The New York Times, December 15. Accessed September 14, 2023. https://www.nytimes.com/2009/12/16/us/16roberts.html.

Selvidge, Marla J., 1999. "Kathryn J. Kuhlman: 1907–1976." State Historical Society of Missouri. Missouri: Missouri Encyclopedia. Accessed August 2, 2023. https://www.missouriencyclopedia.org/people/kuhlman-kathryn-j.

Semple McPherson, Aimee., n.d. "The Angelus Temple." PBS. Accessed July 11, 2023. https://www.pbs.org/wgbh/americanexperience/features/sister-angelus-temple/.

Bibliography

Seven, John, 2018. "Why Did Benedict Arnold Betray America?" New York, New York: A&E Networks, July 17. Accessed June 9, 2023. https://www.history.com/news/why-did-benedict-arnold-betray-america.

2018. "Seymour, William Joseph." Encyclopaedia.com, June 8. Accessed July 5, 2023. https://www.encyclopedia.com/people/history/us-history-biographies/william-joseph-seymour.

Shelton, P. L., 2018. "Cesar Chavez: 1927–1993, Labor Leader." Encyclopedia.com, May 23. Accessed October 13, 2023. https://www.encyclopedia.com/people/social-sciences-and-law/labor-biographies/cesar-chavez.

Slosser, Bob, 2022. "The Prophecy." CBN, December 10. Accessed October 8, 2023. https://www2.cbn.com/article/relationships/prophecy.

n.d., "Stan Hollis and the D-Day Victoria Cross." London: Imperial War Museums. Accessed September 7, 2023. https://www.iwm.org.uk/history/stan-hollis-and-the-d-day-victoria-cross.

Sterne, Gary, 2020. "Nuts! The Story behind the Famous American Reply to the German Surrender Ultimatum at Bastogne." September 15. Accessed September 9, 2023. https://militaryhistorynow.com/2020/09/15/nuts-the-story-of-the-famous-american-reply-to-the-german-surrender-ultimatum-at-bastogne/#google_vignette.

2010. "Stock Market Crash of 1929." New York, New York: History.com, May 10. Accessed July 7, 2023. https://www.history.com/topics/great-depression/1929-stock-market-crash.

Summers, Jerry, 2020. "Jerry Summers: Johnny Cash Meets Walker County Sheriff Ralph Jones." Chattanoogan.com, January 8. Accessed October 3, 2023. https://www.chattanoogan.com/2020/1/8/401757/Jerry-Summers-Johnny-Cash-Meets-Walker.aspx.

Swift, J., 2023. "Battle of Moscow." Chicago, Illinois: Encyclopedia Britannica, September 23. Accessed September 25, 2023. https://www.britannica.com/event/Battle-of-Moscow.

2016. "The 1904 Welsh Revival." Cardiff, Wales: The Bible College of Wales, May 21. Accessed July 4, 2023. https://www.bcwales.org/1904-welsh-revival.

2014. "The Atlantic Wall: 11 Key Facts about the Nazi Defenses at Normandy." Military History Now, June 14. Accessed September 1, 2023. https://militaryhistorynow.com/2014/06/04/the-atlantic-wall-11-amazing-facts-about-the-nazi-defences-at-normandy/.

n.d., "The Birth and Rise of Rock 'n' Roll in the 1950s and 1960s." History Skills. Accessed October 1, 2023. https://www.historyskills.com/classroom/year-10/rock-n-roll-reading.

Bibliography

2007. "The Diary of Tanya Savicheva." Pravmir, June 28. Accessed August 4, 2023. https://www.pravmir.com/the-diary-of-tanya-savicheva.

2023. "The Fall of Singapore." Chicago, Illinois: Encyclopedia Britannica, July 18. Accessed August 11, 2023. https://www.britannica.com/event/World-War-II/the-fall-of-Singapure.

2019. "The Founding Fathers." New York, New York: History.com, January 30. Accessed June 10, 2023. https://www.history.com/topics/american-revolution/founding-fathers-united-states.

2010. "The Great Migration." New York, New York: History.com, March 4. Accessed July 1, 2023. https://www.history.com/topics/black-history/great-migration.

2018. "The Harlem Hellfighters." History.com, August 21. Accessed October 1, 2023. https://www.history.com/topics/world-war-i/the-harlem-hellfighters-video.

2023. "The Holocaust." New York, New York: History.com, April 11. Accessed August 3, 2023. https://www.history.com/topics/world-war-ii/the-holocaust.

n.d., "The Legacy of Hope Began." Houston, Texas: Lakewood Church. Accessed September 12, 2023. https://www.lakewoodchurch.com/about/history.

2023. "The Legacy of TBN." Trinity Broadcasting Network. Accessed October 20, 2023. https://www.tbn.org/about/tbn-legacy.

The Martin Luther King Jr. Research and Education Institute, Stanford University, n.d. "Chapter 1: Early years." The Martin Luther King Jr. Institute, Stanford University. Accessed October 16, 2023. https://kinginstitute.stanford.edu/publications/autobiography-martin-luther-king-jr/chapter-1-early-years.

2016. "The Modesto Manifesto: A Declaration of Biblical Integrity." Billy Graham Evangelistic Association of Canada, October 24. Accessed September 16, 2023. https://www.billygraham.ca/stories/the-modesto-manifesto-a-declaration-of-biblical-integrity/.

2022. "The Reverend Robert Hunt: The First Chaplain at Jamestown." *Historic Jamestown.* Washington, DC: National Park Service, September 4. Accessed June 3, 2023. https://www.nps.gov/james/learn/historyculture/the-reverend-robert-hunt-the-first-chaplain-at-jamestown.

2023. "The Story of TBN: 50 Years in the Making." Trinity Broadcasting Network. Accessed October 19, 2023. https://www.tbn.org/about/history.

2015. *The West Point History of World War II: Volume 1.* New York: Simon & Schuster.

Bibliography

2023. "This Was the Secret War Off the US Coast during World War II." Team Mighty, February 16. Accessed August 3, 2023. https://www.wearethemighty.com/mighty-history/nazi-u-boat-war-off-north-carolina-kept-secret-us-government/.

2023. "Thomas Andrew Dorsey." Chicago, Illinois: Encyclopedia Britannica, June 27. Accessed July 7, 2023. https://www.britannica.com/biography/Thomas-Andrew-Dorsey.

2023. "*Titanic*." New York, New York: History.com, June 29. Accessed July 10, 2023. https://www.history.com/topics/early-20th-century-us/titanic.

Tolentino, Cierra, 2023. "Who Invented the Typewriter? A Brief History of the Typewriter and Its Numerous Inventors." Chicago, Illinois, November 8. Accessed November 12, 2023. https://www.historycooperative.org/who-invented-the-typewriter/.

Toll, Ian W., 2015. *The Conquering Tide: War in the Pacific Islands 1942–1944.* New York: W. W. Norton & Company.

Trueman, C. N., 2015. "The French Resistance." London: The History Learning Site, May 18. Accessed September 2, 2023. https://www.historylearningsite.co.uk/world-war-two/resistance-movements/the-french-resistance.

2023. "United Farm Workers." Chicago, Illinois: Encyclopedia Britannica, March 20. Accessed October 14, 2023. https://www.britannica.com/topic/United-Farm-Workers.

The Rise and Fall of the American Empire

2019. "US and Mexico Sign the Mexican Farm Labor Agreement." History.com, October 7. Accessed October 14, 2023. https://www.history.com/this-day-in-history/us-mexico-sign-mexican-farm-labor-agreement-bracero-program.

2022. "US Entry into World War I." New York, New York: History.com, August 30. Accessed July 3, 2023. https://www.history.com/topics/world-war-i/u-s-entry-into-world-war-i-1.

2021. "US Recognition of the State of Israel." National Archives. Educators Resources, August 2. Accessed October 1, 2023. https://www.archives.gov/education/lessons/US-Israel#background.

Van Engen, Abram C., 2020. *City on a Hill: A History of American Exceptionalism.* New Haven, Connecticut: Yale University Press.

Vergun, David, 2020. "Submarine Warfare Played Major Role in World War II Victory." Washington, DC: US Department of Defense, March 16. Accessed August 15, 2023. https://www.defense.gov/News/Feature-Stories/Story?Article/2114035/submarine-warfare-played-major-role-in-world-war-ii-victory/.

2015. "Vernon and Gladys Presley: Elvis Presley's Mother and Father." Elvis Australia Official Elvis Presley Fan Club, January 24. Accessed October 4, 2023. https://biography.

Bibliography

elvis.com.au/gladys-and-vernon-presley.shtml.

Vision Video, 2020. "*Cross and the Switchblade* (1970)./Full Movie/Pat Boone/Erick Estrada/Jacqueline Giroux." YouTube, April 26. Accessed October 8, 2023. https://www.youtube.com/watch?v=fWA5BNIz7dM&t=12s.

Vnutrennikh, Narodniy, n.d. "The Penal Battalions." Accessed August 4, 2023. https://stalingrad.net/russian-hq/the-penal-battalions/ruspenalbat.html.

Voices of Oklahoma, 2018. "The Friendship of Oral Roberts and Billy Graham." Youtube, February 22. Accessed September 12, 2023. https://www.youtube.com/watch?v=NDZ-bLT1a5ZY&t=121s.

Voight, Larry, n.d. "The Evangelist: Oral Roberts." Words of Life. Accessed September 12, 2023. http://www.lgvoight.com/hs/hs64.html.

Wagner, Margaret E., 2017. *America and the Great War.* New York: Bloomsbury Press.

2023. "War of 1812." New York, New York: History.com, April 24. Accessed June 12, 2023. https://www.history.com/topics/19th-century/war-of-1812.

Warren, Steven, 2021. "Marcus Lamb, Founder of Daystar Television Network, Has Died." Christian Broadcasting Network, November 30. Accessed November 1, 2023.

https://www2.cbn.com/news/news/marcus-lamb-founder-daystar-television-network-has-died.

2007. "Was Daniel Boone an Ancestor of Pat Boone?" Genea Musings, August 31. Accessed October 7, 2023. https://www.geneamusings.com/2007/08/was-daniel-boone-ancestor-of-pat-boone.html.

Welt Documentary, 2021. "The Pacific War: Japan versus the US Full Documentary." YouTube, September 5. Accessed August 15, 2023. https://www.youtube.com/watch?v=RHvh2ly1-18.

2012. "What Happened to the 'Lost Colony' of Roanoke: How Could 115 People Just Vanish?" New York, New York: History.com, October 3. Accessed June 1, 2023. https://www.history.com/news/what-happened-to-the-lost-colony-of-roanoke.

Wilentz, Sean, 2018. "A Battle for the 'Soul of America'? It's as Old as America, one Historian Notes." The New York Times, May 21. Accessed October 10, 2023. https://www.nytimes.com/2018/05/21/books/review/jon-meacham-soul-of-america.html.

n.d., "William Ashley (Billy) Sunday: 1862–1935." Canton, Ohio: Christian Hall of Fame. Accessed July 2, 2023. https://christianhof.org/sunday/.

Bibliography

Wilson, Linda D., 2010. "Oral Roberts University." The Encyclopedia of Oklahoma History and Culture, January 15. Accessed September 13, 2023. https://www.okhistory.org/publications/enc/entry?entry=OR001.

Windsor, Pam, 2022. "Don McLean Tells the Story of 'American Pie' & Explains the Lyrics in New Documentary." Forbes, July 19. Accessed October 10, 2023. https://www.forbes.com/sites/pamwindsor/2022/07/19/don-mclean-tells-the-story-of-american-pie--explains-the-lyrics-in-new-documentary/?sh=307002dad07b.

Zielinski, Adam E., 2020. "Fighting for Freedom: African Americans Choose Sides during the American Revolution." Washington, DC: American Battlefield Trust, November 30. Accessed June 10, 2023. https://www.battlefields.org/learn/articles/fighting-freedom-african-americans-during-american-revolution.

Zimmerman, Carle, 2007. *Family and Civilization.* Wilmington, North Carolina: ISI Books.

ONOMASTIC INDEX

Abraham	12, 36,
Adam	12
Adams, John	39, 54
Adams, Samuel	51
Alden, John	24
Allman, Robert	357
Anderson, Major Robert	86
Andre, John	58
Andrew	119
Anne, Queen	70
Anson, Cap	109
Antichrist	50, 237, 378
Archilla, Reverend Rogelio	280
Arnold, General Benedict	51, 58
Asberry, Richard and Ruth	92, 134, 135
Azusa Street	135-140
Barnett, Luke	186
Barnett, Matthew	173
Barnett, Tommy	173
Barrows, Cliff	278
Barry, Rick	318
Bean, Orville	299
Beauregard, General Pierre GT	89
Beecher, Lyman	62
Beemer, Richard	316
Bell, L Nelson	273
Bering, Vitus	32, 41

Bethany, Reverend and Mrs. Edgar	361
Biden, President Joe	337
Bigler, Henry	72
Billington, Dallas	183
Binion, David and Nicole	368
Block, Adriaen	28
Bonaparte, Napoleon	64-67
Bon Barton, Bill	128
Boone, Archie Altman	307
Boone, Cherry, Lindy, Debby, Laury	309, 317
Boone, Daniel	307
Boone, Judy	307
Boone, Margaret Virginia	307
Boone, Marjorie Ann	307
Boone, Nick	307
Boone, Patrick Charles Eugene	283, 285, 288, 304-318, 372
Boone, Shirley Lee Foley	307
Booth, John Wilkes	65
Bopper, The Big	322
Bouvier, Jacqueline	328
Bradford, William	23, 24
Bradley, Five Star General Omar	226, 236, 237, 238, 245,
Brewster, William	23
Bright, Tim	355
Buckingham, Jamie	188
Buckmaster, Captain	215
Bunyan, John	75
Burgoyne, General John	56
Burt, William Austin	70
Campbell, Glen	288

Onomastic Index

Capone, Al	152
Carter, Ezra	294
Carter, "The Carter Family"	294-295
Carter, President Jimmy	295
Carter Cash, June	294–295
Carter, Maybelle	244
Cartier, Jacques	27
Cash, J. R. Johnny	288-296, 303–305
Cash, Ray and Carrie Cloveree	288
Cash, Roy, Margaret, Louise, Jack	288
Cash, Reba, Joanne, Tommy	288
Cash, Vivian and daughters	291–294
Chaplain, Samuel de	28
Chapman, Jay Wilbur	111
Chavez, Cesar	331-337
Chavez, Cesario	331
Chavez, Dorotea	331–332
Chavez, Helen Fabela	333
Chavez, Juana Estrada	331
Chavez, Librado	331
Chavez, Rita	331
Chilton, Mary	19
Churchill, Clementine	244
Churchill, Gladys	353
Churchill, Winston Spencer	60, 85, 188, 189, 193, 194, 196, 199, 218, 221, 247, 283, 376,
Clark, Lewis	65-66
Clay, Henry	81
Cleveland, James	145
Columbus, Christopher	12-14, 361
Copeland, Kenneth	272
Copley, John Singleton	40

The Rise and Fall of the American Empire

Corbin, Margaret Cochran	52
Cornwallis, Lord	59
Coronado	31
Corte Real, brothers	30
Corte Real, Joao Vaz	30
Cortes, Hernan	30
Crosby, Bing	307
Crouch, Andrew and Sarah	360
Crouch, Janice Bethany	361
Crouch, John Mark	360
Crouch, Matthew	361
Crouch, Paul Franklin Sr.	359
Crouch, Paul Jr.	359
Crouch, Reverend Philip	360
Crudup, Arthur "Big Boy"	300
Cruz, Nicky	317
Curtain, Prime Minister John	207
Cyrus	85
Dahl, Arlene	316
Daigle, Lauren	373
David, King	335
Davis, Confederate President Jefferson	91
Dawes, William	51
Day, Doris	313
Dean, James	322
De Gaulle, General Charles	223
Deweese, Robert	267
Digiorgio, Family	333
Domino, Fats	285
Doolittle, Colonel James	208
Dorsey, Thomas	99, 145-151
Dorsey, Rev. Thomas and Etta	146

Onomastic Index

Douglas, Camp	97
Douglas, Kym Bankier	419
Douglas, Stephen A.	81-82
Douglass, Frederick	69
Dryer, Emma	97
Durham, William	167-168
Dylan, Bob	296, 322
Edison, Thomas A.	70, 105
Eisenhower, President General Dwight	221, 225-226, 233, 236-238, 241, 244-245
Elijah	183
Elisha	183
Elizabeth, Queen	329
Enoch	12
Erik the Red	12
Erikson, Leif	12
Estrada, Eric	317
Evans, Jimmy	368
Farrow, Pastor Lucy	132
Ferdinand, Archduke Franz	115
Ferdinand, Sophie	115
Finney, Charles Grandison	61-63
Fitzgerald, John Francis	328
Fletcher, Rear Admiral Frank Jack	213
Floyd, General John B.	90
Foley, Red	150, 307
Foley, Shirley Lee	307
Ford, Glenn	313
Franklin, Benjamin	39-41, 46, 54, 105

The Rise and Fall of the American Empire

Franklin, Jentezen	366
Fritz, Harvey	276
Frye, Theodore	149
Gabor, Zsa Zsa	313
Garret, Thomas	69
Gates, General Horatio	56
Geyer, General	227
Godfrey, Arthur	308
Goliath	335
Graham, Dr. the Reverend Billy	43, 113, 125, 184, 251, 268, 270, 272-282, 290, 295, 306, 345, 358
Graham, Franklin	272, 282
Graham, Ruth Bell	273
Grant, Amy	373
Grant, General Ulysses S.	88-90
Grant, Marshall	291
Greene, Nathaniel	56
Groves, Lieutenant General Leslie	247
Gulliford, Helen	179
Hagee, John	186, 367
Hagin, Reverend Kenneth E.	183, 184, 251-260, 267, 268
Hagin, Kenneth Jr. and Patricia	258, 259
Hagin, mom and grandfather	258
Hagin, Oretha Rooker	258
Halleck, Henry W.	88
Halsey, Vice Admiral William "Bull"	211
Ham, Mordecai	273
Hamblen, Stuart	276

Onomastic Index

Hamilton, Alexander	54, 56
Hammond, Dr. Bill	377
Handel, George Frideric	148
Harper, Nettie	147, 150
Hartner, Maggie	182
Hayes, Benjamin	344
Hearst, William Randolph	277-278
Herjolfsson, Bjarni	13
Hinn, Benny	165, 185
Hirohito, Emperor	201, 248
Hitler, Adolf	85, 189-196, 201, 221, 222, 227, 235, 237, 239, 243, 244, 325, 341,
Hollis, Sargeant Major Stanley	231
Holly, Buddy	285, 322
Holton, Samuel	96
Hood, General John Bell	93
Hooker, General Joseph	91
Hoover, Herbert	159-160
Hopkins, Elizabeth	25, 26
Hopkins, Oceanus	25, 26
Houghton, Israel	373
Howard, John	25
Hudson, Henry	28
Huerta, Dolores	335
Hunt, Reverend Robert	19
Hutchins, Pastor Julia	133
Ingstad, Helge and Anne	13
Isaac	12
Ishmael	12

Jackson, Andrew	80
Jackson, Reverend Jesse	336
Jackson, Mahalia	146, 149, 150, 269, 348
Jackson, Brigadier General "Stonewall"	89, 91
Jacobson, Edward	283
Jagger, Mick	322
Jakes, T. D.	366
James	119
Jefferson, Thomas	39, 54, 65, 66
Jerusalem, mayor of	103
Jesus Christ	19, 50, 61, 104, 110, 119, 120-126, 137, 140, 145, 164, 166, 167, 170, 178, 179, 182, 184, 252-254, 259, 261, 262, 264-266, 272, 275, 276, 279, 281, 295, 342, 351, 357, 363-365, 372, 373, 375, 376, 379, 380, 385
Job	254
John	119
John, Elton	305
Johnson, Lyndon B.	328
Johnson, House Speaker Mike	372
Jones, Bob	113, 273
Jones, Captain Christopher	26
Jones, Commander John Paul	57
Jones, Sheriff Ralph	295
Kai-Shek, ROC Generalissimo Chaing	218

Onomastic Index

Kaku, Rear Admiral Tomeo	216
Keisker, Marion	300
Kennedy, Carolyn	330
Kennedy, John F.	321, 323, 324, 330, 331,
Kennedy Jr., John F.	225, 227
Kennedy, Joseph Patrick	323,328, 329, 330
Kennedy Jr., Joe	326
Kennedy, Mildred Ona	166, 170
Kennedy, Robert F.	336,
Kennedy Jr., Robert F.	225
Kennedy, Rose	328, 330
Kerr, Phil	181
Kieffer, Philippe	232
Kimball, Edward	96
King, Alfred Daniel	339
King, Bernice	345
King, Christine	339
King, Coretta Scott	345
King, Dexter Scott	344, 345
King, James Albert and Delia	339
King Jr., Martin Luther	69, 104, 322, 334 339-349,
King Sr., Martin Luther	341-349
King III, Martin Luther	345
King, Yolanda	345
Kuhlman, Emma Walkenhorst	175-188
Kuhlman, Joseph Adolph	175
Kuhlman, Kathryn	175
Kuhlman, Myrtle	176, 177
La Fayette, Marquis Gilbert du Motier	56
Lamb, Jonathan	367

The Rise and Fall of the American Empire

Lamb, Marcus Daron	364-368
Lamb, Rachel	367
Lamb, Rebecca	367
Latham, Arlie	109
Lazarus	256
Leclerc, General Philippe	238
Lee, Edward S.	134
Lee, Richard Henry	54
Lee, General Robert E.	90-92
Lenin, Vladimir	117
Lennon, John and the Beatles	322
Lewis, Jerry Lee	285, 292, 303-304
Lewis, Merriweather	65
Lillian	302
Lincoln, Abraham	73, 75-94,143, 144, 331, 349
Lincoln, Mary Todd	79, 80, 86, 88
Lincoln, Nancy, Sarah, Thomas Jr.	76
Lincoln, Robert Todd	79
Lincoln, Sarah Bush Johnston	77
Lincoln, Thomas	76-77
Lindbergh, Charles A.	153, 154
Lindsay, Gordon	259
Lindsey, Hal	372
Livingston, Robert R.	64
Luce, Henry	277
Luke	121
Luther, Martin	240
MacArthur, General Douglas	201, 207
Mack, Ted	308
Madison, James	39, 54, 66
Maiden, Dr. Pastor Michael	186, 373

Onomastic Index

Malay, Paul	41
Malay, Pierre	41
Maloney, Matthew J.	181
Mansell, Gains	299
Manson, Charles	322
Maravich, Pete "Pistol Pete"	187
Mark	119
Marshall, James W.	72
Martin, Roberta	146
Mason, James	316
McAuliffe, General Anthony	242
McCain Sr., Admiral John S.	217
McCarthy, Senator Joseph	287
McClellan, General George B.	88
McDowell, General Irvin	89
McCluskey, Commander Wade	214
Mclean, Betty Ann	322
Mclean, Don	322
McPherson, Aimee Semple	165-173
McPherson, Harold Stewart	168
McPherson, Rolf Potter Kennedy	168
Meade, General	88
Mikawa, Vice Admiral Gunichi	216
Mills, Henry	70
Model, Walter	239
Monroe, James	64
Monroe, Marilyn	286, 310, 315-316
Montgomery, Field Marshall Bernard	221, 225, 226, 241
Moody, Dwight Lyman	95-101, 103, 104, 111
Moody, Edwin and Betsy Holton	95
Morgan, James	166

The Rise and Fall of the American Empire

Moses	12, 139
Mouse, Mickey	142
Mozart, Wolfgang	148
Munizzi, Martha	368, 373
Murillo, Mario	185
Nagumo, Vice Admiral	210-213
Nelson, Ricky	310, 312
Ness, Elliot and the "Untouchables"	152
Newport, Christopher	20
Nicholas II, Czar	117
Nimitz, Admiral Chester	211, 218
Nix, W. M.	147
Nixon, E. D.	245
Nixon, President Richard	328
Noah	12, 124, 164
Nobel, Alfred	106
Obama, President Barack	336
Oppenheimer, Robert	247
Osborne, T. L.	259
Osteen, Dodie	373
Osteen, Pastor Joel	373
Osteen, Pastor John	186, 258, 373
Osteen, Lisa	373
Osteen, Paul	373
Otis, George	314
Owens, Jesse	340
Owens, Mary	79
Ozman, Agnes	131
Paine, Thomas	55
Parham, Charles F.	130-132, 136-138

Onomastic Index

Parker, Colonel Tom	305
Parks, Rosa	345
Parrott, Everett Benjamin	176, 177, 183
Parrott, Myrtle Kuhlman	183
Patton, General George	233, 236-238, 241, 244
Paul, the apostle	375
Pemberton, General John C.	63
Perkins, Luther	202, 211
Pershing, General John J.	91
Peter, Simon	119
Peter, the Great	32
Philip, Prince	329
Phillips, Sam	292, 293, 300
Pickett, General George	92
Pillow, General Gideon	90
Polk, James K.	81
Prescott, Samuel	51
Presley, Elvis Aaron	150, 285, 288, 292 293, 296-306, 310-312, 322
Presley, Jesse Garon	300, 301
Presley, Gladys Love Smith	297
Presley, Lisa Marie	303
Presley, Priscilla Beaulieu	303
Presley, Vernon	297-299, 303
Presley, Vester	297
Princip, Gavrilo	115
Pring, Martin	15
Pringle, Reverend Steve	267
Putin, Vladimir	249
Rainey, Gertrude "Ma"	147, 148

The Rise and Fall of the American Empire

Randle, DJ Bill	310
Reagan, President Ronald	314, 315, 352, 356
Renner, Pastor Rick	367
Revere, Paul	51
Roberts, Reverend Ellis and Claudius	260
Roberts, Elmer and Jewel	262
Roberts, Evelyn	263, 267, 270, 272
Roberts, Oral	175, 183, 186, 251, 260-272,
Roberts, Richard	183, 271
Robertson, Abigail	254
Robertson, Absalon Willis	353
Robertson, Adelia "DeDe" Elmer	359
Robertson, Gordon	352
Robertson, Pat M. G.	352-359
Robertson, Willis Jr.	353
Robinson, Captain	40
Rochambeau, Count de	59
Rodney, Cesar	54
Rommel, Field Marshall Erwin	221, 222, 227, 236, 243,
Roosevelt, Eleanor	161
Roosevelt, President Franklin Delano	160, 161, 195, 207, 221, 244-246, 286,
Roosevelt Jr., Brigadier General Theodore	228
Ross, Araminta	68
Ruder, Lieutenant Colonel James	229
Rundstedt, General Gerd von	221,227, 239
Ruth, Babe	154
Rutledge, Ann	79
Sacagawea	65
Sands of Time, The	7

Onomastic Index

Sanford, Frank	130
Sankey, Ira	98, 99
Savicheva, Tanya	196
Scott, Colonel John	109
Scott, General Winfield	88, 109
Schaffner, Franklin J.	315
Semple, Robert James	167
Semple, Roberta Star	167
Serra, Father Junipero	31
Seymour, Jenny Evans Moore	139
Seymour, Simon and Phyllis	131
Seymour, William J.	131-139
Shakarian, Demos	129, 372
Shea, George Beverly	278
Sheridan, Phillip	88
Sherman, Roger	54
Sherman, William T.	88, 93
Sholes, Christopher Latham	70
Sinatra, Frank	329
Singer, Agnes	128
Smale, Pastor Joseph	130
Smith, Clettes	297
Smith, Gladys Love	297
Smith, Michael W.	373
Smith, Reverend James	149
Smith, Willie Mae Ford	149
Sons of Liberty, the	51, 52
Spalding, A. G.	109
Spruance, Rear Admiral Raymond	213-215
Stalin, Joseph	194-195, 199, 217, 221, 227, 245, 247, 286, 291
Standish, Miles	24

The Rise and Fall of the American Empire

Stanton, Edwin M.	88
Statue of Liberty	104
Stimson, Secretary of War Henry	246
Stone, Chief Justice Harlan F.	246
Stone, Perry	273, 367
Sullivan, Ed	304
Sunday, Helen Amelia "Nell" Thompson	110-113
Sunday, Mary Jane Corey	108
Sunday, William Ashley	108-109, 113
Sunday, William Sr.	108
Sutter, John Augustus	72
Taylor, Elizabeth	285
Taylor, Zachary	81
Terry, Neely	133
Thomas, George H.	88
Tindley, Charles	147
Todd, Mary	79-86
Truman, Bess Wallace	170
Truman, President Harry S.	245
Truman, John and Martha	245-250, 283
Truman, Mary Margaret	245
Tubman, Harriet	68-70
Tubman, Robert, Moses, Henry, Ben	68
Turri, Pellegrino	70
Tryggvason, King Olaf	13
Valens, Ritchie	332
Vanderbreggen, Cornelius	352
Vaus, Jim	276
Verne, Jules	316
Vespucci, Amerigo	13
Villa, Pancho	364

Onomastic Index

von Bethmann, Theobald	117
von Steuben, Baron Friedrich Wilhelm	56
Wainwright, General	207
Wallnau, Dr. Lance	368
Waltrip, Burroughs	179
Washington, Booker T.	343
Washington, President George	50, 54-58
Wavell, British Commander	205
Webster, Daniel	81
Weiss, Dr. Doug	367
Weiss, Joni Trammel	367
Welles, George Orson	372
Wesley, Charles	44
Wesley, John	43, 44
Whitefield, George	40, 43-47
Wilhelm, Kaiser	85, 115
Wilkerson, Pastor David	186, 317
Williams, Reverend Adam Daniel	339
Williams, Alberta	339
Williams, Jennie	340
Willy, Lieutenant Wilford J.	326
Wilson, Grady	278
Wilson, President Woodrow	116
Winters, Jonathan	313
Winthrop, Governor John	35
Woodward, Joanne	316
Wright, Wilbur and Orville	153
Xi, Chinese President Jinping	249
Yamaguchi, Rear Admiral Tamon	215-216
Yamamoto, Admiral	208, 216

Yeardley, Governor	21
Z, Joseph	368
Zamperini, Louis	458
Zimmerman, Harvard Professor Carle C.	145, 287